SNIPERS & SHOOTERS

SNIPERS & SHOOTERS

The kill shot out of nowhere

BILL WALLACE

Futura

FUTURA

First published in Great Britain in 2011 by Futura

A CIP catalogue record for this book
is available from the British Library.

ISBN 978-0-7088-6698-6

Typeset in Great Britain by Omnipress Limited
Printed and bound in Great Britain

Futura
An imprint of
Little, Brown Book Group
100 Victoria Embankment
London EC4Y 0DY

An Hachette UK Company
www.hachette.co.uk

www.littlebrown.co.uk

Photo credits: Getty Images

The views expressed in this publication are those of the author. The information and the interpretation of that information is presented in good faith. Readers are advised that where ethical issues are involved, and often highly controversial ethical issues at that, they have a personal responsibility for making their own assessments and their own ethical judgements.

Contents

PART THREE: ASSASSINATIONS

PART FOUR: CELEBRITY SHOOTINGS

Introduction

The gun – invented by the Chinese in the twelfth century, and, without doubt, the deadliest implement that a human being can hold in his or her hand. Bombs can, of course, wreak considerably more damage, but in a one-on-one situation, the gun is the most lethal of all weapons.

Through the centuries the gun has evolved from what was effectively a portable hand-held cannon to lethal implements of death such as automatics and self-loaders with telescopic and laser sights, accessories that allow the user to see in the dark and a wide variety of bullets that create varying degrees of damage to a target whether human, animal or inanimate. Of course, humans being what they are – greedy, cowardly and insecure – the gun is used maliciously more often than for good, although it is difficult to know where to place wars in such considerations. But there are occasions when a gun has to be used for a good reason.

Police snipers, for instance, although present at many scenes of crime, are most often used only as a last resort or when an extreme situation warrants it –

namely, when lives are in danger. The FBI Standard Rules of Engagement make this clear: 'Agents are not to use deadly force against any person except as necessary in self-defence or the defence of another when they have reason to believe they or another are in danger of death or grievous bodily harm. Whenever feasible, verbal warning should be given before deadly force is applied.' In 1992, at Ruby Ridge, where the survivalist Weaver family was in a stand-off with the authorities, these standard rules were replaced with a more expedient set of rules that, in reality, made it open season on the Weavers. Of course, there was huge criticism of this temporary change of the rules and it served to foment even more unrest amongst the people who were supportive of the Weavers' stand – the extremists, white supremacists and apocalyptic survivalists – and would eventually result in the deaths of 168 people at the hands of Timothy McVeigh in Oklahoma City.

But more often than not, of course, these rules are adhered to and a dangerous situation where lives are at stake can be dealt with quickly and with the minimum loss of life. When James Huberty was shooting at will in a San Ysidro McDonalds fast food restaurant in July 1984, he had to be stopped and the only way to do so was with a bullet fired by police sniper Chuck Foster. Twenty-one people were already dead inside, including women and children, but the angry and paranoid Huberty was denied the chance to claim any more victims by that well-aimed bullet.

In war, the gun has played a major role since its invention, but particularly in the last three hundred years. The real master of the gun in warfare, however, is the sniper. Men like Vietnam veteran Carlos Hathcock, Second World War marksman, Vasily Zaitsev and First World War shooter, Billy Sing were different to their comrades. They were soldiers who were responsible between them for the deaths of hundreds, but to these men it was just their jobs. They had been born with the necessary skills and the skills of the sniper are, indeed, considerable. They include the patience to wait through endless hours, often in uncomfortable conditions, for a victim to appear; the ability to remain still for long periods of time, knowing that one slight movement could mean death or capture, although for the much-hated sniper, those two more often than not mean the same thing; the talent of concealment; and the ability to gauge from his surroundings just what is going to affect the bullet when it leaves the barrel of his gun. As ace

Vietnam sniper, Chuck Mawhinney once said, 'You act like an animal, you work like an animal, you are an animal'.

And they are also like animals in the sense that they have to abandon a great deal of their humanity in those moments when they are doing their job. They cannot afford to think of the life they are ending, the family their victim might leave behind. He is a target and that is it. But although they put aside some of their humanity, that does not make them inhuman. Men like Carlos Hathcock who had 93 confirmed kills, or the Finn Simo Haya who had an astonishing 542, could never be described thus.

Not all snipers are good men, of course, fighting for their freedom and the liberty of others. Mark Essex, a man whose brain had become twisted with racial hatred, killed a number of innocent victims and police officers while firing from a Howard Johnson Hotel in downtown New Orleans in January 1973. He had gone hunting for white people some days before and made his last stand at the hotel, firing down from balconies before finally being cornered and shot on the roof.

Essex at least had a reason, perverse though it was. Men such as Thomas Dillon, Garry and Thaddeus Lewingdon and the Random Violence killers, Dale

Hausner and Samuel Dietman, killed simply for fun. Dillon would randomly shoot people he came across in the east-central Ohio countryside. Guns for him were merely a means of doing harm to people, but people he did not even know. He drove rural roads, fuelled by alcohol, taking potshots and convincing himself that he had found the way to commit the perfect murder. As he said to a friend one day: 'Do you realise you can go out into the country and find somebody and there are no witnesses? You can shoot them. There is no motive. Do you realise how easy murder would be to get away with?' By that time he had already got away with several murders but he would eventually be caught.

Hausner and Dietman were a couple of losers who were angry at their ex-wives and a society that had not treated them as well as they would have liked. They vented their anger at night on the streets of Phoenix, Arizona, pumped on methamphetamine and booze and randomly shooting victims as they drove past them or encountered them on the streets. The Lewingdon Brothers also murdered randomly, often killing their victims in their homes but not for robbery or personal gain because they stole little. It remains fairly unclear why they did it and we are unlikely to know as they have both since died in prison.

Random shooters are, of course, the worst kind for police investigators. Every type of criminal profiler in the business was called in to try to solve the mystery of who was behind the random killing of people in the Washington area in 2002 when the police investigation was failing to come up with an answer. Even the geographic profiling of the Canadian inventor of this investigative technique, Dr Kim Rossmo, was found wanting. That was mainly because the perpetrators, John Allen Muhammad and Lee Boyd Malvo were moving like ghosts around the area, using Washington's ring road, the Beltway, to travel from murder to murder. They had no particular base, using the vehicle from which they fired their shots as their centre of operations as well as their residence and, indeed, when they were eventually caught, as a result of the alertness of an eagle-eyed truck-driver, they were sound asleep in their Chevrolet Caprice at a rest stop.

If men like those had no real reason to kill, assassins would argue that they have all the reason in the world and the gun, used effectively, provides them with the most effective way of achieving their objective, whether it is political or just to make themselves famous. In the case of the four American presidents who have been assassinated – Abraham

Lincoln, James Garfield, William McKinley and John F. Kennedy – their assassins had, to their own minds at least, good reason. Lincoln was killed by John Wilkes Booth, wielding a small derringer pistol, because the South had been defeated in the American Civil War and he detested Lincoln's politics; Garfield died at the hands of Charles J. Guiteau, a man who was probably insane and who was driven to kill the president by a life of disappointment, the ultimate one being a deranged belief that he had somehow helped Garfield get elected and deserved a reward for it; McKinley was murdered by one of the many anarchists that existed at the turn of the nineteenth century, a man who simply believed he was righting injustice and striking at the heart of a callous, corrupt system by killing the president; and Kennedy was, of course, shot by Lee Harvey Oswald, a man with communist sympathies who may or may not have been working on behalf of a wide range of people, from Fidel Castro to the Mafia, if the conspiracy theorists are to be believed.

These men with guns were clearly pursuing political aims, as were the killers of American black activist Malcolm X and Italian Prime Minister, Aldo Moro and Indian premier, Indira Gandhi.

Malcolm X was in trouble with everyone, from

his own former colleagues in the black separatist movement, the Nation of Islam, to government agencies wary of his leftist tendencies and the Mafia, irritated at his efforts to clean up black inner-city areas, promote black pride and eliminate their lucrative trade in drugs in the ghettos.

Aldo Moro was a victim of the murky world of Italian politics, a world of smoke and mirrors and, at the time, bribery and corruption. It is little surprise that organisations such as the Brigati Rossi – the Red Brigades – emerged with violent aims that included striking at the beating heart of Italian politics.

Indira Gandhi was a victim of the extremely volatile situation in her country at the time that had been caused by the occupation of the Golden Temple at Amritsar by Sikh militants and its violent ending when the Indian army moved in to clear the temple compound. She stubbornly refused to dispense with her Sikh bodyguards, despite warnings from those around her, and those same bodyguards shot her dead.

It remains unclear, however, why James Earl Ray shot Martin Luther King on his hotel balcony on 4 April 1968, although, in spite of the obfuscation of Ray at the time, it seems likely that racial and political reasons were behind it. Whether he acted alone or was sponsored by some shadowy individual or group is unlikely ever to be known.

The celebrity stalker is an entirely different type of killer. Like Mark Chapman, the killer of John Lennon, he can be an obsessive fanatic who in his twisted mind craves the kind of fame that his target has achieved or perhaps feels slighted by some action of their erstwhile hero. Chapman predicted to a fellow worker five years before he killed Lennon that one of their group was going to be very famous in five years' time. Of course, he meant none other than himself.

Naturally, there is always a fascination with anything involving celebrities, even their murders, whether they are the victims or the perpetrators. Phil Spector had for many years been a shadowy has-been in the music world. Granted, his joyous musical achievements in the nineteen-sixties will undoubtedly grace the airwaves forever, but since then he had increasingly become better known for waving guns around drunkenly in recording studios. What was less well known was his penchant for keeping women he had dated in his house at gunpoint long after they had expressed the desire to go home. Lana Clarkson was shot at his house in 2003 and Spector became known as a murderer as well as the inventor of the 'wall of sound'

Of course, we have a morbid fascination for celebrity death, especially when that death is shrouded in mystery. Headline writers sharpen their wits and fans scour the media, devouring every column inch in a desperate search for the slightest hint of what might actually have happened. When movie director William Desmond Taylor was found shot dead in his Hollywood villa in 1922, the list of possible killers was extensive and, indeed, speculation continues to this day about who actually fired the bullet that brought his glittering career to an end. But killers can also be celebrities. Men such as Wild Bill Hickok, Jesse James and John Dillinger became stars through their nefarious activities and their deaths all caused a sensation at the time.

Bugsy Siegel was a handsome, starlet-dating Hollywood A-lister who built the Flamingo Hotel and laid the foundations for the gambling paradise of Las Vegas, but he was also a psychopathic killer, a gangster who had been a leading light of Murder Inc. – the Mafia's enforcement arm – with his childhood friend, Meyer Lansky. When a bullet found him, it was not fired by a stalker or a fan; far from it. The shooter who lurked in the bushes outside his house was a professional hitman contracted by his former Mob colleagues as punishment for what they believed to be Siegel's appropriation of monies they had loaned to him to build the hotel.

Snipers and Shooters looks at four different types of shooting deaths, those caused by the random maniac, the military or police marksman, the assassin and the celebrity shooter. The gun is responsible for all of these and for tens of thousands of deaths in the United States, alone, every year. However, perhaps the slogan often rolled out by the gun lobby has at least an element of truth to it – 'Guns don't kill people; people kill people'.

PART ONE

RANDOM SHOOTERS

HOWARD UNRUH

In German, the name 'Unruh' means 'unrest', an appropriate title for the creator of the mayhem wrought on the quiet Cramer Hill area of Camden, New Jersey on 6 September 1949 and horrified America and the world. Twenty-eight-year-old Howard Unruh's fifteen minutes of carnage was the first instance of single episode mass-murder in US history, but it was an episode that would in later years be joined by names like Columbine and Virginia Tech in the annals of crime.

It had been building up for some time. He felt as if he was being constantly slighted by neighbours, that they were talking about him behind his back. Increasingly reclusive, he was considered to be a 'mama's boy', and neighbourhood teenagers teased him, calling him a homosexual and generally making fun of him. The night before that fateful day, he had gone to the twenty-four-hour Family Theater in Philadelphia and watched a double feature three times. Leaving the theatre at three in the morning, he went home. On arriving there, however, he discovered that the outside gate a friend of his mother's had installed the previous day had been stolen. The gate had been needed because the only other way to gain access to the apartment he shared with his mother, Freda, was by using the gate owned by their neighbours, Rose and Maurice Cohen. The use of the gate had become a matter of some contention because Rose Cohen claimed that Howard often left it open and when they argued about it, the Cohens escalated the issue, threatening to stop him using the gate altogether if he did not stop playing loud music at night.

Unruh was furious. 'When I came home last night and found my gate had been taken,' he said, 'I decided to shoot all of them so I would get the right one.'

When he woke up at eight o'clock the following morning, his mother felt there was something wrong, but, as ever, he remained tight-lipped about what was on his mind. She later described him as seeming to be in a trance of some kind and at one point she felt frightened when she surprised him in the living room and he spun round wielding a wrench as if he was about to strike her with it. She had been frightened of her son for some time, scared most of all by the look that sometimes came into his eyes. She felt as if when he stared at her, he had no idea who she was.

That morning, she left the house, walking to the home of some friends with whom she would share her fears about her son. Unruh, meanwhile, continued with his preparations, checking the 9mm Luger that he had purchased for just $37.50 at a sporting goods store in Philadelphia. He had only thirty-three rounds of ammunition, but he reckoned that would be enough for him to do what he wanted to do.

Shortly after nine o'clock, he left the house.

He walked towards town, coming upon a bread delivery truck at the corner of Harrison and 32nd Street. The driver was sitting at the wheel filling in some paperwork as Unruh approached. He pushed the Luger through the window, but the driver quickly tumbled backwards into the pile of breadboxes behind him. Unruh pulled the trigger but missed. He turned and walked on. When the driver cautiously raised himself up again, he saw two children playing in the street. He ran out, grabbed them and threw them into the back of the truck. He then drove off down the street, hoping to be able to warn others about the madman who was suddenly in their midst.

Unruh, meanwhile, was walking up 32nd Street that would take him back in the direction of the house in which he and his mother lived. He had a few scores to settle on the way, however, and he would also take care of anyone else who happened to get in his way.

The first establishment he came to was a shoe repair shop. Inside, twenty-seven-year-old John Pilarchik was working on a child's shoe. Unruh walked up to him and from a distance of about a yard, pumped two bullets into him, one in the stomach and one in the head. Pilarchik fell to the ground dead as a terrified little boy, also in the shop, scurried to safety behind the counter. Ignoring the boy, Unruh turned and left the shop. The bread delivery man had been a bonus; Pilarchik had been on his list.

Out on the street, screams began to echo off the shop fronts, as people started to realise that the noises they were hearing were not a car backfiring. Unruh, meanwhile, had turned his attention to the barbershop owned by thirty-three-year-old Clark Hoover. Hoover was leaning over a young boy whose hair he was cutting, his mother seated nearby. The gunman walked in, pointed his gun at Hoover, said, 'I've got something for you,' and fired twice. His first bullet hit the boy in the head, killing him and the second killed the barber. The boy's mother began to scream while the other children in the shop panicked and ran into the street.

Outside again, Unruh fired at a boy looking out

of the upstairs window of a nearby building, but missed. He tried the door of the local bar but its occupants had been quick-witted enough to lock it and were now cowering in fright behind upturned tables inside. The owner of the bar ran upstairs to his apartment to find the .38 pistol he kept there.

The nearby restaurant was also locked and that left the pharmacy owned by his next-door neighbours, the hated Cohens. Just as he was about to enter it, insurance agent, James Hutton, on the way out, blocked his path. He greeted Unruh and the killer replied, 'Excuse me, sir.' Hutton hesitated for a split second too long and Unruh opened fire. As he later said, 'That man didn't act fast enough. He didn't get out of my way.'

Realising what was going on, the Cohens fled upstairs from their shop to their apartment. Rose attempted to hide in a closet in the bedroom but Unruh pumped three bullets through the closed door. Then he opened it and shot her in the head at point-blank range. Maurice Cohen's sixty-three-year-old mother had run to the telephone to call the police but Unruh found her and shot her twice.

Maurice, meanwhile, had leapt from a window on to the roof of a porch. Unruh leaned out of the window and shot him and he fell to the ground below. Unruh turned and ran down the stairs and outside finished off the wounded man with another shot. At least the Cohens' twelve-year-old son had survived, though, bundled into a closet upstairs before Unruh had arrived.

He entered the home of the Harries, nearby, wounding both Mrs. Harrie and her sixteen-year-old son, Armond.

Back out on 32nd Street, he saw a vehicle pulled up alongside James Hutton's body. Before the driver Alvin Day could do anything, Unruh leaned through the window of his car and shot him dead.

He was his tenth victim of the morning but others quickly followed.

A car was stationary at a traffic light across the street. Unruh calmly walked over to it, shooting dead its woman driver and her mother who was seated next to her. A twelve-year-old boy in the back seat was seriously wounded. He walked back alongside the car to the one behind it and shot its driver, Charlie Peterson, but only wounding him. As Peterson crawled from his vehicle in search of help, Unruh was firing at a grocery store.

At that point, the bar owner, Frank Engel leaned out of his upstairs window and shot at Unruh, believing he hit him. But it did not seem to make much difference to the shooter who moved on relentlessly to the tailor's shop, owned by a man called Zegrino. The tailor's new wife – they had only been married for three weeks – fell to her knees and pleaded with him not to shoot her. She was wasting her breath. He pulled the trigger, shooting her at point blank range.

His last victim was a two-year-old boy, Tommy Hamilton, who had the misfortune to be looking out the window as Unruh passed. He tried the restaurant again but still could not gain entry. In the distance he could make out the sound of approaching sirens. It was time to go home and wait.

Twelve people had been killed in the space of just fifteen horrific minutes – a number that would become thirteen in a few hours when another victim died in hospital – and four were badly wounded.

Inside his apartment, he barricaded the door and reloaded his gun. As police officers began to arrive on the scene, neighbours identified him as Howard Unruh. An armed cordon was established around the building at 3202 River Road, officers taking up their positions having to dodge the occasional bullets that Unruh fired at them from the windows of the apartment. Sharpshooters crawled up onto nearby roofs, hoping to get a clean shot at the killer.

Meanwhile, a crowd of close to a thousand people began to gather at a safe distance behind the police cordon.

Police officers began to fire into the building in what was described by one newspaper as a 'rain of gunfire'. At one point, an officer claimed that he had hit him. But still Unruh remained inside.

Remarkably, a newspaper reporter managed to place a telephone call to Unruh. When asked how many people he thought he had killed, he replied, 'I don't know yet – but it looks like a pretty good score.' When asked why he was killing people, Unruh replied, 'I don't know. I can't answer that yet.' He finished by saying that a couple of friends were coming to get him and hung up the phone. No one ever knew who those people were or if they even existed.

Eventually, police began tossing tear gas canisters through the windows and Unruh was forced to leave get out of the house. Marksmen tensed as he emerged but he unarmed and surrendered quietly. As he was led through the crowd, they bayed for blood, threatening to lynch him.

Naturally, the first thought was that he was insane, but his army records suggested otherwise. He had served for three years during the war seeing action at the Battle of the Bulge and elsewhere. The only strange thing about his military service was that he kept a diary of all the Germans he had killed, recording how they were shot and what they looked like when dead.

His childhood had been fairly normal although he was reportedly introverted and moody. But he went to church every Sunday, a practice he continued until several months before he embarked upon his rampage. He had only ever dated one girl but there were reports that he was depressed after being involved in 'homosexual liaisons' in a movie theatre. His main interest, however, was guns and he spent hours target shooting in his basement.

He was interrogated for hours and it was only when he stood up after this that it was noticed that his right side was covered in blood. He had been hit, but whether by Frank Engel or the policeman could not be ascertained as doctors were unable to remove the bullet.

Howard Unruh was sent to the New Jersey Hospital for the Insane where he remained until his death aged eighty-eight in 2009.

His last public utterance about that dreadful day in September were, 'I had been thinking about killing them for some time. I'd have killed a thousand if I'd had bullets enough.'

Charles Whitman

Although he had been through some rough times, Charlie Whitman seemed, on the surface, to be a pillar of the community. Working as a bill collector for a finance company and then as a bank teller in order to fund his architectural engineering studies at the University of Texas, he filled his leisure hours by volunteering with a local Boy Scout group. While a teenager, he had, in fact, been one of the youngest-ever Eagle Scouts. The journals he kept, however, told a somewhat different story. The inadequacies he felt led to him devising numerous self-improvement schemes, all designed to help him become the kind of man his domineering and violent father always wanted him to be.

C. A. Whitman was a plumber who prided himself on having worked hard to earn everything he had. And, indeed, the family were fairly well off and were liked by their neighbours in Lake Worth, Florida. But inside his home, C. A. was a strict disciplinarian, not averse to beating his wife while his three sons lived in fear of his temper and his impossibly high expectations of them.

Charlie had finally escaped his difficult upbringing in 1959 when, aged eighteen, he had enlisted in the United States Marine Corps after his father had almost killed him by beating him and throwing him in the family swimming pool after he had come home drunk one night.

He was assigned to Guantanamo Naval Base and began his military career with flying colours, passing exams, winning a Good Conduct Medal and the Marine Corps Expeditionary Medal as well as becoming an excellent marksman. Sadly, that would come in useful later. Having been awarded a scholarship through the Naval Enlisted Science Education Program, he was admitted to the University of Texas at Austin. The aim of his course was to teach engineers who were officer potential.

Whitman was soon in trouble, however. He was arrested for poaching deer, and he was also gambling heavily and neglecting his college work. Things improved when he married fellow student Kathy Leissner in August 1962, but the Navy had had enough of him and his scholarship was withdrawn. He was sent to Camp Lejeune in North Carolina while his new wife remained behind in Austin to complete her studies.

By now, he was sick of the Navy and furious

when he found out that his time at university did not count towards his active duty enlistment. He began to seriously go off the rails, eventually being court-martialled for gambling, loan-sharking, for possessing a gun and threatening a colleague who owed him money. He was convicted, sentenced to ninety days hard labour and demoted from lance corporal back to private.

Given an early release from the Navy in December 1964, largely thanks to his father pulling strings, he returned to Austin to resume his studies.

While at university, he was financially dependent on Kathy as well as his father who often sent him money and expensive gifts. But this dependence infuriated him and emphasised to him even more the extent to which he was a failure. He would take it out on Kathy, beating her in the same way that his father had with his mother. Eventually, Kathy suggested that he needed help and insisted that he should seek counselling.

His mental state deteriorated further with the news that his father and mother had separated. Eventually, they would divorce. He agreed to see a doctor who prescribed him Valium and recommended that he see a psychiatrist.

Dr Maurice Heatly recognised that Charles

Whitman was an angry man, but although Charlie described a fantasy in which he climbed to the top of the tower on the university campus and took pot shots at people below with a deer rifle, the psychiatrist did not consider him to be a danger. It was of little importance, however, because Charlie failed to turn up for the follow-up session.

He was now working as a research assistant as well as studying and it was taking its toll. In order to remain awake, he started taking the amphetamine, Dexedrine. It was to little avail, however, and his studies began to suffer. More worryingly, his violent fantasies were becoming stronger. He was beginning to live in terror of his own mental state.

Eventually, he snapped.

On 31 July 1966, he purchased binoculars, a Bowie knife and a supply of canned meat. He picked up Kathy from work and they went to see a film before visiting friends. These friends later said that nothing seemed amiss although Charlie was very quiet. Kathy returned to work at six in the evening and Charlie returned home to 906 Jewell Street.

There, he wrote a letter that was to be found after he had committed the acts he talks about in it. 'I don't quite understand what it is that compels me to type this letter. Perhaps it is to leave some vague reason for the actions I have recently performed.' He described the perilous state of his mind: 'I've been having fears and violent impulses.' He added that he wanted people to know what drove him to do what he did. 'After my death, I wish an autopsy to be performed to see if there's any mental disorder.' He then gave details of the horror he planned to perpetrate in the next twenty-four hours. He knew he was going to die, he said, and did not want his wife or his mother to go on living alone after he was gone, knowing what he had done.

At 9.30 pm, he picked Kathy up from work. The night was hot and he called his mother to ask if they could come over and share her air conditioning, but Kathy was tired and decided to go to bed. Whitman left for his mother's apartment at around midnight.

He killed her after a brief struggle by strangling her with a length of rubber tubing and then stabbing her with a knife. He also struck her on the back of the head with an unknown object.

Returning home, he walked into the bedroom and stabbed his wife three times in the chest as she slept. He sat down with the letter he had begun earlier. '3 am,' he wrote. 'BOTH DEAD.' He continued, blaming his actions on his father and composing individual notes to him and his two brothers.

At around nine the following morning, Whitman went shopping, buying:

> .30 M-1 carbine, a 12-gauge shotgun, and a foldaway trolley. His arsenal already consisted of a .35 calibre Remington rifle, a 6mm Remington rifle with a scope, a .357 Magnum Smith & Wesson revolver, a 9mm Luger pistol, and a Galesi-Brescia pistol. He packed a trunk with tinned food, a radio, water, petrol, a notebook and pen, a compass, a hatchet, a hammer, food, two knives, a flashlight and 1,000 rounds of ammunition.

He put it all in his Chevrolet and drove to the University of Texas campus.

Dressed in grey overalls and posing as a maintenance man, he got into the 307-foot tall tower with his trolley and trunk filled with all his equipment. He ascended to the twenty-seventh floor where he accosted receptionist Edna Townsley and bludgeoned her to the floor with the butt of one of his rifles. He pulled his trolley onto the observation deck but as he did so, a group of visitors poured out of the lift. Three blasts from his sawn-off shotgun killed Marguerite Lamport and teenager Mark Gabour and seriously wounded Mark's mother and brother. Whitman barricaded the door and then shot the still-breathing Mrs. Townsley in the head before finally going out onto the deck. The plaza below was busy as people went about their normal business. It ended at 11.45 when Whitman's first shot rang out, hitting student Alex Hernandez in the leg. Another three shots and another three students crumpled to the ground. Someone immediately called the police telling them that there was a gunman on the tower.

The first respondent was traffic cop Billy Speed who had been busy nearby, but jumped in his patrol car as soon as the dispatcher put out the message. He pulled into the campus soon after the shooting had started. He leapt from his vehicle but as he was running towards the tower, Whitman brought him down with one lethal shot. The bullet hit Officer Speed in the shoulder but travelled down into his chest, killing him instantly.

For the following twenty minutes, the bullets flew regularly and accurately, Whitman making full use of his Navy training. Pregnant eighteen-year-old Claire Wilson fell to the ground wounded, the bullet killing her unborn child; her friend, Thomas Eckman, trying to ascertain if she was alright, was killed by a bullet in the chest as he kneeled over her; visiting physics professor, Dr Hamilton Boyer, was killed by a bullet in the back and Peace Corps trainee, Thomas Ashton, was killed by one to the chest.

By now, the plaza resembled a battlefield with wounded people strewn across it and others screaming and diving for cover, cowering behind whatever shelter they could locate.

More police arrived, sealing off the tower and evacuating as many of the wounded as they safely could. Charlie Whitman, meanwhile, turned his attention to nearby Guadalupe Street, shooting father of six Harry Walchuk who would later die during surgery. Paul Sonntag had taken cover with his girlfriend, Claudia Rutt, but stood up at one point, shouting to her that he could see the gunman. He was killed by a bullet in the mouth. When Claudia tried to help him she was killed by a shot to the chest.

Electrical repairman Roy Dell Schmidt died running towards his truck and seventeen-year-old student Karen Griffith survived for a week before succumbing to a shot in the lung. Police tried to get a shot at Whitman from a light aircraft and from a helicopter but they were unsuccessful. Three police officers succeeded, however, in making it safely across the plaza to the tower. An ex-serviceman, Allen Crum, who was hiding there, was given a rifle. The four men took the lift up to the floor on which the observation deck was situated and then crept their way along to where Whitman was holed up.

They split into two groups and circled the deck in opposite directions, believing that they had Whitman trapped somewhere between them. Just before reaching the southwest corner of the deck, Crum somehow accidentally discharged his weapon. At that moment, however, Officer Ramiro Martinez leapt around the corner and discharged all six rounds from his .38 pistol at the shooter who was roughly fifty feet away. Officer Houston McCoy emerged from behind Martinez and fired two shots with his 12-gauge shotgun that hit Whitman in the neck, head and left side. Martinez tossed his empty revolver to the ground, snatched McCoy's shotgun and ran towards Whitman, firing point-blank into his upper left arm. He threw the shotgun to the ground and began screaming, 'I got him!'

Sixteen people lost their lives as a result of Charles Whitman's actions that day while another thirty-two were wounded.

Whitman got his wish when an autopsy was carried out on his body. He was found to have been suffering from a brain tumour. Results from the subsequent Governor's report investigation revealed the tumour was a glioblastoma, a type of tumour that, according to the report, 'conceivably could have contributed to his inability to control his emotions and actions'.

Mark Essex

Africa greets you. On 31 December 1972, aprx. 11 pm, the downtown New Orleans Police Department will be attacked. Reason – many, but the death of two innocent brothers will be avenged. And many others.

P.S. Tell pig Giarrusso the felony action squad ain't shit.
Mata

The handwritten note on which this was written, had been delivered to New Orleans television station WWL sometime after 2 January 1973 but had not actually been opened and read until 6 January. By that date, the letter's writer, Mark Essex, had been killed by more than 200 bullets fired by marksmen in a Marine helicopter and nine people, including five police officers, had been killed while thirteen others had been wounded.

Mark James Robert Essex was born in Emporia, Kansas, in 1949 and after dropping out of Emporia State University, had enlisted in the United States Navy as a dental technician in January 1969. While many of his contemporaries were sent to fight in

Vietnam, he was given a relatively comfortable assignment at Imperial Beach Naval Air Station in San Diego. Essex was not happy, however. Soon after arriving at Imperial Beach, he began to complain about racial discrimination and was on the wrong end of disciplinary action on several occasions after getting into fights with white sailors.

It was a time of change in the struggle for civil rights in America. The non-violent approach to civil rights protest as advocated by the recently assassinated Martin Luther King had given way to a more militant style of protest at the forefront of which was the revolutionary African-American political grouping, the Black Panthers. When Essex became interested in this movement, his attitude seemed to change almost immediately. Finally, after less than two years in the navy, he could stand it no more and went absent without leave. Having returned to base, he was court-martialled in January 1971 and discharged a month later.

He headed for New York City where he hooked up with the Black Panthers, immersing himself in their beliefs and culture, devouring their publications about how to wage urban warfare and learning about the types of weapons that were most practical for the urban guerrilla. He returned to Emporia for a while, but was unable to settle there, although he did buy a couple of guns – a Colt .38 revolver and a Ruger Model .44 Magnum carbine.

By August 1972, he had decided that he was finished with Emporia. He packed his bags, including his guns, and headed south, to New Orleans.

He was ready for action.

A few minutes before 11 pm on Sunday 31 December – New Year's Eve – Essex parked his blue 1963 Chevrolet in the 2800 block of Perdido Street, leaving the keys in the ignition, ready for a quick getaway, if necessary. It was about a block from the headquarters of the New Orleans Police Department.

The building known as Central Lockup, the location where prisoners were processed when they were arrested, was at the corner of Perdido and South White Streets. At this time of year it was a busy place and if you were hunting police officers there were few better places.

He was carrying his Colt .38 from which he had filed off the serial number, a gas mask, a couple of strings of firecrackers – for diversionary purposes – a roll of electrical wire, a couple of cans of lighter fluid, a pair of work gloves, a ton of ammo and his Ruger .44 Magnum rifle.

He crept along Perdido Street, keeping to the shadows, his rifle held down parallel with his leg to keep it from sight if anyone passed him, and made his way into a dark vacant lot directly across from the Central Lockup. About a hundred yards away was the gate to the Lockup and he had a clear view of it as he got down on the grass in the lot, rested his rifle butt on his shoulder and levelled the gun, ready to fire.

At almost eleven o'clock, he opened fire, bullets flying amongst the police officers milling about inside the entrance to the building. As they scattered and scrambled for safety, a bullet smashed into the chest of nineteen-year-old unarmed police cadet, Alfred Harrell. He would die in hospital later that night. The bullet travelled through his body and out again, ricocheting into the ankle of another officer who collapsed to the floor.

The Ruger only held five bullets and with four of them spent, Essex leapt to his feet and retreated into the darkness at the rear of the vacant lot. He failed to notice, however, that he had dropped his .38. After running a short distance, he stopped, reloaded and fired another couple of times but failed to hit anything. He then ran towards the expressway behind the lot, scaling a link fence and running across the interstate. He entered the area of Gert Town across the road, a rough neighbourhood where even police officers had to be careful.

He tried to break into a warehouse, firing into the lock but failing to dislodge it. Instead, he ran across the street into the Burkhart building, a single-storey warehouse and factory. He smashed a window and clambered in. The police were alerted by the alarm company that a break-in was in progress and a patrol car was dispatched immediately.

At around quarter past eleven, officers Edwin Hosli and Kenneth Blappert arrived at the Burkhart building, little realising that the killer from earlier at Central Lockup was waiting about thirty feet from them with the barrel of his rifle resting on the windowsill.

As Officer Hosli stepped out, Essex took aim and shot him in the back. More bullets shattered the car's windscreen as Hosli's partner threw himself across the front seat. Then all was silent and by the time backup arrived there was no sign of the sniper. Officer Hosli would die in hospital two months after that horrific night.

Amongst other things, a trail of unused cartridges were found that led officers to the 1st New Saint Mark Baptist Church on South Lopez Street. It seemed obvious to some of the more experienced officers present that it was a trap and that the sniper had deliberately laid the bullets and was waiting to pick them off. Suddenly, however, orders were issued to abandon the search. The residents of Gert Town were becoming antagonised by the officers' search tactics leading senior officers to become concerned that rioting might break out.

Two days after the shooting at the Central Lockup, on Tuesday, 2 January, at around 6 pm, Essex walked into Joe's Grocery Store, about three blocks from the church. He bought a razor but the owner, his suspicions aroused, called the police. The following day there was another tip-off that he was hiding in another church on South Lopez. When officers arrived on the scene, they found substantial amounts of evidence that their suspect had been there – bloodstains from a cut hand and a bag of .38 bullets – but Essex was long gone.

On 7 January, he returned to Joe's Grocery Store where he shot the white owner who had spoken to the police but failed to kill him. Outside on South White Street, he came upon a 1968 Chevrolet Chevelle with the engine running. He ordered the owner out at gunpoint, hissing at him 'I don't want to kill you. I'm just killing honkies today…'

He sped to the Howard Johnson Hotel at 330 Loyola Avenue, a seventeen-storey, concrete rectangle of a building constructed in the 1960s. It consisted of a ground floor reception area, six floors of car park and then, above those, ten floors of hotel rooms. Essex dumped the car on the fourth floor of the car park and, rifle in hand, ran up the fire escape. To his dismay, he discovered that the fire doors that led off the fire escape could not be opened from the outside, but on the eighteenth floor, he found a door wedged open. He ran through it, startling three black housemaids but shouted to them not to worry, again insisting that he was only after white people.

In the corridor, in front of room 1829, he bumped into two white people – twenty-seven-year-old Dr Robert Steagall and his wife Betty who were on their way downstairs to check out of the hotel at the end of a holiday. After a brief struggle, Essex shot Dr Steagall in the chest and then, as she crouched down to help her husband, he placed the barrel of his .44 carbine against Betty Steagall's head and shot her dead.

He went into their room, sprayed lighter fluid around and set fire to it. Then, as he ran out again, past the Steagalls, he dropped a red, green and black African flag to the floor beside their bodies.

He hurried down to the eleventh floor, lighting fires in a number of rooms en route and then shot the hotel's assistant manager in the head when he came to investigate. The hotel's general manager, Walter Collins, was gunned down on the tenth floor as he, too, came to find out what was going on. He would die three weeks later in hospital.

As police officers and firefighters started to arrive on the scene, responding to numerous calls, Essex entered the eighth floor pool and patio area where he shot guest Robert Beamish. Beamish fell into the pool where he floated for two hours before being found. Astonishingly, he survived.

On the eighth floor, Essex looked out over one of the balconies and saw a firefighter, Tim Ursin, climbing a ladder. Behind him were two policemen, armed with shotguns. Essex leaned over and shot Ursin in the arm. One of the policemen raised his shotgun and blasted it at the gunman, but Essex had ducked back inside.

Police now converged on the area around the hotel and occupied vantage points on nearby high-rises trying to get a bead on the shooter. Essex, meanwhile, remained on the eighth floor, firing intermittently down into Loyola Avenue and at the nearby buildings. From a distance of about 150 feet away and firing at a difficult angle, Essex hit Police Officer Ken Solis on the back of his right shoulder as he tried to control the crowds that had gathered below. When Sergeant Emanuel Palmisano ran to Solis's aid, he too was hit in the back. Two other officers arrived on the scene in their patrol car and in a deadly display of marksmanship, Essex hit and killed one of them, Officer Philip Coleman, with a bullet to the head as he stepped out of his vehicle to help his fallen colleagues.

Essex moved up to the sixteenth floor, still firing at random on people down below. He wounded an ambulance driver and a civil defense fire chief and he killed Officer Paul Persigo with a bullet in the head. He took the stairs all the way to the roof but was unable to blast the lock open. Starting to descend again, he heard police officers coming up from below. He waited for them on the sixteenth floor.

The first man to appear was Deputy Chief of Police Louis Sirgo. Essex shot down at him, killing him with a bullet in the back. He then ran to the other side of the building, once again aiming to get out onto the roof, but this time found an open door and at last gained access.

Police were convinced that there was more than one sniper and two police teams were ordered to go up and isolate them. They would search each floor room by room and hopefully push the snipers onto the roof.

A team eventually burst through onto the roof but the first officer to emerge through the door was shot by Essex who immediately ran for cover in a concrete cubicle above the stairwell. The entire building, apart from the roof, was now secure and senior police officers were relieved to at last know where the sniper was.

Like the rest of the country, Lieutenant General Chuck Pitman was watching the story unfold on the television news. He put a call in to senior officers in New Orleans, offering them the use of a CH-46 military helicopter, an offer they accepted enthusiastically. At 8.50 pm the helicopter was loaded with marksmen and sent into the skies above the city.

As they reached the hotel, the sniper momentarily came into view beneath them, but quickly disappeared again. He had gone back to his hiding place in the alcove at the top of a stairwell. A metal water pipe ran up the back wall of the alcove and each time the aircraft hovered into view, he climbed to the top of the pipe to a position where he could not be seen.

Pitman, flying the helicopter, manoeuvred it away from the building, trying to give the gunman the impression that they were giving up. As it moved away, Essex ran out onto the roof and fired at the helicopter but Pitman adroitly turned it round and flew over the roof once more, a searchlight illuminating a wide area. Caught in the beam, Essex raised his rifle again and fired a bullet into the craft's transmission. Pitman knew they had been hit, but not how bad. Nevertheless, he continued to hold a steady position over the hotel, hovering at ten feet above the roof less than fifty feet from the gunman.

The searchlight beam suddenly captured Essex in its beam and the marksmen in the helicopter opened up. For a few moments, his body seemed to dance as it was riddled by a fusillade of bullets. Then, he crumpled to the ground.

The autopsy would later reveal that he had been hit by more than 200 bullets.

DAVID BERKOWITZ

'SON OF SAM'

It was something of an anti-climax. On 10 August 1977, police had been staking out a building at 35 Pine Street in Yonkers. A man walked out of the building, carrying a paper bag, and walked nonchalantly towards a Ford Galaxie parked on the street. He opened the car door, put the bag on the seat and climbed in. Just as he was about to turn the key in the ignition, however, a police officer appeared from the rear of the car, carrying a gun. As he reached the front of the vehicle, he yelled 'Freeze!' at the driver and pointed the gun at the man's head.

The driver turned slowly to face him, a stupid grin spreading slowly across his face. He was ordered out of the Galaxie and told to face the car with his hands on the roof.

'Now that I've got you,' said the officer, patting him down, 'who have I got?'

'You know,' replied the man in a soft voice.

'No I don't,' said the officer, 'You tell me.'

The driver breathed deeply and still smiling, said slowly, 'I'm Sam. David Berkowitz.'

At last, it was over. The city of New York had been terrorised for more than a year by a killer and now it could breathe a sigh of relief and feel safe again. People – especially young courting couples – had been afraid to walk the streets or sit talking in their cars in case he was out there. During that time, David Berkowitz had randomly murdered six people and wounded seven others, some receiving injuries that would affect them for the remainder of their lives.

His start in life had been difficult. Born Richard David Falco in Brooklyn, New York, he was adopted before he was a week old by hardware store owners, Nathan and Pearl Berkowitz. They called him David.

Always big for his age, the boy was in trouble from an early age, a habitual thief who was also an arsonist. His mother died of breast cancer when he was thirteen and his home life became even more difficult when his father remarried. He and his stepmother did not hit it off. David became introverted and reclusive but when his father abandoned him and moved with his new family to Florida, he was devastated. He responded to his abandonment by slipping deeper into the bizarre fantasy world that he had created for himself.

A spell in the army did not help, ending with an honourable discharge in 1974. His life became meaningless and he became increasingly paranoid, believing people were out to kill him. Meanwhile, his pyromania developed and prior to launching his career as a murderer, he set 1,488 fires in New York, the exact number known from the diary he kept in which he recorded each one.

As his paranoia got worse, he locked himself away in his apartment, covering the walls with crazed messages. Demons in his head were ordering him to kill and telling him that the Cassaras family, from whom he rented his apartment, were also demons. The head of the family, Jack Cassara, the voices in his head told him, was the head of a pack of devil dogs that roamed the streets of New York. Mr Cassara's own dog was named Sam and from him Berkowitz would take his nickname – 'Son of Sam'.

It began at around one in the morning of 29 July 1976. As two girls, eighteen-year-old Donna Lauria and her nineteen-year-old friend, Jody Valenti, sat talking in Jody's car outside the Bronx apartment building where Donna lived with her parents, Donna suddenly noticed the figure of a man standing beside the car's passenger door. He pulled out a pistol from a paper bag and, crouching down, fired five bullets into the vehicle's interior. Donna was hit in the neck but Jody, who was hit in the thigh, slammed her palm down on the car's horn and the shooter took to his heels. The two girls were rushed to hospital, but Donna sadly did not survive the attack.

For investigators, it was the worst possible kind of murder. There was no apparent motive and precious little evidence. They wondered if it had perhaps been a case of mistaken identity, or maybe a gangland killing gone wrong. Their darkest fear was that the murder had been the work of a lone psychopath.

Three months later, he struck again, this time in Queens. Twenty-three-year-old Cal Denaro had parked his Volkswagen Beetle close to the house of Rosemary Keegan whom he had driven home from a party. As they talked, the side window of the car exploded and bullets ripped into the interior. Carl was wounded in the head, but Rosemary had sufficient presence of mind to turn on the engine and slam her foot on the accelerator, speeding away from their mysterious assailant. Carl survived with a piece of his shattered skull replaced by a metal plate.

A month later, after sixteen-year-old Donna DeMasi and her friend, eighteen-year-old Joanne Lomino, got off a bus close to Joanne's house, Donna noticed a man walking behind them. She whispered to Joanne to walk faster but the man gradually came closer to them. As he reached them, he started to ask a question, but he failed to finish the sentence, instead pulling a gun from beneath his coat. He shot the two girls and then emptied the gun by firing randomly at the nearby buildings.

Donna was fortunate. The bullet that hit her had missed her spine by only a few inches. Joanne was less fortunate and would never walk again.

At just after midnight on 30 January 1977, twenty-six-year-old Christine Freund and her fiancé, John Diel, had just got into their car after leaving a wine bar in Queens when their windscreen was shattered by two gunshots. Christine was hit by both bullets and died in hospital a few hours later.

The police departments in the different boroughs in which the shootings had been carried out had been slow in linking them to one perpetrator. Now, having realised they were the work of one man, but finding that there was absolutely nothing to connect the victims, investigators concluded that the shootings were the work of a lone psychopath. A task force was assembled to pursue him.

It mattered little to Berkowitz, however. On 8 March, he shot and killed nineteen-year-old Barnard College student, Virginia Voskerichian, at close range as she walked home from college in the upmarket Forest Hills Gardens area. As he fled the scene, he ran past a man who had witnessed the incident. 'Hi, mister!' he said, smiling, as he ran past the terrified witness.

The bullet was identified as the same as the others and as New Yorkers panicked and stopped going out at night, the police were in turmoil. They had no idea how to prevent such random incidents. No one knew where he might pop up next. A description was issued that said he was a white male, aged between twenty-five to thirty-six, six feet tall, of medium build and with dark hair but it was too vague and could have been any one of hundreds of thousands of men.

On 17 April, a courting couple were sitting in their car close to the Hutchinson River Parkway at three in the morning when a car pulled up alongside them. Valentia Suriani, aged eighteen, and her twenty-year-old boyfriend, Alexander Esau were both shot dead by a man firing from the other vehicle.

This time, the killer left a horrifically crazed message lying on the road, addressed to one of the investigating officers, Captain Joseph Borelli:

Dear Captain Joseph Borrelli,

I am deeply hurt by your calling me a wemon hater. I am not. But I am a monster. I am the 'Son of Sam'. I am a little brat. When father Sam gets drunk he gets mean. He beats his family. Sometimes he ties me up to the back of the house. Other times he locks me in the garage. Sam loves to drink blood. 'Go out and kill,' commands father Sam. 'Behind our house some rest. Mostly young – raped and slaughtered – their blood drained – just bones now. Papa Sam keeps me locked in the attic too. I can't get out but I look out the attic window and watch the world go by. I feel like an outsider. I am on a different wavelength then everybody else – programmed too kill. However, to stop me you must kill me. Attention all police: Shoot me first – shoot to kill or else keep out of my way or you will die! Papa Sam is old now. He needs some blood to preserve his youth. He has had too many heart attacks. 'Ugh, me hoot, it hurts, sonny boy.' I miss my pretty princess most of all. She's resting in our ladies house. But I'll see her soon. I am the 'Monster' – 'Beelzebub' – the chubby behemouth. I love to hunt. Prowling the streets looking for fair game – tasty meat. The wemon of Queens are prettyist of all. It must be the water they drink. I live for the hunt – my life. Blood for papa. Mr Borrelli, sir, I don't want to kill anymore. No sur, no more but I must, 'honour thy father'. I want to make love to the world. I love people. I don't belong on earth. Return me to yahoos. To the people of Queens, I love you. And I want to wish all of you a happy Easter. May God bless you in this life and in the next.

The legend of 'Son of Sam' was born.

A psychological profile of the killer that was compiled was surprisingly accurate – a paranoid schizophrenic, possibly suffering from the delusion that he was in possession of a demonic power; a loner who was unable to make and maintain relationships with women.

Sam next wrote to Jimmy Breslin, a well-known reporter. He promised more mayhem: '*Sam's a thirsty lad. He won't let me stop killing until he gets his fill of blood.*'

It was not long in coming.

Early in the morning of 26 June, twenty-year-old Sal Lupo and his seventeen-year-old girlfriend, Judy Placido, were sitting in their car near the Elephas discotheque in the Bayside area of Queens where they had spent the last few hours. Suddenly, the car was filled with bullets but although both were hit – Judy by three bullets – they survived.

The city waited with baited breath for the anniversary of Sam's first attack, expecting him to mark it somehow, but when it passed without incident there was a sense of relief. It was a false dawn. Two days later, at around 2.35 in the morning of 31 July, Bobby Violante and his girlfriend, Stacy Moskowitz, both aged twenty, were kissing in their car in Brooklyn when a man approached from the other side of the vehicle. He fired into the car, hitting both in the head, before disappearing into a nearby park. Violante survived although he was left almost blind but Stacy died thirty-eight hours later in hospital.

It was his last murder. That night, a woman, Cecilia Davis was walking her dog near the scene of the crime, when she saw two policemen put a parking ticket on a Ford Galaxie parked across the road from her. Shortly after, she watched as a man came running up to the vehicle and, angrily grabbing the ticket, threw it away before leaping into the car and driving off at speed. When she heard about the shooting nearby, she told the police who traced the ticket and the car registration to which it had been made out. The car belonged to David Berkowitz.

Gary and Thaddeus Lewingdon

THE .22-CALIBER KILLINGS

They were the most difficult of all crimes for police to deal with – a series of ten seemingly indiscriminate but brutal murders with little evidence to go on. The difficulty of the investigation was not helped by a false confession and singularly unsuccessful attempts to find some sort of linkage between the victims.

The murders that came to be known as the '.22-caliber Killings' began around 2.30 am on 10 December 1977 when two women, thirty-seven-year-old Joyce Vermilion and thirty-three-year-old Karen Dodrill, were killed by multiple gunshot wounds as they left by the rear door of Forkers Café in Newark, Ohio, where they worked.

The bodies were discovered at eight the following morning after Joyce Vermilion's husband reported her missing, frozen into a snow bank and surrounded by shell casings from a .22-caliber weapon.

Police were baffled by the killings. There seemed to be no reason, not even robbery. They were relieved, therefore, when a twenty-six-year-old go-go dancer,

Claudia Yasko, turned up at a local police station and told officers that the murders had been committed by two men and she had been there at the time.

Yasko was arrested and charged with murder and the two men that she had mentioned were also arrested and charged. It seemed as if they could close the file on this one.

Two months later, however, the killer or killers struck again. On 12 February 1978, three people were found gruesomely murdered in a house at 4187 Ongaro Drive which was situated in a rural area near the city of Columbus in Ohio. Fifty-two-year-old Robert 'Mickey' McCann had been shot twice in the forehead and once in the mouth, head and right leg; his girlfriend, twenty-six-year-old Christine Herdman had been shot in the cheek, the shoulder and twice in the forehead and his seventy-seven-year-old mother Dorothy had been shot a number of times in the mouth as well as in the head and in the right leg. The telephone lines had been cut and the only trace of the killers were shell casings from a .22-calibre gun. Again, there was no motive and an absence of leads.

On 8 April, seventy-seven-year-old Jenkin T. Jones became the next victim. He was shot six times, including two bullets to the head, at his isolated home just outside Granville, Ohio. The killer or killers had also shot dead each of his four dogs. The now-familiar .22 shell casings were found at the scene.

Reverend Gerald Fields was killed during his hours as a part-time security guard at a private club in northwest Fairfield County known as the Wigwam. Again there were .22 shell casings to prove that this murder was almost certainly linked to the others. That fact was confirmed when ballistics tests showed the same weapon had been used in each of the murders committed in 1978. The 1977 murders at Forker's Café had been omitted from these tests as no one made the connection, but there was little doubt that a serial killer, or a team of serial killers, was on the loose.

It seemed logical to investigators to attempt to find links between the victims. It was rare, after all, for a series of crimes such as these to be committed without any connection at all between victims and it was hard, therefore, for investigators to believe they could be random. They investigated whether they might have perhaps been on a jury that had found someone guilty and now either that person or his or her associates were taking terrible revenge. No jury connection came to light, however. Their backgrounds were meticulously investigated to discover whether they perhaps all belonged to the same club or frequented the same bars, cafes, banks, churches or even petrol stations. Again, however, there seemed to be not a single thing to connect them.

Licking County Sheriff, Max Marston, could only answer reporters' questions with the words, 'To the best of my knowledge it is a complete mystery.' All he could suggest was that the motive might have been robbery, but there was little to support that view.

Two more victims were added to the body count three weeks after Gerald Fields was gunned down. Forty-seven-year-old Jerry L. Martin and his fifty-year-old wife, Martha were found dead in their house at 3823 Morse Road in Franklin County. They had each been callously shot in the head a number of times and the usual .22 shell casings added to the disquiet of investigators. They began to wonder if the killings might be the work of a gang or a cult, like the Charles Manson Family who had created mayhem in the Los Angeles area in 1969. At any rate, they began to presume that more than one person was involved in these dreadful murders.

Finally, someone decided to look at old cases and the Forker's Café killings came to investigators' attention. The bullets and casings from that incident were tested and provided a match to the others. It was good news for Claudia Yasko because she and the two men she had implicated had been in custody when the other murders were carried out. They were released, the reason for her confession remaining a mystery until some years later she confessed that she had overheard her boyfriend and Gary Lewingdon discussing the murders and was persuaded that night to go with one of his associates to the murder scene to search for drugs that he believed to be there. Claudia was at the time undergoing treatment for schizophrenia and this, together with her strong recollection of what the murder scene looked like, convinced her that she must have been involved in some way in the killings.

Suddenly, however, the murders stopped. Investigators wondered if the perpetrator(s) had perhaps been arrested and imprisoned for another crime or whether he or she may be dead. They also speculated that they might have come so close to catching them that they had decided to lie low or even bring a halt to their activities. Of course, it could also have been the case that all the victims had been connected after all and they had all been dealt with now. There was no one left to kill.

When a $16,000 reward was put up for information leading to the arrest of the killers, the police department was flooded with tip-offs. They were hard times and a reward such as the one on offer was very tempting for many people. They spent three weeks following up every lead but by the end of that time they were no closer to identifying the murderers and, gradually, officers began to be assigned to other, more recent cases.

They were jolted back to the .22-calibre Killings, however, when another body turned up after a gap of more than six months. On 4 December, fifty-six-year-old Joseph Annick was found dead from five bullet wounds to the chest and stomach. He had been killed while working in his garage and although a different .22 had been used, officers had little doubt that the same person or persons had killed Annick as had killed the previous nine people.

The breakthrough in the case occurred, as is often the way, through a stroke of luck. On 9 December, a seventeen-year-old clerk at Woolco Department Store in Columbus noticed that a credit card being used by a customer was on the list of stolen cards that was kept by the till. She told a managerial trainee, Jeff Slovak, and he managed to detain the man who had proffered the card until the police turned up. The card had belonged to Joseph Annick and was now in the possession of thirty-eight year-old Gary Lewingdon.

Lewingdon had been in the Air Force, serving briefly in Vietnam, but had been discharged in 1962. In the years following, he had been arrested several times for petty larceny, possession of criminal tools, indecent exposure and having a concealed weapon. He had lived with his mother, trying to stay out of trouble but had moved out in 1977 when he married a nightclub waitress. Living in Kirkersville, Ohio, he found work as a repairman for Rockwell International Tool Division in Columbus. He was perfectly situated in Kirkersville, midway between Columbus and the crime locations at Newark and Granville.

While investigators waited for a warrant to search his house, Lewingdon surprised them by launching into a confession to the murder of Joseph Annick. He added that he and his brother Thaddeus had been involved in nine other killings.

Thaddeus, a divorcee with three children, living in nearby Glenford, Ohio, was a graduate of the Cleveland Institute of Electronics and possessed a first-class Federal Communications Commission engineer's licence. He worked as a maintenance man for Columbus Steel Drum and, like his brother, had a record for petty crime.

Thaddeus was brought in and he, too, seemed happy to speak about the murders. He explained how Gary would select a victim and how when they killed they would wear ski masks and gloves and used a homemade silencer on their .22 pistol. He told them that after the killings of Jerry and Martha Martin, he had had enough and started to refuse to take part in attacks on the next few victims suggested by his brother. The two began to argue and eventually fell out. Consequently, he knew nothing about the shooting of Joseph Annick.

Meanwhile, a search of the brothers' homes revealed weapons and several items stolen from the homes of the murdered people, although it still appeared that robbery was not the motive.

On 14 December 1978, Gary and Thaddeus were charged, Gary with twenty felony counts, including ten of murder and Thaddeus with seventeen felonies and nine of murder.

Thaddeus was sentenced to six terms of life imprisonment but died in prison of lung cancer in 1989. Gary received eight life sentences but after his trial, he became psychotic and was sent to the state hospital for the criminally insane. He died of heart failure in 2004. After their initial confessions, neither brother spoke in such detail about their crimes again and their motive for killing ten random people remains unclear to this day.

Michael Ryan

It was a beautiful summer's day in the small market town of Hungerford, situated an hour's drive to the west of London in the lovely Berkshire countryside. With a population of around 5,000, it is a neat, quiet place boasting quaint antique shops and cosy tearooms on its high street.

This particular day, Wednesday, 19August 1987, would change that idyllic view of Hungerford forever. No longer would it be known as a lovely little town near the River Dun. From that day on, it would be notorious as the place where Michael Ryan lost his mind and shot dead sixteen people in the incident that became known as the Hungerford Massacre.

Ryan was an unemployed labourer and antiques dealer who had been born at Savernake Hospital in Marlborough, Wiltshire, not far from Hungerford, in 1960. An only child, and his father having died in 1985, he shared a house with his mother, Dorothy, who worked at the local primary school as a dinner lady. He had been a sullen, quiet child who had been subjected to bullying because of his small stature for his age and his refusal to join in with other children.

At the John O'Gaunt School, which he attended from the age of eleven, he was a poor student and often played truant. Moving on to a technical school, aged sixteen, he fared little better, dropping out to become a caretaker at a girls' school. Meanwhile, his mother spoiled him, buying him cars, and providing him with his first gun, an air rifle.

Ryan had a near-obsession with firearms and survival-ism. He had been issued with a shotgun certificate in 1978 and in 1986 he obtained a firearms certificate that covered the ownership of two pistols. This was extended several times and in July 1987 he applied for and was granted the right to purchase two semi-automatics. By this time, he owned an extensive arsenal of guns that included a Zabala shotgun, a Browning shotgun, a Beretta 92 semi-automatic 9 mm pistol, a CZ ORSO semi-automatic .32 pistol, a 'Type 56' 7.62 x 39mm semi-automatic rifle (a Chinese copy of the Kalashnikov AK-47) and an M1 Carbine .30 7.62 x 33mm semi-automatic rifle (a rare 'Underwood' model). He would use the Beretta and the Type 56 and M1 rifles on the day of the massacre.

By 19 August 1987, Ryan had become irritable and morose. His mother could not get to the bottom of it but thought that it was just the way he was and had always been. That morning, she left home to do some shopping before going to work.

At around noon that day, thirty-five-year-old Susan Godfrey was finishing a picnic in Savernake Forest, a popular local beauty spot, with her children, four-year-old Hannah and two-year-old James. As she packed up, ready to take the children to visit her grandmother who was celebrating her ninety-fifth birthday, she noticed a man watching her from a nearby parked car. He suddenly got out of the car and walked towards Susan and the children. He was dressed entirely in black and had a grim expression on his face. He was carrying a pistol and he was aiming it at her.

Pointing the gun at her, he ordered her to put the children in the car and she hurriedly did as she was told, fumbling with their seatbelts. She turned to the man who ordered her to walk, picking up the groundsheet she and the children had been using.

No one knows what happened after that, apart from the fact that he took her into the woods and pumped thirteen bullets into her body. Dropping the groundsheet, he ran back to his car, driving away and leaving the children to wait for their mother.

After a while, the oldest child, Hannah, unfastened their seatbelts and went to look for their mother. They were found wandering a little later by a woman who called the police when Hannah told her what had happened. An officer found Susan's body 250 yards from the car. As his Vauxhall Astra GTE was low on petrol Ryan pulled into the Golden Arrow Service Station where Kakoub Dean, wife of the owner, was at the cash desk behind a safety glass screen. As Kakoub served another customer, she noticed Ryan outside going to the rear of his car. To her horror, she watched him take a rifle from the boot and drop into a firing position, leveling the weapon directly at her. As he fired she had the presence of mind to duck and the bullet ripped through the glass and ricocheted around the space behind the counter. She dropped to the floor out of sight.

Ryan came into the station and aimed at her again but as she pleaded with him not to fire, his rifle clicked, failing to fire. Three times he pulled the trigger and three times she heard the click. Ryan simply turned round, went out to his car and drove off at speed. She dialed 999.

At around 12.45 pm, Ryan arrived at his house at 4 South View, one of a row of houses in a dismal terrace. People outside heard what sounded like muffled shots coming from inside the house – he was shooting his dogs. Shortly after, he emerged wearing a flak jacket and a headband and carrying a bag filled with food. He climbed into his car and turned the key in the ignition but nothing happened. Incandescent with rage, he got out and pumped four bullets into the boot. He then walked back into the house, emptied a five-litre gallon tank of petrol around the rooms and set fire to it. Within moments, the house was ablaze and threatening the others in the terrace.

Out on the street again, he walked off, the AK-47 dangling from his shoulder and the Beretta in his hand. He immediately saw two of his neighbours, Roland and Sheila Mason chatting. He shot them and both fell to the ground dead. He spotted another neighbour trying to hide in her house and wounded her through a window. He jogged up and down the street, looking for more targets, but he is reported at one point to have told several children to go inside. He walked on, ignoring an elderly woman who had innocently come out to warn him about making so much noise. He walked on.

Encountering fourteen-year-old Linda Maidenhall, he shot her four times, but failed to kill her but then killed Ken Clements who was walking towards South View with his family. He continued on his way, the remainder of the family hiding behind whatever they could find. Police were now searching for him and a police helicopter hovered directly above him issuing instructions to officers to set up roadblocks to prevent traffic from entering the area. Even the fire engine racing towards the blazing buildings in South View was unable to get through.

A police officer, Roger Brereton, was next to die when Ryan opened fire on his patrol car and then fired at another vehicle but only succeeded in wounding its occupants. A man who was gardening on the corner of South View and Fairview Roads was shot dead. Abdul Khan had heard what was happening and had rushed home to make sure his family was alright. He appeared in front of Ryan and was shot three times but lived.

A vehicle approached, carrying the husband of the woman that Ryan had earlier wounded through the window of her house. Ryan fired into the car hitting Ivor Jackson, the woman's husband in the chest and the head. He lived but his work colleague who was driving the car was killed.

At that moment, Ryan's mother returned from work to find her street ablaze and, shortly after, her son standing in front of her, holding a gun. She managed to push her way through and stood in front of him asking him why he was killing people. She was heard to say, 'Don't shoot me,' just before he fired two bullets, hitting her in the leg and the stomach. She fell to the ground and Ryan coolly walked up to her and shot her twice more in the back, killing her.

Police were reluctant to intervene, preferring to wait, instead, for the specialist Tactical Firearms Unit which was en route for Hungerford. Meanwhile, they carefully followed his every move and warned the people of Hungerford to stay indoors.

Ryan now walked across the nearby school playing fields, firing randomly as he went. He wounded an elderly woman and then shot dead twenty-six-year-old Frances Butler as she walked her dog. The M1 was empty now. He threw it to the ground and started using the Beretta and the AK-47. A boy cycled past but his shot missed him. A taxi driver on the way to see his newborn son in hospital had a piece of his skull blown off but survived the assault. A car passed and he killed its two occupants, a man and a woman. It later emerged that they were the parents of the police officer who had paid a visit to Ryan to check him out before he received the licence that permitted him to own more powerful weapons.

The twelfth person to die was a van driver, Eric Vardy, and shortly after, twenty-year-old Sandra Hill was shot dead as she drove past him.

He crossed the road and started firing at a house

at 60 Priory Road, blasting the front door while its elderly occupants, Victor and Myrtle Gibbs cowered inside. As Ryan entered the house, Victor threw himself across Myrtle who was in a wheelchair. Ryan opened fire and Victor died instantly while Myrtle passed away several days later in hospital as a result of her wounds.

He shot from inside at people out in the street, wounding several and then killed the driver of a passing car, Ian Playle, who had circumvented a roadblock by taking a side street as he headed into the centre of Hungerford with his family.

Michael Ryan had now killed fourteen people in just fifteen minutes from the time he had left his blazing house.

Leaving the Gibbs' house, he headed for the place where he had suffered so much when he was younger – John O'Gaunt school. En route, he shot and wounded a man in his garden.

He disappeared from sight at this point for several hours, although it seemed certain that he was in the school. Its third storey offered a terrific vantage point for a shooter, offering a good view of the town. Police converged on the building and waited.

As they tried to establish communication with him they noticed that he had tied a white handkerchief to his rifle and thrown it out of the window, leaving him with only the Beretta. Gradually, they persuaded him to talk and he let them know during these conversations where he had dropped the M1 rifle. He told them he was sorry for shooting his mother and his dogs and said he would not come out until they told him whether his mother was dead. The officer in charge refused to do this, however.

By this point, marksmen positioned around the school had Ryan in their sights and he was ordered not to appear at the window holding a gun or he would be shot. They hoped to take him alive.

He threw the Beretta's magazine out the window but informed them that he still had one bullet. It was clear to them what that bullet was for. The day wore on and as the afternoon turned into evening, they desperately tried to persuade him to give himself up.

At around 6.45, he was heard to say, 'If only my car had started,' as if he would have escaped and so would all of his victims. Then he added the words that have since become famous: 'I wish I had stayed in bed.'

At 6.52 pm, as they waited in grim silence, police officers heard a muffled shot. After waiting for three hours, they entered the building to discover Michael Ryan dead behind a filing cabinet, his gun between his knees.

DAVID GRAY

Sometimes it is the small, trivial things that push us over the edge. One day we will brush them aside and get on with our lives. At other times, they become insurmountable, they take over our minds and our lives and we snap. For David Gray, living in the small, tranquil coastal town, of Aramoana, a settlement of just 261 inhabitants, twenty-seven kilometres north of Dunedin on New Zealand's South Island, it took only a two dollar bank charge levied on him for cashing a cheque to push him over the edge.

Gray was born in 1956 in Dunedin and was brought up in Port Chalmers, a suburb of Dunedin as well as its main port. His father David worked in a factory and his mother was a machinist. At Port Chalmers Primary School and later at the Otago Boys' High School, Gray was a quiet, fairly average student. 'There was nothing frightening about him then,' a fellow pupil said. Since primary school, however, he had been something of a loner, working occasionally as a farmhand, but in the few years leading up to 1990, he had been largely unemployed.

He was deeply affected by the deaths of his parents – his father in 1978 and his mother in 1985. Following his mother's death, he moved from Port Chalmers to the Gray holiday home in Aramoana.

He was a regular customer of Galaxy Books and Records in Dunedin where he purchased military and survivalist books as well as *Soldier of Fortune* magazine, a monthly publication devoted to the worldwide reporting of wars. Its subjects included conventional warfare, low-intensity warfare, counter-insurgency, and counter-terrorism. He also collected guns and possessed a large arsenal that he kept at his house.

In the months leading up to 13 November 1990, Gray's mental state had deteriorated. He had alienated the few friends he had and became increasingly reclusive. He had even been barred from Galaxy Books the previous February after threatening a shop assistant with what appeared to be a shotgun in a cardboard box.

That morning he had travelled into Dunedin to cash a cheque at a bank. When he was charged two dollars for doing so, he was furious and had left the bank in an angry mood. He next visited a gun shop where he placed a hundred dollar deposit on a gun he wanted to buy and that he would collect the following week. His next stop was at a coffee bar, but he was still in a dark mood following his experience at the bank. He got into an argument there and ominously told the owners as he left, 'I'll be back, I'm going to get you. I'll blow you away.'

At about 7.30 that evening, with his mood no better, he got into an argument with his next-door neighbour, Garry Holden. Gray detested Holden mainly because Holden's pets kept dying and Gray was a huge animal-lover.

This particular argument was over a complaint by Gray who claimed that one of Holden's daughters had trespassed on his property. It was not unusual for the two to argue, but on this particular night there was no calming Gray down. Suddenly, he turned and stormed off into his house, returning a few minutes later carrying one of his huge collection of guns, a Chinese-made Norinco AK-47 assault rifle. Without a moment's hesitation, Gray aimed it at a shocked Holden and pulled the trigger. Holden collapsed to the ground dead.

Gray stomped into Holden's house, looking for his daughters. He found nine-year-old Chiquita and shot her, the bullet passing through her arm and then into her chest and finally her abdomen. She now believes that the force of the bullet knocked her through a door allowing her to make her escape, despite the blood flowing from her wounds. She ran to the house of a neighbour, Julie Ann Bryson, passing the body of her father. She later said she had no doubt at that point that he was dead.

She told Julie Bryson that Holden had shot her father and her and that her sister, eleven-year-old Jasmine and Holden's girlfriend's adopted daughter Rewa, also eleven, were still in the house. Bryson jumped in her car and drove to the Holden House, Chiquita beside her, using a towel to staunch the flow of blood. As they approached, she could see smoke billowing from it and realised that Gray had set fire to it with, she feared, the two little girls still inside. Gray, standing outside the blazing building, levelled his weapon and began firing at the car. She put her foot down and drove past, managing to escape.

His shooting spree now became random; he was shooting at anyone who came within range. A utility vehicle was passing the house when the driver spotted the blaze. He stopped to help but when he started to get out, Gray opened fire on him.

Another vehicle approached, a car belonging to the Percy family, inside which were twenty-six-year-old Vanessa, her forty-two-year-old husband

Ross, their six-year-old son Dion and their daughter, four-year-old Stacy. Dion's six-year-old friend, Leo Wilson and a family friend, forty-one-year-old Alek Tali had accompanied them on the fishing trip from which they were returning. Gray spun round, directing a fusillade of bullets at the car, killing Ross, Vanessa and Dion Percy as well as Leo Wilson and Alek Tali. Stacy, seriously wounded, was the only one to survive.

Gray walked off, coming to the house belonging to sixty-nine-year-old Tim Jamieson. He pushed the front door open and walked in, shooting dead a shocked Jamieson and a friend who was visiting, seventy-one-year-old Victor Crimp. As he walked out, he caught sight of forty-five-year-old Jim Dickson who was out searching for his dog Patch who had run off earlier in the evening. Gray raised his rifle and Dickson crumpled to the ground dead.

He had now claimed the lives of eleven people.

Helen Dickson, Jim's mother and another neighbour, sixty-two-year-old Chris Cole, came running out into the street to find out what all the noise was. As soon as he saw them, Gray opened fire and they dived for cover, but he succeeded in hitting Chris Cole.

Helen Dickson who had hidden herself in a ditch

at the front of her house, used its cover to crawl back to the house to phone for help. Courageously, she then crawled back along the ditch to console the wounded Chris Cole who, sadly, would later die from her wounds in hospital. They waited for the sounds of sirens, but none came. Helen Dickson once again made the perilous journey back to the house on her stomach to once again dial the emergency number. She was reassured that help was on its way.

By this time, darkness was falling but police officers were at last beginning to converge on the scene. Amongst the first was Sergeant Stewart Guthrie, the officer in charge of the Port Charles police station. Guthrie, armed with a .38 Smith & Wesson police revolver, and the local fire chief, Russell Anderson, who had borrowed a rifle from one of the residents, made their way cautiously towards Gray's house. As they got closer, Sergeant Guthrie signalled to Anderson to cover the front of the house while he took care of the rear. Behind the two men, other officers began to quietly move towards the house, forming a tight cordon around it.

Guthrie, concealed in some sand dunes at the back of the small building, caught sight of Gray in the house and warned everyone to be careful and to remain alert. Gray unexpectedly emerged at the rear of the house and Guthrie shouted a warning to him before firing a shot. Gray screamed, 'Don't shoot!' and Guthrie, relieved, thought that the gunman was at last bringing an end to the carnage. Suddenly, however, Gray opened fire in the direction of the policeman, a bullet hitting Guthrie in the head and killing him instantly.

Officers of the Armed Offender Squad (AOS) had arrived by this time and they began to seal off the settlement. But the night wore on and Gray remained at large.

The Special Tactics Group (STG), New Zealand's counter-terrorist force arrived at Dunedin Airport in the early hours of the following morning and were rushed by helicopter to Aramoana, making sure they hovered out of range of a bullet from Gray's rifle, a lesson learned after he had fired on a low-flying news helicopter earlier. They landed and split into two groups, mingling with the officers of the AOS who had been in position now for several hours and being brought up to speed on the horrific events of the previous evening.

A stun grenade and tear gas canister were tossed at Gray's window, but he had cleverly placed a mattress up against the window to deal with just such an eventuality and they bounced harmlessly to the ground outside the window. Meanwhile, Gray, walking from window to window was firing randomly at the out-side world.

At 5.50 in the evening of 14 November, almost twenty-two hours after Gray had shot Garry Holden, he suddenly burst out of the door of the house, carrying the assault rifle with which he had done so much damage the previous day and screaming, 'Kill me! Fucking kill me!'

The officers had been told that if Gray was seen armed, he was to be shot and as soon as he appeared, there was a fusillade of bullets in which he was hit five times – in the eye, neck, chest and twice in the groin. Incredibly, however, he had still not given up despite the blood seeping from his wounds and fought strenuously with the officers who tried to put handcuffs on him. He cursed them for failing to kill him. Twenty minutes later, however, he got his wish when he died from his extensive wounds.

David Gray had shot dead eleven people and Holden's daughter Jasmine and his girlfriend's adopted daughter, Rewa, had both died in the blaze at Holden's house.

Three days after the incident, Gray's house was mysteriously burnt to the ground. His family re-

Thomas Dillon

'I am the murderer of Jamie Paxton ... Jamie Paxton was a complete stranger to me. I never saw him before in my life and he never said a word to me that Saturday. The motive for the murder was this – the murder itself ... Paxton was killed because of an irresistable (sic) compulsion that has taken over my life. I knew when I left my house that day that someone would die by my hand. I just didn't know who or where ... Technically, I meet the defintion (sic) of a serial killer (three or more victims with a cooling off period in between) but I'm an average looking person with a family, job, and home just like yourself. Something in my head causes me to turn into a merciless killer with no conscience. Five minutes after I shot Paxton I was drinking a beer and had blacked out all thoughts of what I had just done out of my mind. I thought no more of shooting Paxton than shooting a bottle at the dump.'

They were the worst kind of murders for police to investigate. Each of the five victims had been alone when he was murdered. There were no witnesses and no one saw any vehicles in the vicinity at the times of the killings. The men who died were absolutely unconnected with each other and they seemed to have been chosen at random, each in a different county in east-central Ohio.

The above letter was delivered to a Belmont County newspaper, the *Times Leader* around the first anniversary of the pointless murder of twenty-one-year-old Jamie Paxton, who was killed while out hunting deer on 10 November 1990. It taunted investigators with the words, *'Don't feel bad about not solving this case. You could interview till doomsday everyone that Jamie Paxton ever met in his life and you wouldn't have a clue to my identity … With no motive, no weapon, and no witnesses you could not possibly solve this crime.'*

Water department draughtsman, Thomas Dillon, enjoyed an elaborate fantasy life in which he was a multi-millionaire, or a Superbowl-winning quarterback, or the lead singer of The Beatles. More dangerously, he also fantasised, during the hundreds of miles that he drove on weekends, that he was a special-forces soldier who was out stalking enemy targets.

He killed for the first time near the small town of New Philadelphia, a hundred miles south of Cleveland, on 1 April 1989. Thirty-five-year-old Donald Welling was out jogging in the countryside when Dillon shot him dead. He claimed he did it in response to a voice in his head that urged him to shoot Welling. Later, he told investigators that Welling spoke to him as he pulled up alongside him. 'What's up?' he said and from just five feet away, Dillon fired.

He next killed Jamie Paxton, about whose murder he wrote to the *Times Leader*, in November 1990, outside St. Clairsville, a small settlement close the border with West Virginia.

Just over two years later, on 14 March 1992, Dillon shot dead thirty-year-old Massachusetts hunter and father of three, Kevin Loring, in Muskingum County but it would be almost four months before he again felt the urge to kill. Forty-nine-year-old Claude Hawkins was fishing in Coshocton County when Dillon drove past him. He claims that he heard a voice inside his head urging him to 'go back and get him'. Dillon followed the urge and shot the unsuspecting fisherman 'right in the back'.

A month later forty-four-year-old Gary Bradley was also shot dead while fishing, close to Noble County. Police noted that each of the men, apart from Kevin Loring, had been gunned down during a weekend. Loring had died on a Wednesday – during a vacation that Dillon had. They had each been killed with a high-powered rifle, fired in all probability from a nearby road. Apart from that, however, there was precious little else to go on, no forensic evidence at the murder scenes and the killer had been careful not to leave behind spent shell casings. The first break came a year after Paxton's murder with the letter sent to the newspaper which had been put into the mail outside a post office in Martins Ferry.

In the absence of any other developments, the FBI's Behavioural Sciences Unit was called in to try to piece together a profile of the perpetrator. They deduced that he was an educated white male – in this detail they were correct as Dillon possessed a college degree. He enjoyed killing animals and probably also liked setting fires. Dillon later confessed to killing more than a thousand household pets and farm animals and to being responsible for more than a hundred fires.

They wrongly surmised that he lived close to the sites of the murders; Dillon actually lived as far away as 150 miles. The age they predicted was also wrong – they said he would be in his twenties and Thomas Dillon was in his early forties. They acknowledged that the letter described him as an ordinary family man, but they said that he would be a loner, probably with a drinking problem and a history of vandalism. The killings, the report went on, would be committed while he was drunk. It was a fairly accurate picture of Thomas Dillon.

In August 1992, a friend of Dillon's, suspecting that he might be the man responsible for the killings, contacted the police and told them of his suspicions.

On the surface, Dillon did not appear to be the type. A husband and father, he had worked in the same job for twenty-two years in the city of Canton and lived quietly in a middle class ranch-style house in southern Stark County's Pike Township.

Another picture of him emerged, however – a gun fanatic whose hearing had been damaged through the shooting of so many guns in his life. He was remembered at high school as intelligent, but had been a loner who, even back then, was interested in guns and was known to shoot dogs. He even kept a tally on a calendar at home of the number of dogs he had killed. By the early 1980s, he reckoned to have killed 500 animals.

He became a serious gun-collector, regularly visiting gun shows. He also began to like firing crossbows on his murderous sprees across the countryside.

The informant told police that on one occasion, after Dillon had told him he had stopped killing animals, he had asked him, 'Do you realise you can go out into the country and find somebody and there are no witnesses? You can shoot them. There is no motive. Do you realise how easy murder would be to get away with?' On their way to a gun show on another occasion, Dillon asked his friend, 'Do you think I've ever killed somebody?' The friend told him that he did not and tried to laugh off the question, but he remembers being scared by the look on his friend's face and began to think that it might just be possible that he had killed.

When police officers began to look into Dillon's background, it seemed at first as if this might just be another tip-off that led nowhere. After all, his work record was good and his boss spoke highly of him.

Moreover, they found only a couple of instances when he had been in trouble with the law. In 1969, while still a student, he had been investigated for possessing an antique Russian mortar. It was decided, however, that it was a collector's item rather than a weapon and no charges were brought. In 1991, he had been arrested for target shooting and a .22 calibre pistol was found in his car with a silencer. This was a federal violation but he made a plea bargain in which he promised not to purchase any more weapons.

When they began to interview his co-workers, however, they learned that Dillon had been nick-named 'Killer' because of his persistent boasting about shooting dogs and cats. They revealed another link between Dillon and the murders – he kept maps of the areas in which they occurred. When they looked into his gun-buying history, they learned that he had purchased eighteen weapons in the past few years and amongst his purchases were four .30 calibre rifles and two Mausers of the kind that had been used in the murders of four of the dead men.

One officer who began to carry out surveillance on Dillon, discovered that he was responsible for the shooting of a dog in Tuscarawas County. The bullet matched a weapon that he had owned. Now, the task force that had been formed to catch the killer focused on him. They watched him from the air, following him to gun-fairs and on his long drives over Ohio's country roads. He was seen buying beer, sometimes as early as 7.15 in the morning.

On one occasion, they saw him shoot out four electric meters on some oil well pumps while on another he threw a brick through the window of a car that was for sale at the side of the road. On 11 November they lost him as he drove home from Belmont County. Next morning, two cows were found that had been shot with a crossbow. The arrows matched those that Dillon used.

Finally, on 21 November, matters came to a head when he began buying guns at gun shows. They decided to arrest him for violating the terms of his plea bargain before he could kill anyone else.

Searches of his home, vehicles, camper van, office and a safe deposit box belonging to him turned up nothing, but on 4 December, just when investigators were beginning to despair, a man from Stark County informed them that he had purchased a Swedish Mauser from Dillon at a gun show on the same day that Gary Bradley, his last victim, had been killed. Ballistics tests proved that it was the gun used in Bradley's murder.

On 27 January 1993, in return for the state dropping its call for the death penalty, Thomas Dillon pled guilty to five counts of murder and was sentenced to five consecutive terms of life imprisonment.

After sentencing, it emerged that Dillon was terrified of going to the Southern Ohio Correctional Facility in Lucasville which had a few years previously been the site of a terrible riot. The families of his victims launched a petition to have him sent there and more than 8,000 residents of Ohio signed it. The State of Ohio obliged.

Martin Bryant

Born in Tasmania, Martin Bryant is remembered as a quiet and well-mannered child but there are memories of him pulling the snorkel from another boy while they were diving and he is reported to have set himself on fire when he was seventeen. His teachers were concerned about how distant and unemotional he seemed and psychological reports note the pleasure he took in torturing animals, always a sign of trouble ahead.

He became increasingly disturbed throughout his adolescence and possessed an IQ of only sixty-six, equivalent to that of an eleven-year-old boy. He was thought to be possibly suffering from autism and when he left school, a psychiatrist wrote, 'Cannot read or write. Does a bit of gardening and watches TV … Only his parents' efforts prevent further deterioration. Could be schizophrenic and parents face a bleak future with him.' He was put on disability benefit that he supplemented by doing a bit of gardening.

One of the people for whom he gardened and did odd jobs was wealthy fifty-four-year-old eccentric recluse, Helen Harvey. Eventually, Bryant moved into Harvey's house and the two began to spend large sums of money, including the purchase of thirty cars in three years. Around this time there was a reassessment of Bryant's eligibility for his pension and it was noted by a doctor that, 'Father protects him from any occasion which might upset him as he continually threatens violence … Martin tells me he would like to go around shooting people. It would be unsafe to allow Martin out of his parents' control.'

When Helen Harvey died in a car crash for which some thought Bryant might have been responsible – he had a habit of lunging for the steering wheel – he was the sole beneficiary of her will, inheriting more than $550,000. A year later, he inherited another $250,000 when his father also died.

With his father and his benefactor dead, Bryant became increasingly lonely. He wondered if travel might improve his life and set off on a couple of years of globe-trotting, visiting Singapore, Bangkok, Sweden, Los Angeles, Frankfurt, Copenhagen, Sydney, Tokyo, Poland, and Auckland and travelling to the United Kingdom several times. He still found it impossible to make friends, however, and began drinking heavily, eventually wondering if suicide might be the answer.

But he also began to think about murder.

He awoke early on the morning of 28 April 1996, which was unusual as he had no work to go to and nothing to get up early for. His girlfriend left for work at eight and Bryant walked out the door at around nine-fifty, carrying a large blue sports bag filled with the guns about which he was passionate – an AR-15 rifle, a .30 caliber gun and a 12-gauge shotgun.

He drove his yellow Volvo to a shop where he bought a cigarette lighter and the first sign of his odd mood manifested itself. He paid with a large denomination note and left without picking up his change.

At a Shell petrol station at Focett Village, he purchased a cup of coffee. He had a brief conversation with the man behind the counter, telling him that he was going surfing. A bit further down the road, he pulled into another petrol station and filled the Volvo's tank.

He drove on, stopping and parking at the Seascape Guest House, a building which held a particular meaning for him. A few years previously, his father had tried to buy the guesthouse but before he had been able to raise the money, it had been snapped up by David and Noelene Martin. His father had become depressed after losing the property and finally committed suicide. Bryant blamed it on the Martins.

All we know about this part of the day is that Bryant went inside the guesthouse, found David Martin and tied him up and gagged him before stabbing him to death. The same fate befell his wife, Noelene.

He left the guesthouse and drove off in the direction of Port Arthur, one of Tasmania's most popular tourist and leisure sites, a collection of harbour-side restaurants, bars and cafés that marked the location of a nineteenth-century penal colony.

He paid his fee at the gate to enter the area and parked close to the Broad Arrow Café. Getting out of the car, he walked towards the Broad Arrow carrying his sports bag and a video camera.

The café was busy, with around sixty people enjoying lunch. Bryant, with his long, blond hair looking every inch the surfer, walked in, sat at a table on the balcony and ordered his food. At one point, he is reported to have uttered the words to no one in particular, 'There's a lot of wasps around today,' referring not to the insects, it is presumed, but to the 'White Anglo-Saxon Protestant' kind. He also observed that there were not many Japanese tourists.

Finishing his meal, he picked up his heavy bag and walked into the café's main area. He bent down, unzipped the bag and, reaching inside, pulled out the AR-10 which he levelled at a young Asian couple seated at a table nearby and opened fire, hitting the man in the neck, killing him instantly. He swung the rifle round to the dead man's table companion and fired a bullet into her head. Next, he shot at another group of diners seated at a table nearby. One man felt a bullet sting his scalp as it narrowly missed him. Falling instinctively to the floor, he was horrified to see Bryant shoot his girlfriend in the back of the head. Three people had been killed in just seconds and the restaurant was in uproar.

Terrified people threw themselves under tables and behind the counter. As they did so, Bryant continued firing, coldly selecting his victims. A twenty-eight-year-old winemaker, Jason Winter, tried to distract him by throwing a tray at him but was shot as his wife and fifteen-month-old son looked on. Another three men, seated with their backs to the shooting, and with no inkling of what was going on, were brutally gunned down.

Bryant moved quickly to the restaurant's door, firing all the time, killing a couple of men seated nearby from almost point blank range. Their wives hid under the table as their husbands died. He shot a couple seated near the door, walking over to the woman and finishing her off with a bullet to the head.

One woman, Sarah Loughton, ran across the room to protect her mother who had been crawling amongst the tables, trying to hide from the maniac, but Bryant shot her mother and then leaned down and fired a bullet into Sarah's head. She died and her mother survived.

Fifteen seconds had passed since he had pulled the rifle from his bag and already twelve people lay dead. More were shot as he walked deliberately towards the gift shop section of the café. He walked up to Nicole Burgess and fired a bullet into the terrified woman's head and then shot people trying to hide behind a flimsy screen. A man and a woman died.

After another minute or so, during which time he continued to walk around the room firing indiscriminately at people, he left the building.

Ninety seconds had passed and twenty people lay dead.

There was chaos on the harbour-front outside the café. People who had fled the carnage inside were screaming at passersby to take cover, but Bryant began to stalk people around the parked cars and coaches, shooting a driver who would later die in hospital. He shot people hiding on coaches, before returning to his own car to change weapons.

He re-emerged after a few moments, shooting an already wounded woman who was bleeding on the ground and then shot dead a woman on a coach. A man, the husband of his last victim, suddenly encountered him and tried to flee, running onto a coach. Bryant followed him, uttering the chilling words, 'No one gets away from me,' as he aimed his gun at him and fired. The man was hit in the neck but was lucky enough to survive.

He walked back to his Volvo, climbed in and drove out of the car park. Approaching the tollbooth at the gate, he spotted a woman, Nanette Mikac and her two daughters, one aged six and one three. He ordered Nanette to kneel down and then shot her in the temple. He then shot dead one of her daughters but the other ran off, taking cover behind a tree. Bryant went after her, put the barrel of his gun to her neck and callously shot her dead.

He shot two more men at the tollbooth, going up to the BMW of the second man and dragging out the two female occupants whom he shot dead. He transferred his bag and video camera to the BMW, preferring the faster car, and sped off, taking a potshot at an approaching car as he did so. He stopped a Toyota Corolla at a petrol station close to the tollbooth and tried to drag a woman from the passenger seat. When the driver jumped out and attempted to stop him, Bryant pointed his gun at him instead and ordered him to climb into the BMW's boot. He then turned back to the Toyota and pumped a bullet into the woman he had first tried to abduct, killing her.

He sped off in the direction of the Seascape Guest House where it had all begun such a short time ago. He was still shooting, however, hitting two cars en route and wounding the woman occupant of a Frontera. Arriving at Seascape, Bryant handcuffed his hostage to the banisters before dousing the BMW with petrol and setting fire to it. He was going to make his last stand here.

Police arrived at around 2 pm and started to place a cordon around the building. As they did so, Bryant fired at them from a window. They were able to make contact with him through a cordless phone in the building and, calling himself 'Jamie', he demanded a helicopter to take him to a plane that was to fly him to Adelaide. As negotiations continued into the night, however, the telephone's battery ran out and all communication with him ended.

Next morning, officers suddenly noticed flames pouring from the building and shortly after Bryant came running out, his clothes on fire. He was taken to hospital, suffering from burns, ironically the same hospital in which a number of his victims were fighting for their lives while others were still being treated for their wounds. His hostage, it emerged, had been shot dead during the standoff with the police.

Interrogation proved fruitless. Bryant denied everything and claimed not even to have been at Port Arthur that day. He denied ownership of the guns, apart from the shotgun that he had left behind in his Volvo.

In court, as the judge read out the thirty-five charges of murder, Bryant laughed hysterically. He was given thirty-five sentences of life imprisonment and the judge added a further 1,035 years to his sentence for the countless other charges that arose from the incidents of that day.

He is currently serving his sentence in Hobart's Risdon Prison where he has tried six times to commit suicide. In 2006, he was moved to Hobart's Wilfred Lopes Centre, a secure mental health unit from which he will never be released.

THE BELTWAY SNIPERS

The two men who would go on to become notorious as the Washington Snipers or the Beltway Snipers, launched their campaign of deadly attacks on 1 August 2002. At about 8.20 pm, John Gaeta was shot for no apparent reason in Hammond, Louisiana. The bullet pierced Gaeta's neck and exited his back, just below the shoulder. Fortunately, however, doctors found he had avoided damage to his spine and arteries and he was released after an hour.

About five weeks later, at 10.30 on the night of 5 September, fifty-five-year-old pizzeria-owner, Paul LaRuffa was shot six times in the chest as he locked up his pizza parlour in Clinton, Maryland. Like Gaeta, LaRuffa lived and police surmised that as his laptop computer was taken, the incident could probably be put down to a simple robbery.

Sixteen days later, liquor store clerk, Claudine Parker, became the first person killed by the pair. She was gunned down while they robbed the store where she worked in Montgomery, Alabama.

The shootings had been carried out by forty-one-year-old former soldier John Allen Muhammad and seventeen-year-old Lee Boyd Malvo. They were en route to Washington where they planned to execute an audacious and deadly plan dreamed up by Muhammad. They would kill six white people a day for thirty days, using the Capital Beltway, the interstate highway that rings the capital to make their getaway or to move to the next location. They would then move up to Baltimore where they planned to shoot a pregnant woman in the stomach before shooting dead a Baltimore police officer. At the policeman's funeral, they would detonate explosive devices, killing a large number of police and other mourners. They would then offer to stop their actions if the government agreed to give them several million dollars, this money to be used to create a utopian society for 140 black homeless children somewhere in Canada.

Muhammad and Malvo had met when Muhammad had become friends with Malvo's mother, Una, in Antigua and Barbuda in 1999. Later, when Una moved illegally to Florida, she left her son with Muhammad, hoping that he would be able to follow later. He arrived in 2001, but he and his mother were arrested as illegal immigrants in Bellingham, Washington. Malvo was released on a $1,500 bond and had soon re-connected with Muhammad.

On 2 October, a bullet smashed the window of a craft store in Aspen Hill, Maryland. No one was hurt in that attack, but an hour later, fifty-five-year-old James Martin fell to the ground dead in the parking lot of a grocery store in Glenmont.

This was just the beginning. The following day brought mayhem to the streets.

At 7.41 that morning, thirty-nine-year-old landscaper, James 'Sonny' Buchanan was killed by a single shot to the chest while mowing the lawn at the Fitzgerald Auto Mall, near Rockville, Maryland.

At ten past eight, fifty-four-year-old taxi driver Prem Kumar Walekar was shot as he filled his tank with petrol at a gas station in Aspen Hill. He managed to stagger across to a nearby minivan, but did not survive.

Twenty-five minutes later, thirty-four-year-old housekeeper Sarah Ramos, was shot dead as she read a book while waiting for a bus at the Leisure World Shopping Centre in Aspen Hill. A witness told police that he had seen two men speeding away from the area in a white box truck. It gave investigators their first lead, but, sadly, it proved to be a false one.

Time passed, but just as emergency services were beginning to breathe a little more easily, at 9.58

another call came in. Twenty-five-year-old Lori Ann Lewis-Rivera had been gunned down as she vacuumed her Dodge Caravan at a gas station in Kensington, Maryland.

All went quiet, but this dreadful day had one more horror in store. At 9.15 that night, seventy-two-year-old retired carpenter, Pascal Charlot was shot on Georgia Avenue in Washington, dying from his wounds in hospital an hour later.

In a little over thirteen hours, five people had been shot dead.

The authorities were baffled. Each of the five victims of 3 October had been killed by a single shot fired from a distance. This sniper was an excellent marksman who rarely seemed to miss. Each one of them had been felled with frightening accuracy. The area was in deep shock and terrified of what the following day might bring.

They would not have to wait long to find out.

At 2.30 in the afternoon of 4 October, forty-three-year-old Caroline Seawell was busy loading her purchases into her car at a Michaels craft store at Spotsylvania mall in Spotsylvania in Virginia when a shot rang out. She was wounded in the lower back, but she was one of the few lucky ones – she survived.

The sniper's next victim caused a storm of outrage. On 7 October, thirteen-year-old Iran Brown was just arriving at school – Benjamin Tasker Middle School – in Bowie, Maryland when he was shot in the chest. He survived but his injuries were serious. Police recovered a .223 cartridge shell from a wooded area about a hundred and fifty yards from the scene as well as a Tarot card, the one signifying death. On the front was scrawled *'Call me God'* while the back carried instructions to the police: *'For you mr. Police. Code: Call me God. Do not release to the press.'*

On 9 October, fifty-three-year-old civil engineer, Dean Meyers swung his car into a gas station in Manassas on the way home from work. A single bullet in the head made him the seventh person to die from a bullet fired by the mysterious sniper.

Two days later, another gas station was the location for the shooting dead of the tenth victim. At 9.30 am, another fifty-three-year-old, Kenneth H. Bridges, was hit just outside Fredericksburg, Virginia. Once more, investigators were misled by a report of a white van speeding away from the scene. After this incident, gas stations began to hang large tarpaulins across their frontages to prevent the sniper from being able to see customers as they filled their cars. The area was in a heightened state of panic.

Nothing happened over the weekend, but on Monday, 14 October, FBI analyst Linda Franklin was gunned down and killed as she left a store in Falls Church, Virginia with her husband.

Around this time, Muhammad and Malvo made a mistake. Not content with merely causing chaos in the Washington area, they began phoning the police and taunting them about it. In one such call, they referred to the robbery they had carried out in Montgomery in September and on 17 October, a fingerprint found at the liquor store was matched to one found at Benjamin Tasker Middle School. Records showed that it belonged to Lee Boyd Malvo. Further investigation revealed his connection with John Allen Muhammad. They knew they were travelling in a blue 1990 Chevrolet Caprice, the number plate of which they publicised through the media.

Meanwhile, a man survived being shot as he left a restaurant in Ashland, Virginia and then on 22 October, they claimed their last victim. Thirty-five-year-old bus driver Conrad Johnson was standing on the steps of his bus in Aspen when he was hit in the abdomen from a distance. He was rushed to hospital but later died.

It was a member of the public who gave the police the break that would lead to the capture of the Beltway Snipers. Trucker Ron Lantz called them to say that he had found the Chevy Caprice at a rest stop on Interstate 70, northwest of Washington. He told them that he had parked his rig across the rest-stop exit to stop the car from making an escape, but there was no movement inside the car. When police arrived they found Muhammad and Malvo sleeping like babies inside.

Ballistic tests run on the .223 rifle they found in the vehicle proved to be a match for the bullets used in all the sniper attacks. They had cleverly modified their car, carving out a hole in the trunk through which a rifle with a sight could protrude. To access the boot space without leaving the car, they had cut a hole in the rear interior. They just crawled into position and took aim. It was chillingly efficient.

Ten people had been killed and three others wounded during the dreadful three weeks that Muhammad and Malvo had waged their hate-filled war on ordinary Americans going about their business. They were found guilty of murder and Muhammad was sentenced to death. He was executed by lethal injection on 10 November 2009.

Lee Boyd Malvo, too young to be executed, is currently serving six life sentences at the Red Onion State Prison with no possibility of parole.

Dale Hausner and Samuel Dietman

The 'Serial Shooters'

'Random Recreational Violence' was their name for it, a murderous game of death in which people were mown down at random over a two-year period by two men fuelled by drink and drugs and with a twisted hatred for the world inside them.

Thirty-six-year-old Dale Hausner had been a janitor at Phoenix's Sky Harbor International Airport since 1999 but also worked part-time as a barman, comedian, commercial actor and even as a boxing photographer. He was divorced and had a seriously ill child. On the two nights a week when he had custody of his daughter, he had to keep a close eye on her.

There had been other tragedy in Hausner's life. In 1994, a car in which he and his wife and two sons were travelling left the road when his wife Karen Ledford, who was at the wheel, allegedly fell asleep. It plunged into a creek and the boys drowned despite Hausner's desperate efforts to save them.

He was overwhelmed by grief and became severely depressed, which led to Karen eventually walking out on him.

Karen Ledford later made a number of accusations about Hausner – that he was, in fact, bisexual and that he had been violent towards her. She claimed that after she left him, he had become insanely jealous when he heard that she was dating someone else. He drove her out into the desert near the town of Wickenberg, she claimed, and threatened to kill her, a threat that was interrupted only by a couple of motorcyclists who drove past them at just the right moment.

Hausner was something of a ladies' man and tried to use his numerous romantic liaisons as alibis for the times of the murders. However, after Karen left, a great deal of his time was spent drinking and cruising aimlessly around town with his brother, Jeff.

One night, in early 2006, Jeff Hausner was drinking in a bar when he got talking to the man on the adjacent barstool. Samuel Dietman was, it transpired, a like-minded lost soul. He had spent his childhood moving back and forward between Minnesota and Arizona after the divorce of his parents. In 1992, he married in Arizona and had two children, but in 2001 his wife left him and went back to Minnesota. Like

Hausner, he sank into a deep depression and, also like Hausner, he considered killing his wife, planning to bury her body in the desert.

He started using drugs and his life began to unravel. Thrown out of his apartment, he moved in with his mother and stepfather but they, too, threw him out in 2005. Jeff introduced Dietman to Dale who let him sleep on his sofa.

Soon, the two of them dreamed up a scheme to make money. Dietman would steal booze and CDs from stores and Hausner would sell them on to co-workers at the airport. They would split the money evenly.

He also began to travel with the brothers on their aimless drives around town in Dale's silver Toyota Camry, pumped up on methamphetamine and looking to cause trouble. They amused themselves by setting rubbish bins on fire and shooting out car tyres with BB gun pellets.

But Dale had already proved to be a man of an unusually violent nature. What were called the 'Serial Shooter' killings had started six months previously when he had shot dead twenty-year-old David Estrada in Tolleson. He had since killed another three men – Nathaniel Shoffner, Jose Ortiz and Marco Carillo.

Soon, he was carrying out acts of random violence in front of the others. One night, the three drove up to a woman on the street who they assumed was working as a prostitute. Dale asked her a question but before she could answer, he pulled out a gun and shot her in the chest at almost point-blank range. In April 2006, Jeff stabbed a man when the other two were present.

Dietman later claimed that he felt pressure to emulate the dreadful acts of the two brothers and his turn came on 2 May 2006 after Dale shot a man with a shotgun. He handed the gun to Dietman, indicating that it was his turn. Fifteen minutes later, twenty-year-old Claudia Gutierrez Cruz was shot dead as she waited at a bus stop in Scottsdale. The three men celebrated with rum and coke at Dale's house.

Dale and Dietman now became regular companions on the cruises along Phoenix's streets and avenues. Armed with Hausner's shotgun and a .22 calibre rifle, they shot at anyone who came within range. Eight people died in the course of this rampage and seventeen were wounded. They are also thought to have shot dead at least ten animals.

They targeted areas where Hausner could work out his anger with the homeless and with prostitutes but in reality anyone was likely to become a victim and the inhabitants of Phoenix became terrified to walk anywhere in their city.

In June 2006, they shot Paul Patrick who was innocently strolling along a Phoenix street late one night. Hausner used his shotgun, spraying Patrick with hundreds of pellets. He was lucky; he survived, but only just and he is now confined to a wheelchair as a result of his injuries.

Seventeen-year-old Kibil Tambadu was shot in the abdomen, after which Hausner and Dietman stood over him laughing as he doubled over in terrible pain.

Raul Garcia was shot dead while riding past Hausner's Toyota on a bicycle. Hausner was furious at the time because Dietman had been caught shoplifting.

Their last murder occurred on 30 July 2006. Hausner who was with Dietman at the time, shot twenty-two-year-old Robin Blasnek who was walking to a friend's house from her parents' house following an argument with her boyfriend.

It has been alleged that the Serial Shooters were in competition with another Phoenix serial rapist, robber and killer of the time, the Baseline Killer. Named thus because his first crimes took place around Baseline Road in South Phoenix, the Baseline Killer, later identified as a man named Mark Goudeau, killed nine times, committed fifteen sexual assaults and carried out eleven kidnappings. He was also responsible for a number of armed robberies. Phoenix police were stretched considerably by these two strands of murder.

The breakthrough came in the Serial Shooter case when a man named Ron Horton contacted police. He was a drinking-partner of Dale Hausner and his wife Debbie Dryer sometimes gave Dietman a lift home from the bar. On one such occasion, a drunken Hausner boasted about his crimes and Horton called the police to tell them about it.

They put Hausner and Dietman under surveillance, following them on their middle of the night cruises and tapping their phones. They taped the two men bragging about the murders and even heard them comparing favourite methods of killing and arguing callously about the number of victims they had claimed.

By August, they had enough evidence to condemn them and a raid on Hausner's apartment uncovered his collection of newspaper clippings about the murders and even a map that detailed the locations of each one.

In custody, Hausner was arrogant and surly, refusing to cooperate. Dietman, on the other hand, immediately confessed, providing interrogators with even more evidence against his partner in crime. Hausner denied everything and claimed to merely be a gun collector and that the only time he fired his weapons was when he went out shooting in the desert. He maintained that for the night of each shooting he had a clear alibi. He had been looking after his sick daughter or had been on a date with one of his many girlfriends. He went as far as to suggest that Dietman had probably borrowed his guns and his car and gone out while he was asleep.

Hausner's lawyers argued, when the case came to court, that Dietman's testimony could not be relied upon as it was part of a plea bargain but in March 2009, the jury, relying on the surveillance evidence and believing Dietman's testimony, found Dale Hausner guilty of more than eighty crimes that included murder, attempted murder, aggravated assault, drive-by shooting and animal cruelty. They acquitted him of two murders and one of the attacks in which the victim survived.

He still insisted that he was innocent, but ordered his attorneys not to fight the death penalty, stating that his execution would provide solace for the families of the victims. His punishment was six death sentences and two life sentences. There were also hundreds of years of imprisonment for the less serious charges of which he had been found guilty.

Three months later, Jeff Hausner was found guilty of aggravated assaults in two stabbings and was sent to prison for eighteen years.

Samuel Dietman had confessed and pled guilty but friends and family came forward to provide a portrait of a man helplessly addicted to drugs who had fallen into bad company and had been bullied by the overpowering Dale Hausner. He told the judge that he had considered turning Hausner in earlier but had been afraid of the consequences.

Dietman, as the murderer of one of their victims and having been present when another was killed and three were wounded, was sentenced on 29 July to life without parole.

HERIBERTO 'EDDIE' SEDA

In the late 1960s and early 1970s, a serial killer known as the Zodiac Killer operated in Northern California, killing five people (he claimed to have actually murdered thirty-seven) and taunting police with letters that he sent to the Bay Area press. Although numerous suspects had been named by the police over the years, the Zodiac Killer was never caught and his last communication with the media had been in 1974.

Suddenly, however, in New York, in 1990, it seemed as if the Zodiac was back in business, but this time on the east coast. Letters began to arrive at media outlets with the sign-off *'This is the Zodiac'*.

However, this was not the old Zodiac making a comeback. It was twenty-two-year-old Herbert 'Eddie' Seda, an unemployed young New Yorker who lived with his mother and half-sister, Gladys 'Chachi' Reyes in East New York.

Seda was a tidy, clean-cut, good-looking young man who had been forced to drop out of high school after being found carrying a weapon. And, indeed, he did like guns. They were his hobby and he devoured magazines like *Soldier of Fortune* as well as books about serial killers. Amongst his heroes was the clean-cut rapist and serial killer, Ted Bundy, but the killer he had most time for was the Zodiac Killer. He had never been caught after all and to Eddie's mind, he had made a fool of the cops. He read everything he could about him and resolved to model himself on him.

He launched his campaign by sending letters to East New York's 75th Precinct. The first, arriving on 17 November 1989, bore the heading *'This is the Zodiac'* and contained a drawing of a circle with lines through it, dividing the circle into twelve sections, each part representing a sign in the zodiac but with the sign 'Virgo' missing and the message, *'the first sign is dead'.* It warned that there would be twelve murders, one for each sign of the Zodiac. It read:

This is the Zodiac.

The First Sign is dead.

The Zodiac will
Kill the twelve signs in the

Belt when the Zodiacal light is seen?

The Zodiac will spread fear

I have seen a lot of police in Jamaica Ave and Elden Lane but you are no good and will not get the Zodiac.

Orion is the one that can stop Zodiac and the Seven Sister

However, police could find no evidence of the murder that had been claimed and they dismissed the threat as nothing but a hoax.

He struck for the first time in the early hours of the morning of 9 March 1990. Mario Orozco, a forty-nine-year-old kitchen porter was limping home from work in East New York with the help of his wooden cane when a young man wearing a maroon beret emerged from the shadows of a cemetery. He pulled out a 9 mm zip gun and shot Mr Orozco in the back. The shooter walked over to the wounded man, wrapped a note around his gun, laid it on the ground and disappeared into the night. The note bore the legend *'This is the Zodiac'.*

Orozco survived, as did Seda's second victim. At 3 am on 29 March, thirty-four-year-old Germaine Montenesdro was drunk and wandering aimlessly through the streets of East New York. He was tossing up in his mind whether to go home to his girlfriend in the Bronx or spend the night at his father's apartment which was not too far away. As he swayed along the street, he failed to notice that he was being followed. Suddenly a shot was fired, hitting him in the left side of his lower back and going through his liver. He crumpled to the ground and as he lay there bleeding, his assailant went through his pockets. He found his wallet, but left the money. Instead he grabbed his passport before vanishing into the darkness.

At that time, random shootings were a frequent occurrence on New York's dangerous streets but, unfortunately, these two shootings were not connected by any of the officers investigating them.

The first death at Seda's hands was an elderly man living off public assistance in Woodhaven, an area bordering on East New York. Joe Proce liked to walk the streets, even late at night and that was what he was doing at 1.30 on the morning of 31 May, a couple of months after the attack on Germaine Montenesdro. As he made his way home, he was approached by Seda who asked him for a glass of water. Wary of strangers on the streets of the city in the middle of the night, Proce dealt brusquely with the enquiry and walked on. But he had angered Seda, who walked after him. After another brief exchange, Seda pulled out a zip gun and shot the elderly man in the lower back, hitting his kidney. He placed a handwritten note beside Proce's prone body and ran off.

The case was viewed as a robbery and detectives were concerned about the strange occultist note that had been left by the killer. They knew that this case was out of the ordinary. However, the first two shootings had occurred in another borough and this was the days before cases were entered into national databases to ascertain whether any similar crimes had been committed. The shooting of Joe Proce was, therefore, never linked with the shootings of Mario Orozco and Germaine Montenesdro. Furthermore, officers investigating the shooting of Joe Proce had no knowledge of the strange letter that had been sent to the 75th Precinct. To make matters worse, Proce was a hopeless witness, unable to make up his mind even about the ethnicity of his attacker.

Now, however, letters similar to the one found next to Proce began to arrive at newspapers and the offices of television news programmes. They listed the time, place and date of each shooting and gave the victim's star sign. The letters added that they were 'all shot in Brooklyn'. Investigators searched their files but could find no murders that matched those listed. They decided that the letters were a hoax.

One detective, however, crosschecked the dates and star signs with shooting victims who had not died in their attacks and came across Orozco and Montenesdro. He concluded that the killer had failed to realise that he had strayed into the borough of Queens when he shot Joe Proce.

The story broke in the *New York Post* on 19 June with the headline, 'Riddle of the Zodiac Shooter'.

Chief of Detectives Joseph Borelli had worked on the 'Son of Sam' case in the 1970s and the last thing he wanted was a serial killer on the loose that reminded New Yorkers of those dark, terrifying days when people were afraid to walk the city streets. He launched 'Operation Watchdog' to catch the Zodiac quickly.

Some began to wonder if, in fact, the Bay Area Zodiac Killer had relocated to the east coast and New Yorkers felt increasingly nervous. As vigilante groups such as the Guardian Angels stepped up their patrols, Operation Watchdog detectives discovered that there was a pattern to the new Zodiac's attacks. They predicted that he would next strike early on the morning of Thursday, 21 June. That night and into the early hours of the morning, the streets of East New York were flooded with patrols and police cruisers.

They were correct; he did strike that night, but not where they expected.

Larry Parham made ready to sleep on a bench in Central Park that night. Parham was not the usual down and out. He was well dressed and had $4,000 in the bank. He had just been unlucky and had ended up on the street. Now, he was saving hard in order to give himself a good start when he had enough money. He could have been in a shelter that night but believed he was safer in the park.

How wrong he was.

As he slept, a figure crept out of the bushes towards him. He carefully took Parham's wallet out of his pocket, flicked through its contents, leaving the cash untouched and returned it. Satisfied that Parham's star sign was Cancer, he fired a shot into his chest, just missing his aorta.

Parham survived the shooting and the following day, the Zodiac sent an intriguing communication to the *New York Post*. It was filled with the usual occult nonsense, but tried hard to convince that the New York Zodiac and the Bay Area Zodiac were the same person. No one really believed it but he tried again two days later, writing:

This is the Zodiac

The note Sent to the Post not to any of
The San Francisco Zodiac letter you are

Wrong the handwriting look different it is

One of the same Zodiac one Zodiac

In San Francisco killed a man in the park with a

Gun and killed a women with a knife and killed

A man in the taxi cab with gun.

The case went to a new level on 24 June when Seda's second victim, Joe Proce, died in hospital. They were now hunting for a killer.

Police waited for the August attack, knowing exactly when it would happen, but just like the Bay Area Zodiac, Seda decided all of a sudden to stop. He had become worried that the cops were getting closer and he was scared.

Other cases came along and Operation Watchdog

began to be scaled down until there were only eighteen officers working on it.

After a year, however, Seda was bored and decided it was time to make a comeback. This time it would be different, however. He could no longer follow the pattern of his first series and it was too risky to check through his victims' ID. He would simply shoot and flee the scene immediately.

On 10 August 1992, he shot thirty-nine-year-old Patricia Fonti at the Highland Park reservoir. She struggled after he shot her twice but he finished her off by viciously stabbing her more than a hundred times.

On 4 June 1993, he shot forty-year-old Jim Weber in the buttock but failed to kill him. On 20 July, however, forty-year-old Joseph Diacone died after being shot in the neck outside Highland Park. On 2 October, forty-year-old Diane Ballard survived after being shot as she sat on a bench in Highland Park.

On 1 August, he wrote to the *Post* again, the letter containing the eerie line, *'sleep my little dead how we lothe (sic) them'.*

On 18 June, Seda's bad relationship with his sister pushed him over the edge. He had warned Chachi to stay away from the young drug dealers of the neighbourhood and the two argued frequently about it. On June 18, she brought one of those boys home and Seda became increasingly irritated as he heard them having fun through his bedroom wall.

He took one of his zip guns and blasted the wall with it. Infuriated, Chachi ran out of her room and a furious argument erupted in the living room. As Chachi ran out the front door to get help, her brother shot her in the back, but she was able to stagger to a neighbouring apartment. Her boyfriend, meanwhile, cowered in her bedroom.

The police arrived and Seda fired at them from the window for several hours. Eventually, however, Detective Joey Herbert of the 17th Precinct persuaded him to give himself up.

At the station, Seda wrote his statement but at the end of it, he drew the symbols that he had included on each of the Zodiac letters. They could not believe what they were seeing. Could he really be the Zodiac? His fingerprints were immediately sent off to be matched up with those found on the Zodiac communications. They were a perfect match.

In June, 1998, Eddie Seda, the New York Zodiac Killer was convicted of murder and attempted murder. He was sentenced to 152½ years in prison where he now reads the Bible every day. The original Zodiac Killer has still not been caught.

PART TWO

MARKSMEN

Timothy Murphy

Timothy Murphy was born to Irish immigrants in 1751 near the Delaware Water Gap on the border of New Jersey and Pennsylvania where the Delaware River cuts through a large ridge of the Appalachian Mountains. In 1759, the family moved to Shamokin Flats (now known as Sunbury) in Pennsylvania. A few years later, Timothy was apprenticed to a man named van Campen. He moved west with the van Campen family to the Wyoming Valley.

It was in this wild country, the American frontier, that he acquired his skill with a flintlock rifle, learning to shoot from great distances. Allowing an enemy to get too close was a certain way to be killed, especially as it took so long to re-load the flintlock and if you were too close an enemy was likely to be upon you before that had been accomplished.

On 29 June 1775, aged twenty-four, he enlisted in the Northumberland County Riflemen, in Captain John Lowdon's Company, to fight the British in the American Revolutionary War. He took part in the Siege of Boston when the British were besieged in the town from April to March 1776, before withdrawing. He also fought in the Battle of Long Island, fought in August 1776, the first major battle of the war. It was won decisively by the British.

He was promoted to the rank of sergeant in the Continental Army's 12th Pennsylvania Regiment and fought in the battles of Trenton and Princeton. Recognised as a superb marksman, reputed to be able to 'hit a seven inch target at 250 yards,' he was selected in July 1777, as one of 500 riflemen, to join Daniel Morgan's 'Sharpshooter Corps'.

At the Battles of Saratoga, British General John Burgoyne and Brigadier Simon Fraser fought two battles eighteen days apart on the same battlefield, situated nine miles south of Saratoga, New York. Burgoyne had set out with an army of British, Canadian, German and Native American troops from Canada to divide New England from the southern colonies, but after an auspicious start, the fort of Ticonderoga falling without a fight, his campaign had slowed mainly because of logistical problems. The Americans had adopted highly successful tactics that involved ambushing, sniper shooting and guerrilla warfare.

One particular tactic was the 'shooting wall'. The Red Coats started out early in the morning when the ground was generally blanketed with mist making visibility virtually nil. The American militiamen organised a wall of shooters somewhere on their route, placing regular lookouts in the trees along the route, above the level of the mist, so that they could see each other but could not be seen from below. When the enemy passed below a spotter, he would signal silently to the next one and the British troops would be tracked until the moment that the last spotter gave his signal. Then, the riflemen, aiming at the bottom of the tree in which the last spotter sat, would fire blindly into the swirling mist.

It was a devastating tactic, creating total confusion in the British ranks while killing and wounding many of them.

On 19 September, Burgoyne won a small victory over General Horatio Gates and the Continental Army in the first Battle of Saratoga, known as the Battle of Freeman's Farm. It was at a cost, however, as he took significant casualties.

Advancing again, the British were ravaged by American raids, but they finally arrived at the heavily defended fort of Bemis Heights. The American force of local soldiers, led by General Benedict Arnold was slightly inferior in numbers to Burgoyne's but the battle, when it began, swung alternately from one side to the other. Eventually, however, the British seemed to be obtaining the upper hand, pushing the American forces back. It was time to force home their advantage.

Burgoyne decided to reconnoitre the American left flank to see whether an attack there would be possible. As an escort, he took Simon Fraser's Advanced Corps.

Leaving their camp between ten and eleven in the morning, they advanced about a quarter of a mile to Barber's wheat field, situated on a rise above Mill Brook. There they stopped to observe the American position.

Benedict Arnold had been removed from field command and General Gates had assumed command of the American left flank, the right being commanded by General Benjamin Lincoln. Informed by scouts of the movement by the British, Gates sent Morgan's Riflemen – his 500-strong force of sharpshooters, Timothy Murphy amongst them – out to the far left with other companies of militiamen taking the centre. There were more than 8,000 Americans in the field that day.

At between two and two-thirty in the afternoon, the British grenadiers opened fire and made a bayonet charge on the American positions. The

Americans fired on them from close range and the British were routed. On the left things were going equally badly for the British. Morgan's men wiped out the Canadians and Native Americans with ease and now faced Brigadier Fraser's men.

Fraser had been spotted by the Americans; he could hardly be missed on his grey horse, a charismatic figure, encouraging his men to take advantage of any weakness in the American lines. It was obvious that his men were responding to his cajoling. An order was issued to bring him down and several crack American soldiers armed with flintlock rifles were dispatched to try to put him out of action.

One of these early snipers was Timothy Murphy, now a battle-hardened veteran aged twenty-six. Murphy climbed a tree, finding a V-shaped notch in the branches that would support the barrel of the rifle. He was around 300 yards distant from the brigadier.

He cocked his weapon and took steady aim, taking his time in order to get a proper bead on the man on the grey horse. Squeezing the trigger, he let off a first shot that narrowly missed his target. The second grazed Fraser's grey horse but the third was successful, hitting Fraser in the abdomen and blasting him from his horse. Fraser died from his wounds that night.

Then, moments after he had brought down Fraser, Murphy spotted another prime target, another senior British officer, Sir Francis Clarke, who was chief adviser to General Burgoyne, galloping across the Red Coat line, probably carrying an important message. Murphy took aim again and Clarke was killed instantly.

These two deaths represented dreadful news for the British troops, especially the death of Simon Fraser. But British troops were also frightened by the astonishing skill it had taken to kill from such a distance. Were all the Americans that good with rifles, they began to ask themselves and how safe would they be if they advanced any closer to the American lines?

When another 3,000 American troops arrived on the battlefield, the battle was as good as over, the British being outnumbered now by three to one. Their resistance soon collapsed and the Americans won the battle.

We will never know what kind of gun 'Sureshot Tim' used that day to fire his two fatal shots. Some say it was a Goulcher double-barrelled rifle, a Swiss weapon that was not that common in the

Revolutionary War. However, it is more likely that he was armed with a Kentucky long rifle with its extraordinarily long barrel, sometimes more than four feet in length. There is even a possibility, knowing how long it took to re-load, that he carried two rifles.

Timothy Murphy may not have been a sniper in the modern sense of the word, but there is little doubt that he was an extraordinarily good shot. Pulling off two such shots in the heat of battle while fairly exposed in the branches of a tree was no mean feat.

He went on to fight in many more battles of the Revolutionary War but in 1779 he left Morgan's Riflemen and joined a new militia company. At one point later in life, he was captured by Native Americans but managed to escape with a friend who had also been taken. Murphy stabbed to death all eleven of his captors while they slept.

On another occasion with the militia, he was besieged in Middle Fort in the Schoharie Valley, New York, with 200 of his riflemen. It was one of three forts built by the local people as protection against continual raids by the British. As the British attacked the Middle Fort, Murphy was supported by his wife Peggy who busied herself moulding bullets and loading muskets. She is said to have claimed that if the ammunition ran out, she would pick up a spear and fight alongside her husband with that.

The commander of the fort, Major Woolsey was not made of the same stuff. He was ready to surrender and let the British into the fort. But his officers vehemently disagreed with his decision and there was a delay while the matter was discussed.

Murphy knew that ammunition was low and the women had indeed been preparing spears, pitchforks and boiling water to be used in an attempt to fend off the final attack when the bullets ran out. However, he was also well aware what befell prisoners and captives and as a British party approached the fort to discuss a surrender, he fired twice over their heads, forcing them to retreat back to the British lines. When they tried to return, he again fired over their heads. On their third approach, Major Woolsey threatened to shoot Murphy if he tried to fire again. Murphy replied that he would rather die than be taken prisoner. He fired again.

Woolsey now ordered that the white flag be raised above the fort but Murphy declared that he would shoot anyone who dared to do so. There was a tense stand off before Woolsey backed down and went to his quarters where he relinquished his command.

The British eventually abandoned the siege, having found it impossible to get anywhere near the fort with Murphy's sharpshooters lining the walls.

Timothy Murphy reenlisted in 1781 under General Wayne and was present at the final battle at Yorktown. At the war's conclusion, he returned to a life of farming and milling at Fultanham, New York and entered local politics. He died of cancer in 1818, aged sixty-seven.

When a statue was put up in 1929 by the State of New York honouring Timothy Murphy, then-Governor Franklin Delano Roosevelt said: 'This country has been made by Timothy Murphys, the men in the ranks. Conditions here called for the qualities of the heart and head that Tim Murphy had in abundance. Our histories should tell us more of the men in the ranks, for it was to them, more than to the generals, that we were indebted for our military victories.'

The Shooting of Horatio Nelson

Nelson was one of Britain's greatest heroes, providing the nation with some of its proudest and most important moments in battle. While the Duke of Wellington won on land during the Napoleonic Wars, Nelson won at sea, an inspirational leader and a brilliant and innovative naval tactician.

Following the short-lived Peace of Amiens in 1802, the British had imposed a naval blockade on France, trapping the French fleet at Brest, that severely damaged trade and prevented the French from fully mobilising their naval forces. This left the British free to launch attacks on French interests both at home and abroad.

Napoleon resolved to invade Britain but in order to accomplish this he first needed to secure control of the English Channel, preventing the British fleet from attacking any invasion force while it was at sea. He devised a plan, therefore, for the French Mediterranean and the Spanish fleet, based in Cadiz, to breach the British blockade and assemble in the West Indies. They would then sail back across the Atlantic and help the French fleet. When they approached Europe, however, two of their ships were captured in the Battle of Cape Finisterre and French Admiral Pierre-Charles Villeneuve ordered his ships to retreat to Cadiz harbour. Shortly after, however, Napoleon sent orders that he should resume his journey to Brest. In order to do so, Villeneuve would have to do battle against Nelson and the British fleet. They met at the Battle of Trafalgar, fought off Cape Trafalgar in southwest Spain on 21 October 1805, the most important sea battle of the nineteenth century.

Facing Nelson's twenty-seven vessels were the combined fleets of France and Spain, thirty-three ships commanded by Villeneuve outnumbering the British fleet. Villeneuve had already suffered at Nelson's hands, having been captured soon after the Battle of the Nile, but Napoleon considered him to be a 'lucky man' and he kept him in place, despite the misfortune at the Nile.

Nelson had spent weeks honing his tactics for the battle that lay ahead, making his intentions clear over dinner with his captains. The customary way in which a naval battle was fought involved each fleet lining up to form two lines of battle, parallel with each other. They would then let loose with their guns. It was a tactic that did not favour the faster, more accurate gunnery of the Royal Navy and often resulted in battles ending indecisively and with the enemy fleet escaping. Nelson's plan was to create a melee in which its superior weaponry would give the British fleet the advantage.

He planned to split his ships into three sections, the largest of which would engage closely with one part of the enemy fleet and destroy it. Meanwhile, the other two columns would sail towards the enemy line at right angles, preventing it from rushing to the aid of the other ships.

One distinct disadvantage would be the difficulty of communicating from ship to ship. Therefore, rather than direct the progress of the battle in the usual way, with the use of signals, he ensured that his captains understood his plan and informed them that he was giving them greater than ever leeway in carrying out their orders, displaying an astonishing degree of trust in the capabilities of his officers.

The main danger lay in the fact that the French and Spanish ships would be able to fire upon the British fleet, but the British would be unable to return fire. Speed was, therefore, of the essence and Nelson ordered them to make all sail available.

On 16 September, Villeneuve received orders from Napoleon to set sail for Naples where he was to land the soldiers the fleet was carrying and engage with any enemy ships they encountered. There was some dissent amongst his officers about this order and it was not until 18 October that the Combined Fleet finally set sail. Calm weather, however, hampered progress and allowed the British time to organise themselves.

At 5.40 on the morning of 21 October, the British fleet was about twenty-one miles northwest of Cape Trafalgar with the Combined Fleet between them and the Cape. At 6 o'clock, Nelson gave the order to prepare for battle.

Two hours later, Villeneuve ordered his ships to return to Cadiz but it took almost ninety minutes for his inexperienced crews to carry out the order and turn back.

By 11 am, Villeneuve could see Nelson's fleet, which was sailing in two parallel columns. In an hour, the two fleets would be within range of one another and Villeneuve was still struggling to bring his ships into tight order. As they approached each other, tension mounted. The fate of Britain depended upon this battle.

At 11.45, Nelson sent his famous signal, reminding

his sailors that 'England expects that every man will do his duty.'

Battle was finally joined at noon with Nelson's flagship, HMS *Victory*, herself coming under fire from several French vessels. A number of the crew were killed and wounded and her wheel was blown away, so that she had to be steered from below decks.

At 12.45, *Victory* cut through the enemy line between Villeneuve's flagship, the *Bucentaire* and another ship, the *Redoubtable*. *Victory* came close to *Bucentaire*, firing a broadside through her stern that killed many. Nelson moved on to engage *Redoubtable* whose crew and an infantry corps that was on board looked like they might board *Victory* and seize her.

Nelson, meanwhile, was a prime target. With characteristic lack of concern for his own safety, he was issuing orders to his men from the quarterdeck, in full view of everyone. On many occasions, he had been warned not to wear his decorations, or at least to hide them so that the enemy would not be able to pick him out. Sir Thomas Hardy is reported to have warned him about this at Trafalgar, but he stubbornly refused to take off his medals. It was a refusal that later gave rise to speculation that Nelson actually wanted to die at Trafalgar, a notion reinforced by the fact that the sight in his left eye was beginning to fail and, having already lost his right eye in 1794, he was facing eventual blindness. He also suffered considerable pain from the stump of his right arm – he lost that after being shot by a musket at the Battle of Santa Cruz de Tenerife – and an old wound to his side.

Shortly after one o'clock, Hardy realised with a start that the admiral was no longer by his side. Turning, he spied him kneeling on the deck briefly using his one good hand to support himself, before falling onto the deck. Hardy rushed to his side.

Lying on the deck, Nelson smiled and said, 'Hardy, I do believe they have done it at last … my backbone is shot through.'

As he had turned to face the enemy, he had been hit by a sniper, firing from the mizzen top of the *Redoubtable*, from a range of around fifty feet. The surgeon of HMS *Victory*, Dr Beatty wrote a detailed report on the path of the damage the bullet did to the admiral's body:

> *The ball struck the fore part of his Lordship's epaulette and entered the left shoulder immediately before the processus acromion scapulae, which it slightly fractured. It then descended obliquely into the thorax, fracturing the second and third ribs,*

and, after penetrating the left lobe of the lungs, and dividing in its passage a large branch of the pulmonary artery, it entered the left side of the spine between the sixth and seventh dorsal vertebrae, fractured the left transverse process of the sixth dorsal vertebra, wounded the medulla spinalis and, fracturing the right transverse process of the seventh vertebra, made its way from the right side of the spine, directing its course through the muscles of the back, and lodged therein, about two inches below the interior angle of the right scapula.

By now, the men in the *Redoubtable*'s mizzen were the only ones left alive, the ship having been taken, and there is a good chance that the sniper was already wounded. That, plus the distance, a strong crosswind, swirling gun smoke and the movement of the ship, made the shot a difficult one. Dr Beatty insisted that there were only two men left alive on the mizzen and that they had been firing deliberately at Nelson, continuing to shoot at Hardy and other officers for some time following the shooting of the admiral. One of the two men was then shot and as the second attempted to escape, climbing down the rigging, he took a bullet in the back and fell dead to the deck of the *Redoubtable*. Vice Admiral

Collingwood, Nelson's second in command, and a midshipman named Pollard have been given credit over the years for shooting these two men.

Nelson was carried below by a sergeant major of marines and two sailors but even as he was being carried, he was still issuing orders, asking his bearers to stop so that he could advise a midshipman on the handling of the tiller by which the ship was being steered. He then covered his face with a handkerchief, concerned that if the members of his crew recognised him as he was being carried down, they would become alarmed.

When Beatty began to attend to him, Nelson said, 'You can do nothing for me. I have but a short time to live. My back is shot through.' Nonetheless, they made him comfortable and brought him lemonade and water. He asked a number of times to see Hardy but he was on deck issuing orders in Nelson's place. He asked Beatty to remember him to his mistress, Emma Hamilton, and to his daughter and friends.

At around 2.30, Hardy finally came down to see the admiral and was able to give him the good news that a number of enemy ships had surrendered. Nelson told him that he was dying and informed him that he wanted his possessions given to Emma. He feared that a gale was getting up and ordered

Hardy to be sure to anchor. He told him to 'take care of poor Lady Hamilton,' and added the famous words, 'Kiss me, Hardy.' Hardy knelt and kissed the admiral on the cheek. He then kissed him again and Nelson, becoming disorientated, asked, 'Who is that?' On being told it was Hardy, he said, 'God bless you, Hardy.'

In an increasingly weak voice, Nelson continued to murmur instructions to the ship's purser, Walter Burke and the chaplain, Alexander Scott: 'Fan, fan... rub, rub...drink, drink.'

Dr Beatty heard Nelson gasp at one point: 'Thank God I have done my duty.' And then, as Beatty took his pulse, Nelson, by now very weak, looked up at him and then finally closed his eyes. Scott recorded his last words as, 'God and my country.'

He died at 4.30 in the afternoon, three hours after the fatal shot.

Meanwhile, his tactics had worked. Eighteen of the enemy vessels were destroyed and more than 4,400 French and Spanish sailors were killed. Nelson lost 449 men – including himself – but his ships all returned to port safely. More importantly, any chance that Napoleon had of invading Britain was gone and the British Navy would remain in control of the world's oceans for the next century.

Hiram Berdan and 'Berdan's Sharpshooters'

Hiram Berdan was born in the small New York Town of Phelps and worked as a mechanical engineer in New York City. He was also a renowned marksman and, prior to the outbreak of the American Civil war, had been the top rifle shot in the United States for fifteen years.

Berdan's inventions before the war included a repeating rifle and a patented musket ball. He had also devised a machine for separating gold from ore. He had become wealthy and internationally well known as a result of his work.

At the outbreak of war, Berdan strenuously lobbied US President Abraham Lincoln to establish a regiment of sharpshooters, an idea that had originally been dreamed up by Swiss-American marksman Caspar Trepp. Trepp had conceived of special units of marksmen using the best rifles who could develop the art of skirmishing. These men could function as advance scouts or flank skirmishers, providing protection for the rest of the army. Trepp was an immigrant, however, and needed a man of Berdan's influence to advance his ideas. Berdan being the type of man he was, however, swiftly appropriated the idea, making it his own.

Berdan lobbied relentlessly and finally, Lincoln's Secretary of War, Simon Cameron, accepted the idea. On 30 November 1862, Berdan was appointed Colonel, 1st United States Sharpshooters. Cameron instructed him to establish his own specifications, such as personnel, weapons, equipment and uniform.

Flyers and posters were issued calling for volunteers but Berdan was determined to take on only the most able. During the summer of 1861, he and his officers travelled across the Union looking for likely candidates, taking in state fairs, town meetings and sports events. They made particular appeals for European marksmen, calling for Swiss and Germans to join up.

There was always a good turn out at their event, partly due to the glamour attached to the regiment, but mainly because it was believed that the sharpshooters would be the best-paid soldiers in the entire Union army.

Berdan pitched it attractively to prospective recruits:

> *The Government supplies each man with one of Berdan's improved Sharp's rifles which will fire 1¼ miles at the rate of 18 times a minute. We have no drill or picket duty. Our warfare is like the Guerilla or the Indian. Our uniform is green for summer, the color of grass & foliage, and Miller's Grey for fall and winter. You are privileged to lay upon the ground for shooting, picking your position. No commander while firing.*

Such attractive conditions drew many more applicants than there were places. Therefore, each applicant was put through a stringent test of his shooting skills. To be accepted, a man had to fire ten bullets in succession into a ten-inch circle from a distance of 200 yards. Having achieved that, there was then a test of moral character and testimonials and references also had to be provided. The 1,392 officers and men who won through would quickly become known as 'Berdan's Sharpshooters'.

On 24 September 1861, Berdan created the 1st Regiment of United States Sharpshooters which consisted of ten companies – four from New York, three from Michigan and one each from Vermont, New Hampshire and Wisconsin. However, the quality of the applicants had been so good that four days later he was given permission to form the 2nd Regiment of United States Sharpshooters which was made up of 1,178 officers and men in eight companies – two each from New Hampshire and Vermont and one each from Maine, Minnesota, Michigan, and Pennsylvania. It was commanded by Colonel Henry Post.

Berdan now had more than 2,500 of the deadliest marksmen in the United States under his command, men that he boasted were worth 30,000 ordinary troops. They were to be issued with Sharp's 13.2mm calibre breech-loading rifles, a model that fired a cartridge including the bullet and a sack of paper or thin cloth that contained the powder charge. They also occasionally used target rifles that were equipped with telescopic sights.

Characteristically, Berdan wanted his men to stand out on the parade ground. He devised for them uniforms of forest-green wool frock coats and trousers that certainly provided a contrast with the blue uniformed Union Army of the Potomac. However, the green uniform also served as very good cover when the troopers were in woodland or even in open countryside. Their green forage caps often bore black ostrich feathers and their buttons were made of black rubber and not the shiny brass that other Union soldiers' uniforms were made of. And to protect them against the roughness of the terrain, they wore brogan shoes and knee-length leather gaiters. They quickly became known as 'green coats', but the uniform attracted the attention of many and the feelings about it were summed up by a reporter from the New York Post who wrote that Berdan's men reminded him of Robin Hood and his band of outlaws.

They were rigorously trained between September 1861 and March 1862 at a 'Camp of Instruction' north of Washington where they were told never to recklessly expose themselves, to make use of all possible cover and, most importantly, not to waste ammunition.

The camp, in fact, became a great diversion for polite Washington society. Onlookers arrived from far and wide, visiting dignitaries dropped in and even the President himself turned up to observe. Berdan drilled his men daily in front of large crowds of spectators and the displays of shooting proved particularly popular.

At this point, however, demonstrations were all that the Sharpshooters could do. They did not have enough weapons to fight.

The War Department was unwilling to cough up

the money to buy a $45 Sharp's rifle for every man in the two regiments which left these sharpshooters effectively unarmed. Some men had brought their own weapons but this meant that many were left with only ancient muskets with which to fight. They were eventually offered less expensive Colt rifles, perfectly good weapons but not what had been promised. At one point, the War Department wanted to put the Sharpshooters into action, but the officers and men refused to go until they received the proper ordinance.

While Berdan's Sharpshooters were admired by many, the President amongst them, the ordinary Union soldier looked upon them as something of a luxury. It was a view that would persist in the US military for the next 150 years. Snipers would be trained up where necessary, for the Korean War or the Vietnam War, but their role was not really seen by the ordinary infantryman as real soldiering. Their disdain could clearly be seen in their interpretation of the letters USSS that were inscribed on the sharpshooters' cap badges. The letters stood for 'United States Sharp Shooters' but the disgruntled infantrymen said they really stood for 'Unfortunate Soldiers Sadly Sold'.

But the public loved it and saw the glamorous

regiments as the answer to their prayers, believing that the forces of the rebellious South would have no answer to their professionalism and their extraordinary skills.

The war raged on and the Sharpshooters remained unused, partly because there was disagreement about exactly how they should be deployed. Some believed that they should be used en masse, arguing that their long-range fire would devastate the enemy. It was pointed out, however, that one accurate artillery barrage could quite easily wipe out the regiment as it lay in the grass. Eventually, it was agreed that they should be organised into units no bigger than companies and attached to regular regiments while the two best shots in the two regiments should be assigned separate sniper duty, targeting Confederate officers, artillery crews and enemy snipers. These men were issued with heavy 35-pound rifles equipped with a specially devised telescopic sight. Furthermore, they were given authority to select their own targets. It was a forerunner of the type of sniper unit that operated in the twentieth century.

Finally, in March 1862, after months of training, Berdan's Sharpshooters were deployed, the Colt having been temporarily accepted. They were assigned to the Corps commanded by General Irvin McDowell but the Sharp's rifles would finally arrive a few months later.

They saw their first action at the siege of Yorktown, their task being to silence the Confederate cannon. News of their effectiveness in this task led other commanders to request their assistance and they became active on the left flank of the battle after General William Smith had asked for their help. This was a style of warfare very much like that of the First World War fifty-two years later. They occupied water-filled trenches and fired through loopholes, the slightest movement or sound alerting the enemy to their presence. They spent as many as sixteen hours a day up to their knees in muddy, stagnant water.

Now equipped with brand-new Sharp's rifles, the 1st Regiment of Sharpshooters moved on to Williamsburg but morale noticeably declined in the regiment as time wore on, partly because their constant presence in the thick of battle was leading to heavy casualties. Many resigned, including Colonel Post, commander of the 2nd Regiment. The long-simmering resentment between Berdan and Caspar Trepp – the inventor of the sharpshooter concept – who was a lieutenant colonel in the 1st Regiment, was also causing problems.

The Sharpshooters played an important part in the Battle of Gettysburg in July 1863, but Berdan began to believe that his officers were trying to bring him down. One of his problems was suddenly solved, however, when Trepp was killed, ironically by a sniper's bullet, at Mine Run.

A short while later, Berdan was himself wounded, receiving an injury that forced him to retire from military service.

Meanwhile, those of the Sharpshooters who had not been killed or who had not already left the army, fought in the Battle of the Wilderness and at Spotsylvania Courthouse. The attrition had been terrible. For example, of 136 men who had started in Company A of the Sharpshooters, only 26 remained by the end of April 1864. In the three months that remained of their term of enlistment, they fought in no fewer than eighteen engagements and lost a further 14 of their number.

The Sharpshooters proved beyond question that the sniper was a deadly and essential part of any army, killing more Confederate soldiers than any other regiment in the Union force. But of the 2,570 who had started the war, 1,008 were killed or wounded, an appalling casualty rate. Finally, in early 1865, with the war coming to an end, the regiments were broken up.

Hiram Berdan was ultimately disappointed not to receive the recognition he craved and believed he deserved. He died in 1893, aged sixty-eight, and was buried at the national military cemetery at Arlington in Virginia.

BILLY SING

In the spring of 1915, troops from Britain, France, Australia and New Zealand landed on the beaches of the Gallipoli Peninsula in Turkey. They were there to help a naval offensive in the Dardanelles, the strait separating Europe from Asia, and to threaten the Turkish capital, Constantinople (now known as Istanbul). The Ottoman Turks were allied with Germany and its allies in the war that had broken out the previous year.

The hope was that, thus threatened, Turkey would surrender and a supply route could be opened up through the Black Sea to hard-pressed Russia. The Gallipoli campaign turned into a bloody war of attrition and, as in other parts of Europe, most of it took place in muddy trenches. 46,000 Allied troops, mostly from Australia and New Zealand, were killed between April 1915 and January 1916, when the Allies finally withdrew.

The terrain was made for snipers and with the ANZAC and Turkish emplacements overlooking each other, they took full advantage of it. Both sides dispatched snipers into the undergrowth, creeping death machines who, with their spotters selected their prey, like hunters stalking game, and ruthlessly and efficiently eliminated it. Losses to snipers on both sides were high and the Commonwealth troops – the ANZACS – averaged twenty deaths a day to snipers.

Armed with German Mauser rifles, the Turks were highly proficient both at shooting and at concealment, using both man-made and natural camouflage. They also employed effective strategies to get their man. One officer reported that his detachment suffered one casualty per night and it always happened in the same place, just opposite the mess. One evening, he spied something white lying at the side of the road, at the spot where the shootings had occurred. It turned out to be a piece of white cloth.

That night, there were no casualties but the following night he noticed a piece of white paper lying on the ground at exactly the same spot. He removed this and assigned the responsibility of keeping that area free of marks and items to one of his men. There were no further casualties there.

It would appear that the mark was dropped there and every evening the sniper aimed a little to the side of the mark. When it was obscured by something passing in front of it, he fired and invariably hit an ANZAC soldier.

Billy Sing, a soldier in the Australian force that took part in the landings on Turkish soil at Gallipoli in April 1915, during the First World War, was known as 'The Assassin' or 'The Murderer' by his colleagues, so callous was his attitude towards the enemy. There are a number of varying estimates as to his tally of confirmed kills – instances when the spotter who accompanied him in his work actually saw the target fall. According to Brigadier-General Granville Ryrie, the commander of the 2nd Australian Light Horse Brigade, Sing was responsible for 119 kills. Regimental records state that he had 150. On 23 October 1915, however, General William Birdwood, commander of the ANZAC forces, issued a dispatch that complimented Sing on 210 'unconfirmed' kills. His steadily increasing tally of kills was passed along the trenches like a cricket score on a daily basis, helping morale on the Allied side.

His tally was estimated by Major Stephen Midgely as 300 and it had been Midgely who had told General Birdwood about this remarkable marksman. Birdwood had said to Kitchener, 'if his troops could match the capacity of the Queensland sniper, the allied forces would soon be in Constantinople.' Birdwood had first-hand experience of Sing's remarkable ability as a marksman, having joined him as his spotter on one occasion. It gave Billy Sing a chance to display the mordant wit with which he approached the task in hand. It was a windy day when he and the general went out and as a careless Turk showed his head above the parapet, Sing fired, narrowly missing, the wind having pushed the bullet off course. He waited a few moments for the wind to drop and then once again put his eye to his rifle sight. The next bullet struck a Turkish soldier, spinning him out of his trench. The poker-faced sniper turned to the general and told him that he would not add that kill to his tally as he had actually been aiming at another Turk.

Sing was a methodical man with a business-like approach to his grisly job. When asked by Major Midgely how he felt about killing men in what was, after all, cold blood, he replied that shooting them had never caused him to lose any sleep.

William Edward Sing was born in Queensland, Australia in March 1886 to a Chinese immigrant, a drover who had come to Australia from Shanghai and an English nurse who had immigrated from Kingswinford in Staffordshire. He grew up on the family's farm with his two sisters.

At the time, there was a substantial amount of racial prejudice towards Chinese immigrants in Australia and Sing suffered his share. However, one place where he did find respect was at the Proserpine Rifle Club where he distinguished himself with his impressive marksmanship. As well as targets, he also established a reputation for shooting kangaroos around his hometown of Clermont.

He worked hauling timber and was later a stockman and a cane cutter. But, just two months after the outbreak of war in August 1915, he enlisted in the First Australian Imperial Force (AIF). Also enlisting from the North Queensland area was Ian 'Jack' Idriess who would later become a prolific and influential author. But in 1915, he was destined to work with Billy Sing as his spotter.

After a few months of training, Sing sailed for Egypt five days before Christmas 1914. He and the other members of his regiment waited in the Egyptian desert, impatient to get into action and hearing about the troubles of their Australian comrades in Gallipoli. Finally, with casualty numbers rising on the peninsula, Sing and his comrades of the Australian Light Horse were sent to the Dardanelles on 16 May.

For the first few weeks, they fought alongside the infantry battalions in order to gain experience. They had never been to war before, after all. By the middle of June, however, they rejoined their regiment when it moved to the seaward side of Bolton's Ridge. The position was known as Chatham's Post, in memory of a young English-born Light Horse officer who had met his end there. There, Billy Sing would perfect his deadly art.

Each morning, before sunrise, Billy and his spotter would take up their position. The day would then be spent in absolute stillness and silence. Billy would have his Short Magazine Lee Enfield No.1 Mark III calibre rifle aimed and ready for the first sign of movement from the areas he was targeting – a trench 350 yards from his post, a communication trench at about 500 yards' distance and a track in a gully at about 1,000 yards' distance.

The Turks, driven to distraction by the success of the sniper at Chatham's Post, assigned one of their own best marksmen to try to deal with him. Nicknamed 'Abdul the Terrible' by the Allies, he was, like all great snipers, a meticulous man, analysing shootings, trying to separate the everyday shots by ordinary Australian troopers from the brilliant marksmanship of his rival sniper. He reconstructed each fatal shot, working out the bullet's angle of trajectory from the entrance and exit wounds on the victim's body. He then related these to the exact stance and position of the soldier before he was shot and deduced exactly where the bullets were fired from. Eventually he began to decipher a pattern, his eyes continually returning to a hillock on the heights at Chatham's Post. It was on that position that he decided to concentrate his efforts.

Like Billy Sing, Abdul occupied his position before sunrise each morning and also like him, he spent his days watching and waiting, with infinite patience, the essential skill of the sniper.

One morning, as Sing's spotter swung his telescope round the enemy positions, he spotted movement. He passed the telescope to Billy and he raised it to his eye. Pointing it in the direction indicated by the spotter, he found himself staring into the eyes and rifle muzzle of 'Abdul the Terrible'.

As Sing settled his Lee Enfield into his shoulder and prepared to fire, Abdul did the same. Just at that moment, however, a bullet slammed into the Turk's forehead between the eyes killing him outright. Sing had been the quicker of the two.

Shortly after, the aggrieved Turks turned their artillery on Chatham Post and Billy and his spotter were lucky to get out alive.

Sing was wounded in August 1915 when an

enemy sniper spotted him and his spotter of the time, Trooper Tom Sheehan. He fired a bullet that, incredibly, passed through Sheehan's telescope, from one end to the other, and wounded him in the hands before entering his mouth and emerging through his left cheek. The bullet travelled on, hitting Sing in the right shoulder. Sheehan was shipped back to Australia but a barely a week passed before Billy Sing was back in position at Chatham's Post.

Billy Sing's exploits made him famous, stories appearing in London and American newspapers. In March 1916, he was awarded the Distinguished Conduct Medal for conspicuous gallantry as a sniper at Gallipoli.

He joined the 31st Infantry and sailed for England from Egypt. From there, he was sent to France but in the course of the next nineteen months, he was frequently out of the line due to wounds and the recurrence of old illnesses and injuries incurred in Gallipoli. While recuperating, he travelled to Edinburgh where he met and married Elizabeth Stewart, the twenty-one-year-old daughter of a naval cook.

In France, snipers were less necessary but he still performed with courage and dedication. On one occasion, at Polygon Wood, in late September 1917, he led a patrol that managed to wipe out German snipers who were causing a great deal of casualties amongst the Australians. For this action, he was awarded the Belgian Croix de Guerre.

Arriving back in Australia in late 1918 or early 1919, he was greeted by the people of Clermont as a returning hero. They turned out in droves and a large procession led him to the town hall.

However, life at home did not go well. After a few years, his wife left him and Billy became a gold prospector on the Miclere goldfield. In 1942, now aged fifty-six, he moved to Brisbane where he took a labouring job, but his health was failing by this time. On 19 May 1943, he died alone in his room in the boarding house in which he was living.

He left five shillings which was found in his room and six pounds ten shillings and sixpence that he was owed in wages. The most valuable item he left was a hut worth twenty pounds on the Miclere claim.

It was a sad and lonely end to a man whose exploits had once echoed round the world like a bullet from his sniper's gun.

FRANCIS PEGAHMAGABOW AND HENRY NORWEST

Francis Pegahmagabow was the most decorated First Nations soldier in Canadian military history. Awarded the Military Medal three times – one of only thirty-nine members of the Canadian Expeditionary Force to achieve this accolade – he was an expert marksman and scout who is credited with 378 verified kills as a sniper but was responsible for capturing around 300 enemy soldiers.

Pegahmagabow was born on what is now the Shawanaga First Nation Reserve to Michael Pegahmagabow, a member of the Parry Island First Nation and his wife, Mary Contin of the Henvey Inlet First Nation. A member of the Ojibwa tribe, he grew up near Parry Sound in Ontario and until the outbreak of the First World War in 1914, worked as a marine fireman for the Department of Marine and Fisheries on the Great Lakes.

When war was declared, Pegahmagabow, who had enlisted immediately for service with the Canadian Expeditionary Force, was assigned to the 23rd Canadian Regiment (Northern Pioneers), based at the Canadian Forces Base, Valcartier, about sixteen miles north of Quebec City. His army tent there was decorated with traditional symbols, including the symbol of his tribe, the deer.

Finally, in February 1915, 'Peggy', as he was called by his colleagues, sailed for Europe with the 1st Canadian Infantry Battalion of the 1st Canadian Division. They were the first Canadian troops to be sent to fight in the war in Europe. Sadly, only a few would return at the end of the conflict.

The men of the First Contingent, as they have become known in the decades since, did not have to wait too long before seeing action, fighting in the Second Battle of Ypres which took place in April and May of 1915. It was the battle in which the Germans used chlorine gas for the first time. It was during this battle that Peggy began to establish a reputation for himself, as a sniper as well as a scout. As well as his sniping duties, Peggy was tasked with carrying messages along the lines and it was for the courage he showed doing this that he was awarded his first Military Medal. Interestingly, he had initially been nominated by his commanding officer, Lieutenant Frank Albert Creighton, for the Distinguished Conduct Medal but this was downgraded to the MM because, it has been alleged, of Pegahmagabow's ethnicity.

In the horrific Battle of the Somme, fought from July to November 1916, he was wounded in the leg but recovered in time to join his battalion as it moved to Belgium. He earned a bar to his Military Medal at the Battle of Passchendaele in November 1917 and his third came when, in August 1918, he braved heavy machine gun fire to go out into no-man's land and bring back enough ammunition to allow his sniping post to continue firing and help repulse enemy counter-attacks.

Returning to civilian life, Pegahmagabow entered First Nations politics. In 1943, he became Supreme Chief of the Native Independent Government, an early First Nations organisation. He died on the Parry Island Reserve in 1952 at the age of sixty-one.

Another expert First Nations Canadian sniper was Lance Corporal Henry Louis Norwest. Born in Fort Saskatchewan in Alberta of French-Cree ancestry, in his three years as a sniper with the 50th Canadian Infantry Battalion, Norwest officially fired 115 fatal shots, making him the greatest sniper amongst the Canadian forces at the front and quite possibly the best in all of the British forces. He earned the Military Medal and bar, one of around

830 members of the Canadian Expeditionary Force to be accorded this honour.

His reputation was well known amongst the German troops, as was learned from captured German prisoners, and he was greatly feared by them.

He had worked as a saddler and cowpuncher up until the war but on 15 January, a few months after the start of the First World War, he enlisted under his real name, Henry Louie. Three months later, however, he was thrown out for drunkenness. He was briefly employed by the Royal Northwest Mounted Police but re-enlisted in Calgary eight months after his discharge, this time giving Norwest as his surname.

From being a bad influence, Norwest developed into an inspiration to his comrades. One of them wrote of him: 'Our famous sniper no doubt understood better than most of us the cost of life and the price of death. Henry Norwest carried out his terrible duty superbly because he believed his special skill gave him no choice but to fulfill his indispensable mission. Our 50th [Battalion] sniper went about his work with passionate dedication and showed complete detachment from everything while he was in the line … Yet when we had the rare opportunity to see our comrade at close quarters, we found him pleasant and kindly, quite naturally one of us, and always an inspiration.'

His calm demeanour is said to have never deserted him, whatever situation he found himself in. His 'clear and remarkably steady eye' was noted and one colleague added that his eyes were 'like discs of polished marble … enigmatic, yet hypnotic, strangely piercing yet mellowly compassionate, deadly serious, yet humorously twinkling. One could never forget them.'

They nicknamed him 'Ducky' after he explained to his comrades that while in London he had been forced to 'duck' the girls there.

His comrades' respect and admiration for him was interesting because snipers were rarely the most popular men in a battalion. The more successful a sniper was, the more likelihood there was of retribution being brought down on the area in which he was operating, usually in the form of a heavy artillery barrage. Naturally, they were also the most unpopular prisoners when captured by the enemy; in the desire to avenge fallen comrades, action was usually swift and fatal as soon as a sniper fell into enemy hands.

Sniping was, of course, a hazardous occupation. Much of Norwest's time was spent in no-man's land, the empty, but deadly dangerous area between the opposing forces. He would also frequently slip behind enemy lines to make a kill under cover of darkness. But he was born to be a sniper. He was an expert shot, had the ability to remain still for long periods of time and was skilled in the art of concealment, using his knowledge of camouflage techniques to blend in with the surrounding countryside.

Norwest earned his Military medal in 1917 at a hillock on Vimy Ridge that had been nicknamed 'the Pimple'. A huge Allied offensive had been launched and the Canadian Corps were assigned the task of taking the Ridge. It was not the first time the Allies had tried to capture it but all previous efforts had failed. This time, however, the Canadians succeeded and by the end of the first day, 9 April, most of the Ridge had been won. Three days later, the two remaining enemy positions, including the Pimple were also captured, Norwest playing no small part in the action. He was described as having shown 'great bravery, skill and initiative in sniping the enemy after the capture of the Pimple. By his activity he saved a great number of our men's lives.'

A little more than a year later, Norwest once again displayed commendable bravery when, in the Battle of Amiens, the Allies attacked and captured a strategically important salient. Taking the Germans completely by surprise, they advanced nineteen kilometres in just three days. In this time, Norwest destroyed a number of enemy machine gun posts and broke the battalion record for confirmed kills by a sniper.

He would not live to see the end of the war and an Allied victory, however. On 18 August, just three months before the armistice, as he and two other soldiers were hunting for a nest of enemy snipers that had been taking a toll on the Canadian forces, a sniper's bullet hit him in the head, killing him instantly. He was posthumously awarded the bar to his Military Medal for 'Gallantry in the Field'.

Henry Norwest's comrades recognised the skill of the marksman who had finally ended the life of their brave and remarkable comrade. On the temporary grave marker they made for him, they wrote, 'It must have been a damned good sniper that got Norwest.'

SIMO HAYA

It was not for nothing that he was known as the 'White Death' because during the brutal Winter War of 1939–40 between the Soviet Union and Finland, he killed 542 enemy soldiers in just 100 days, a tally to which he would undoubtedly have added had he not been seriously wounded and invalided out of the war.

The Winter War came at the end of several decades of worsening relations between the two neighbours. Finland had for centuries been part of the kingdom of Sweden but in 1809 it was conquered by Russia and made an autonomous buffer state within the Russian Empire, providing protection for the imperial capital, Saint Petersburg. At the end of the nineteenth century, Russia tried to assimilate Finland completely but even though these efforts failed due to the internal strife Russia was undergoing at the time, relations with the Finns deteriorated and self-determination movements began to become influential.

The collapse of the Russian Empire in 1917 gave

the Finns the chance for which they had been waiting and independence was declared. Relations between the two were never completely repaired, however, despite the signing of a non-aggression pact in 1932.

Following the Great Purge in Russia in 1938 and Joseph Stalin's rise to almost absolute power, Soviet foreign policy radically changed. They began to pursue the recovery of the provinces lost during the October Revolution and the Russian Civil War. In 1938 and into 1939, the Soviets started an intensive mobilisation close to the Finnish border. Then, in October 1939, they made territorial demands amongst which was one stating that the border with Finland should be pushed westward to a point thirty kilometres east of Viiprui. The Finns, of course, rejected the demands and, after some skirmishing, on 30 November the Red Army invaded Finland with 450,000 men and bombed the Finnish capital, Helsinki.

It was a brutal war fought in the most dreadful of winter conditions. The Soviets had three times as many soldiers as the Finns but the Finns had thirty times as many aircraft and a hundred times as many tanks. In the three and a half months in which it was savagely fought, 25,000 Finns and 127,000 Russians lost their lives.

The Finns fought with a fiery passion and heroes inevitably emerged. The conditions were perfect for snipers and several astonishing kill rates were notched up. Sulo Kolkka, for instance, approached sniping as if it was a sport. His particular tactic was to sneak behind the Russian lines and strike fear into them by shooting them from behind. He is credited with slightly more than 400 kills in 105 days of combat. He also used a machine gun and killed a further twenty with that. A Russian sniper was sent to hunt him down, but after the two men had stalked each other over the frozen wastes for several days, Kolkka shot him dead from 600 yards.

However, it was the sniper known as the 'White Death' who took the sniper's art to another level and it is no surprise that he is often recognised as the greatest sniper who ever shouldered a rifle butt.

Simo Haya was born in either 1905 or 1906 (the date differs according to which source is used) in Rautajärvi in Finland, a town close to the border with Russia and was thirty-four-years old when the war broke out. Like many of the greatest snipers, he was an outdoorsman who was a practised hunter and stalker. He knew the benefits of concealment, of patience and of a good steady hand when hunting for animals and he brought these skills to his role in the Finnish army. He had served his year of compulsory military service in 1925 when he was twenty years old and during those twelve months had achieved the rank of lance corporal. He had then settled down to a quiet life as a farmer but later enlisted in the Suojelskunta – the Finnish Civil Guard – serving in his local area.

In 1939, he was called up to serve in the 6th Company of JR 34 in the Finnish army on the Kollaa River where he took part in one of the most famous actions of the war when, in temperatures of minus twenty to minus forty degrees, and with the ground covered in several feet of snow, the Finns, under the command of Major General Uiluo Tuompo faced twelve Soviet divisions, some 160,000 men. Red Army losses were staggering as the Finns put up a fanatical defence of this strategically important region. In one famous incident, the battle of 'Killer Hill', 32 Finns are said to have fought against 4,000 Soviet soldiers. The region remained in Finnish hands at the end of the war and this resolute and courageous stand is nowadays known to Finns as 'The Miracle of Kollaa'.

This was the arena in which the 'White Death' operated, waging a one-man campaign against the Red Army. Dressed in all-white camouflage to blend in with the snowy landscape, and armed with a Russian-made Mosin-Nagant M28/30 rifle, he would go out with a day's rations and ammunition and lie in wait for Russians. On one day, he delivered fatal shots to twenty-five enemy soldiers.

Before long, the Russians were all too aware of this man who seemed to be invisible but was decimating their forces. They made a number of attempts to eliminate him. A task force which was assembled and despatched to find him succeeded in finding him but they only realised they had found him when their comrades began to drop like flies beside them. He wiped out the entire task force. He also killed a team of counter-snipers that were sent into the woods to find and kill him. They tried artillery strikes in areas in which they believed him to be operating, but next day another brace of Red Army soldiers would fall to the ground with bullets in their heads, fired from a great distance by a man they had not even seen.

Finnish High Command were so delighted with the work he was doing that they gave him a present to replace his antiquated rifle. It was a custom-built Sako M2/28-30. But, interestingly, he did not use a telescopic sight. He preferred to use the rifle's regular iron sights, mainly because it allowed him to present a smaller target. He also wanted to avoid the chance of light glinting off the sight as would have been possible with a telescopic one. He was only too aware of this because many of the snipers he had killed had been given away by just that oversight.

His luck finally ran out on 2 March 1940 when he was hit in the jaw by an explosive bullet that blew away part of his face. He was dragged from the battlefield in a coma by his comrades, but not, he later claimed, before he had killed the sniper who had shot him. He did not wake up for eleven days, but the day he awoke was an auspicious one – it was the day that the Winter War ended as a victory for Finland over their mighty neighbour.

Simo Haya was awarded five medals for valour, including the prestigious Kollaa Cross. He was also promoted from corporal to second lieutenant. His final tally was 542 but he is reported to have killed 200 more men with a Suomi submachine gun which brings his total kill to well over 700 men in around a hundred days.

He returned to his farm and spent his later years breeding dogs and hunting moose. He died in 2002, aged ninety-six.

Vasily Zaitsev

Between the two world wars, the Red Army was the one that maintained the highest degree of sniper training and preparedness. Of course, they had some practical experience during that time. Just as German pilots were able to hone their bombing and strafing skills during the Spanish Civil War that lasted from 1936 until 1939, so Soviet military personnel were able to see action first hand as they advised Republican forces in that conflict. They had also fought the bloody Winter War against Finland in 1939 and 1940.

The Soviets learned well from the Winter War; just how well can be seen from an incident in September 1941 during the Second World War when the German 465th Infantry Regiment lost 100 men to what were described as 'tree snipers' in a thickly wooded area.

Russian snipers were different to snipers in other armies in that they were expected to be general sharpshooters as well as specialist snipers in both defensive and offensive situations. Consequently, by

1938, six million Russian soldiers had qualified for the 'Voroshilov Sharpshooter' badge, named after the Soviet military commander and bureaucrat, Kliment Voroshilov that was awarded to soldiers passing the sniper's course. Although these soldiers may not have been snipers in the true sense of the word, they were highly trained marksmen – and markswomen.

And, in fact, there were around 2,000 Soviet women snipers, one of the most successful of whom, Ludmilla Pavlichenko, is credited with 309 kills. The team of Nataly V. Kovshova and Maria Polivanova had 300, Liba Rugova 274 and Yekatarina Zuranova 155. Of those 2,000 women snipers, 500 did not survive the war.

One of Zaitsev's trainees was Tania Chernova, a Russian-American who had returned to Russia at the outbreak of war, in order to be close to her beloved grandparents. They were killed, however, along with many others in their town, by the invading Germans, Tania wanted revenge and, concealing her American background, she became a partisan with a mission to kill as many Nazis as she could. She learned from the master, Vasily Zaitsev, also becoming his lover.

Further proof of the seriousness with which the Soviet High Command took sniping can be seen in the astonishing fact that up to 1938, around 53,000 Mosin-Nagant sniping rifles were manufactured but by 1942, 53,000 were being manufactured annually.

Vasily Grigorevich Zaitsev was possibly the greatest of all the Soviet snipers, although many have suggested that the legend that grew around this phenomenal killing machine was in part a creation of the Soviet propaganda machine.

He was born in Yeleninsoye in the chilly Ural Mountains and from the age of four was taught to hunt by his grandfather. He would have learned, therefore, at a very early age many of the skills required by the sniper – the patience and stealth required to stalk prey over a long period of time, as well as the ability to merge with his surroundings. He will also have developed that other necessary skill of the sniper – a cold and unrelenting ruthlessness.

Zaitsev had served in the Russian navy as a clerk in Vladivostok before volunteering for front-line duty after reading about the horrors of Stalingrad.

From August 1942 until February 1943, Stalingrad represented everything that was horrific about modern warfare. A point of great strategic importance on the Volga River, the city was destroyed by invading German forces that were stubbornly resisted by Soviet troops. After failing to capture other Russian cities, Hitler had ignored the advice of his generals, surrounding Stalingrad and trapping tens of thousands of civilians and soldiers inside. He believed that the fall of the city would open up the valuable Soviet oil fields and signal the end of the stubborn but costly Soviet resistance.

The offensive began in August 1942 with an intensive bombing raid by the Luftwaffe. A barrage of artillery fire added to the terror of the city's inhabitants and soon the landscape was an alien one, littered with collapsed buildings and thousands of corpses. Now, some of the bloodiest hand-to-hand fighting of the war began as the Red Army defended the city street-by-street and house-by-house.

Zaitsev had been assigned to the 1047th Rifle Regiment of the 284th Rifle Division that was commanded by general Nikolai Batyuk. He was put in charge of a snipers' training school in a ruined factory where he trained sniping apprentices who became known as zaichata, meaning 'leverets' or baby hares – Zaitsev's surname derives from the Russian word zayats meaning hare. His training, although only a few days – the war meant that troops could not be spared for much longer – included basic instruction on advanced rifle handling, scope shooting, ballistic performance, correct target selection and – most importantly – concealment. His philosophy of 'one shot, one kill' was distinctly different from that of the Germans who wasted vast amounts of ammunition and in the process lost large numbers of men. His zaichata, therefore, were highly prized by the cash-strapped Russians.

Some of them also became great heroes, almost as famous as their teacher, men such as Nikolai Kulikov, who was killed in 1943 and the elusive 'Zikan', both of whom notched up large numbers of victims.

This signalled the beginning of the sniper initiative in the 62nd Army and there were conferences and meetings at which ideas and techniques could be exchanged. It has been said that the snipers trained by Zaitsev were responsible for the deaths of more than 3,000 enemy soldiers.

Zaitsev was not only an unfailingly brilliant marksman. The Soviet authorities quickly learned that he could also be a weapon himself against an enemy whose morale was suspect in the face of the dreadful conflict in which it was engaged. Flyers were printed that detailed Zaitsev's achievements, elevating him into an almost supernatural force against which the Germans had no answer. The psychological effect of this on the exhausted and demoralised German troops was devastating.

For his own people, too, he became an unflagging symbol of the strength and courage that would be needed to defeat the enemy. Igor Danilov, a Russian Commissar and journalist, wrote newspaper articles about Zaitsev, turning him into one of the most famous people in the Soviet Union.

The biography of this Hero of the Soviet Union would be incomplete without the story that cemented his reputation, a story that has been dealt with in film and literature probably more than any other personal, one-to-one combat in the entire Second World War. To what extent it has been embellished by the Soviet propaganda machine and the 2001 film that was made of it, Enemy at the Gates, starring Jude Law, is, of course, impossible to say, but it does help to shed further light on this extraordinary human being.

German High Command, resolved to do something about the sniper who was cutting a swathe through their forces, dispatched one of their own super-snipers to do battle with Zaitsev. We are led to believe that Major Erwin König (some sources name the German sniper as Colonel Heinz Thorwald) was the senior instructor at the Zossen sniper school in Germany.

Zaitsev heard about the arrival of König in Stalingrad and was concerned. Of course, he had eliminated countless enemy snipers but only after putting in a great deal of work on them, observing their routines, knowing how they worked and where they would be likely to strike.

For two days, he and Kulikov searched for some sign of the German, studying the German lines through binoculars. But, as the battle raged around them, they saw nothing untoward.

On the third day, another man accompanied Zaitsev and when this man stood up to point out a soldier in the distance he thought might be König, he was shot in the shoulder. The eagle-eyed Soviet sniper was certain that at last he had found his man, hiding under a sheet of iron near a disabled tank and a pile of bricks.

He had to be sure, however, and to test his theory, he hung a glove from the end of a stick and raised it up above the parapet behind which he was concealing himself. There was a gunshot and when he pulled down the stick, he found that the glove had a bullet hole in it. He was now sure that König was hiding under the sheet of iron.

On the fourth day of his hunt, he and Kulikov waited until the sun was behind them and shining straight at the German's hiding place. Any movement from König was likely to provide a glint of light in the bright sunshine and Zaitsev would be able to take a bead on him. He pointed his rifle at the sheet of iron and waited patiently, as he did most days.

Suddenly the sun bounced off a piece of glass in front of König's hiding place. Zaitsev nodded to Kulikov who slowly raised a helmet over the top of the parapet. König fired once and as he did so, Kulikov rose, screaming loudly as if he had been hit.

The German next made a fatal error. Instead of lying low, he raised his head a little to be able to get a better view of his latest victim. At that point, Zaitsev pulled the trigger of his Mosin Nagant and shot König between the eyes.

Vasily Zaitsev was eventually credited with 242 verified kills. Probably the greatest of all Russian snipers, he survived the war and died in 1991, aged seventy-six.

On 31 January 2006, Zaitsev was granted his dying wish. He was re-interred on Mamayev Kurgan, the hill overlooking the city of Volgograd, as Stalingrad is now known, where a memorial to the defenders of Stalingrad has been erected. On the monument is inscribed Zaitsev's famous quote:

'For us there is no land beyond (the) Volga.'

VIETNAM SNIPERS:

ADELBERT F. WALDRON, CHUCK MAWAHINNEY, CHARLES HATHCOCK

Never was the phrase 'one shot, one kill' used more effectively than in the activities of American snipers in the Vietnam War in the nineteen-sixties. Military marksmen developed their expertise to unparalleled levels, efficiently eliminating an enemy that was often difficult to find, let alone keep in a gun-sight long enough to shoot.

Vietnam was a war unlike any other and required tactics, procedures and weapons that were specially adapted to its unique conditions. The US Army and Marine Corps found themselves having to be constantly innovative and flexible and prepared to jettison old and trusted ideas in the face of an enemy whose tactics ranged from the guerrilla warfare of the Vietcong to huge multi-division offensives by the official North Vietnamese Army.

Of all the innovations and changes to the usual mode of operation one of the most effective was the widespread use of individual sharpshooters or snipers.

In Vietnam, American snipers developed their skills and techniques to such an extent that they could kill an enemy at ranges often greater than 800 metres. And all it took was a single round from a telescopically sighted rifle.

Of course, sniping made good economic sense – one bullet, one body was a pretty good ratio, especially when compared to the cost of some of the lengthy battles in the Vietnam War. And compared to figures from the Korean War when, it is estimated, it took 50,000 rounds of ammunition to kill one enemy soldier, the work of the modern sniper looked even better. Worse still, in Vietnam, the American infantry were expending 200,000 rounds per enemy body.

Lieutenant General John H. Hay Jr., commander of the army's 1st Infantry Division in 1967 wrote after the war, 'The use of snipers was not new in Vietnam, but the systematic training and employment of an aggressive, offensive sniper team – a carefully designed "weapon system" – was. A sniper was no longer just the man in the rifle squad who carried the sniper rifle; he was the product of an established school.'

Astonishingly, however, when the United States entered the Vietnam War, it possessed not a single trained sniper and there were no sniper units or training schools in existence. In previous conflicts there had, of course, been snipers, but at the end of those conflicts, the units had been disbanded and their members discharged or returned to the ranks of the infantry. The Vietnam War made the services think once again about snipers, however.

The Marines deployed sniper teams in 1965 but it took the Army another three years to put theirs into the field. Lieutenant General Julian J. Ewell assumed command of the 9th Infantry Division and took the leadership role in establishing army snipers in Vietnam.

It was a successful innovation. Snipers were cost-effective, used resources well and they were good for morale. Moreover, they were bad for the enemy's morale, as is demonstrated by a Chinese proverb that hangs on the wall of the marine sniper school at Camp Pendleton in California that says: 'Kill one man, terrorise a thousand.'

ADELBERT F. WALDRON

One of the men who became an expert sniper in Vietnam was Sergeant Adelbert F. Waldron, a collected and self-possessed man, who, by the end of the conflict, was the top-scoring American sniper of the Vietnam War with 109 confirmed kills to his credit.

Lieutenant General Ewell told how Waldron was riding along the Mekong River one afternoon on a Tango boat – an armoured troop carrier – when an enemy sniper began taking potshots at it from high up in a coconut tree on the shore about 900 metres away. As everyone on the boat strained their eyes to make out exactly where the shooter was, Waldron picked up his sniper rifle, took careful aim and shot the sniper out of the tree, and this while the boat was still moving.

On another occasion, on 4 February 1969, an official report states, Waldron and his partner had occupied a night ambush position with Company D of the 3/60th Infantry approximately three kilometers south of the town of Ben Tre. The area chosen for the ambush was at the end of a large rice paddy adjacent to a wooded area.

At around five past nine that evening, five Vietcong moved from the wooded area towards

Sergeant Waldron's position. Settling his rifle with its Starlight Scope – a night vision device – and noise suppressor, he shot the first member of the group and killed him. The dead man's comrades all dropped to the ground, remaining motionless for a few minutes. They then stood up again and cautiously started moving forward, seeming not to be aware that the shot that had killed their comrade had come from the rice paddy. Waldron opened fire again and killed all four.

Almost three hours later, at quarter to midnight, another four Vietcong appeared in the rice paddy to Waldron's left. He shot and killed all four. He had eliminated nine enemy troops in the course of a few hours at an average range of 400 metres.

Adelbert Waldron was born in 1933 in Syracuse, New York and joined the Navy in 1953. In 1965, he left the Navy but three years later enlisted in the US Army as a sergeant, the rank he held in the Navy when he left. He was attached to Company B, Third Battalion, 60th Infantry Regiment of the 9th Infantry Division and was sent to fight in Vietnam.

Already an excellent marksman, Waldron was selected to attend the 9th Infantry's in-country sniper school run by members of the Army Marksmanship Unit. The 9th Infantry conducted its operations in the Mekong Delta where it formed part of the Mobile Riverine Force (MRF). Riding shotgun on the US Navy brown water 'Tango Boats' and Patrol Boats, River (PBRs), the job of the MRF was to clean out insurgent units operating in the area. It was into this highly perilous environment that Adelbert Waldron arrived as a sniper.

It took him only until the middle of 1969 to achieve his record-breaking total and he did it using different equipment to his fellow snipers. Everyone else used bolt-action rifles whereas Waldron used a semi-automatic weapon, an accurised M-14 rifle, known popularly as an M-21. The M-21 Waldron used was a National Match quality weapon with a Leatherwood 3X-9X Adjustable Ranging Telescope (ART) and the standard leather M1907 sling. It would become the weapon of choice for US Army snipers until 1988.

Adelbert Waldron was discharged from the Army in March 1970, having been awarded two Distinguished Service Crosses, a Bronze Star and three Silver Stars. He spent the last nine months of his enlistment as a sniper instructor at the sniper school at Fort Benning in Georgia and, always an enigmatic individual, it is rumoured that he had some disciplinary issues. Eventually, his commanders asked him to accept an honourable discharge because they were reluctant to discipline such a highly decorated soldier.

He worked for a while for the noted mercenary, firearms engineer and former CIA agent, Mitchel WerBell III, employed as firearms instructor at his private training schools at the 'Farm' in Powder Springs, Georgia.

He died in obscurity in 1995, aged sixty-two and there is little but unconfirmed rumour concerning the last years of his life.

Chuck Mawhinney

Charles Benjamin 'Chuck' Mawhinney was born in Oregon in 1949, the son of a World War Two Marine Corps veteran. In just sixteen months in Vietnam, he achieved a total of 103 kills as a Marine Corps sniper. He also recorded an astonishing 216 probable kills. These were only listed as 'probable' because it had been too risky at the time to search the bodies of his victims for weapons and documents. Although Adelbert Waldron holds the record for the highest number of confirmed sniper kills by an American soldier, Mawhinney holds the record for a Marine sniper.

Oddly, however, for the two decades following his departure from the Marine Corps in 1970, no one knew about Mawhinney's feats in Vietnam. It was a book by another Marine Veteran that told the world. Mawhinney had always thought that books about snipers – and there were plenty written about his colleagues – were boring and he never even told his closest friends back home in Oregon what he had done in Southeast Asia.

He was in training to be a sniper from an early age, even if he did not know it. When he was young in Oregon he was an enthusiastic hunter, often going out on hunting expeditions alone, unaware that his silent, patient stalking of animals would provide him with many of the skills necessary to hunt and kill human beings in the jungles and rice paddies of Vietnam. In fact, he would later describe his sniping activities as 'the ultimate hunting trip: a man hunting another man who was hunting me.' It was simply his job, he has said, to kill Charlie – the US soldier's slang for Vietcong – before he was himself killed.

He had actually planned to join the Navy after graduating in June 1967 from high school in the remote town of Lakeview, Oregon, but decided on the Marines. His decision seemed to him a good one when he was allowed by the Marine recruiting officer to delay his enlistment until after the end of the deer-hunting season.

Displaying an aptitude for marksmanship, he was sent to the sniper school at Camp Pendleton. On graduation from the school, like every other graduate, he was given a little red book that was described as the sniper's manual. Inside, however, was one single sentence: 'Thou shalt kill.'

He was shipped to Vietnam in early 1968, just after the Tet Offensive that struck military and civilian command and control centres throughout South Vietnam in an effort to spark a general uprising among the population that would then topple the Saigon government and end the war in a single blow.

It was a difficult job. Generally, US troops used semi-automatic rifles that sprayed bullets at the enemy. The Army called the time when these guns were being fired as 'mad minutes'. Snipers, on the other hand, generally used bolt-action rifles that ensured much greater accuracy but would leave them virtually defenceless against automatic rifles at close range. Furthermore, the Vietcong put a bounty on the heads of American snipers and snipers were in no doubt that if captured, they would be treated

Charles Joseph Whitman was a student at the University of Texas in Austin. He was shot down by a policeman in August 1966 after a shooting rampage from the top of a clock tower at the University, which left 16 people dead and many others wounded. (Credit: Time & Life Pictures/Getty Images)

John Allen Muhammad (one of the Beltway Snipers) addresses the court in Manassas, Virginia, after he was given the death sentence for his role in a string of sniper killings around Washington DC in 2002. (Credit: Getty Images)

ABOVE: Deputy US Marshal Larry Cooper (right) testifies at the investigation into the FBI siege at Ruby Ridge, Idaho, in 1995. Next to him is a photo of Deputy US Marshal William Dego who was killed in the shoothout. (Credit: AFP/Getty Images)
BELOW: Irish politician and Sinn Fein leader Michael Collins (centre) was assassinated by the IRA in August 1922. (Credit: Getty Images)

A sign was erected on the site where the assassin Jack McCall was captured in the business district of South Dakota. McCall shot Wild Bill Hickok at Deadwood on 2 August 1876, following an argument between the pair that took place during a poker game. (Credit: Time & Life Pictures/Getty Images)

WANTED BY THE FBI

UNLAWFUL FLIGHT TO AVOID PROSECUTION - MURDER SECOND DEGREE

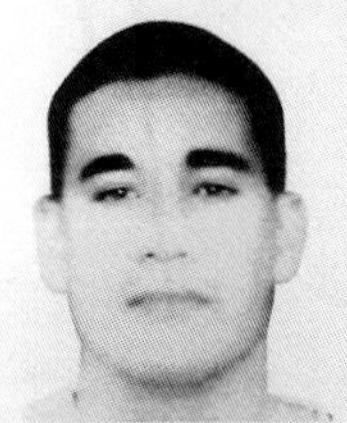

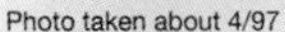

Photo taken about 4/97

Date of Photo Unknown

ANDREW PHILLIP CUNANAN

Alias: Andrew Phillip DeSilva

DESCRIPTION

Date of Birth: August 31, 1969; Place of Birth: San Diego, California;
Race: White; Sex: Male; Height: 5' 9"– 5' 10"; Weight: 160 – 180 pounds;
Eyes: Brown; Hair: Dark Brown.
Remarks: Cunanan may wear prescription eyeglasses. He has been known to change his hairstyle and weight. He allegedly has ties to the gay community. He has portrayed himself as being wealthy.

CAUTION

CUNANAN IS BEING SOUGHT FOR AN APRIL, 1997 MURDER, WHICH OCCURRED IN CHISAGO COUNTY, MINNESOTA. ALSO, HE IS WANTED FOR QUESTIONING IN CONNECTION WITH ADDITIONAL MURDERS, WHICH OCCURRED IN CHISAGO COUNTY, MINNESOTA; CHICAGO, ILLINOIS; AND PENNSVILLE, NEW JERSEY. CUNANAN MAY BE IN POSSESSION OF A HANDGUN.

ARMED AND EXTREMELY DANGEROUS

ADDITIONAL INFORMATION MAY BE FOUND ON THE FBI INTERNET PAGE:
http://www.fbi.gov

FBI Ten Most Wanted Fugitive: June, 1997. FBI/DOJ

FBI wanted poster of Andrew Phillip Cunanan, the man who shot and killed fashion designer Gianni Versace outside his home in Miami in 1997. (Credit: Time & Life Pictures/Getty Images)

From left to right: Sheriff Lillian Holley and prosecutor Robert Estill stand with outlaw John Dillinger in Chicago in March 1934. Dillinger has been described as a gangster who had both charm and style and, rather than being reviled, he was idolised by the public who followed his every move. (Credit: NY Daily News/Getty Images)

Here are just a few of the weapons used by John Dillinger during his many bank raids. This armoury was abandoned after the gangster fled an FBI trap in the Little Bohemia resort near Mercer, Wisconsin. (Credit: Getty Images)

Charles Guiteau (above), the attorney who assassinated American president James A. Garfield (right) on 2 July 1881, was hanged on 30 June 1882 despite strong evidence of his insanity. (Credit: Getty Images)

without mercy. Mawhinney, therefore, always carried a sidearm that he could use to put a bullet in his temple if it looked like he was about to be taken prisoner.

He was an extraordinary marksman and soldier. His squad leader described how he had the capability of running half a mile before standing straight up and shooting someone at a distance of 700 yards. He possessed the innate ability to gauge distance, moisture, weather and terrain, all the factors that affect the trajectory of a bullet. More than anything, however, he had the extraordinary patience required to be a good sniper. He was able to down one enemy soldier and wait sometimes hours afterwards until another crawled out to the body. Then, he would once again do the thing for which he seemed to have been put on the earth.

In one remarkable incident, he downed sixteen enemy soldiers with headshots using an M-14 automatic rifle that he often carried as well as his bolt-action rifle. These sixteen were listed only as 'probable kills' because there was no officer present to confirm them and there was no chance to search their bodies in order to provide evidence of their deaths.

Mawhinney and his partner would venture out

into the jungle every day from the safety of their combat base. The partner was often a rookie who spotted for the sniper, using binoculars and carried an automatic weapon should they have to resort to covering fire. Eventually, the rookie would be ready for his first kill, but it was up to the sniper to decide when that was.

In terrible heat and humidity, they would sometimes stalk the enemy for hours at a time until they could get within range. At other times, they would establish themselves in areas where they knew the enemy was present and would wait for them to pass by.

Mawhinney approached his job with the seriousness and respect it required. When an over-enthusiastic platoon leader pinned up a 'kill board' for snipers, Mawhinney was furious. He and his fellow snipers were, after all, risking their lives in difficult conditions and taking the lives of others in the way they did was anything but a game. They protested to their officers and the 'kill board' was discreetly removed.

Eventually, however, it took its toll on him. One colleague explained later how he feared for his friend's sanity, describing how other snipers would return to base in tears after their day's work, while

Mawhinney would laugh as he talked about his kills. It is suggested that it was a defence mechanism; the laughter was merely a means of hiding his true feelings. Nonetheless, when he had been a sniper for sixteen months, a chaplain informed Mawhinney's commander that he thought he was suffering from combat fatigue. His days in Vietnam were at an end.

He was assigned to Camp Pendleton for a time as a rifle instructor, but life as a trainer did not suit him after his experience of combat. He left the Marine Corps and went home to Oregon where he worked on a road maintenance crew for the Forestry Service until he retired.

In a recent interview in the Los Angeles Times, he summed up his time hunting humans in the jungle: 'You get to the point where you start living like an animal. You act like an animal, you work like an animal, you are an animal. All you think about is killing.'

Carlos Hathcock

He once recorded a kill from 2,500 meters using an M2 .50 caliber machinegun with a side-mounted scope – one of his own innovations. Known as 'Long Tra'ng' – the White Feather – because of the trademark white feather he wore to taunt his enemies, the North Vietnamese feared him so much that when the standard bounty on dead or captured American snipers was eight dollars, a reward of $30,000 is reported to have been put on his head.

Registering 93 kills, he was one of the deadliest snipers in the Marine Corps during the Vietnam War as well as probably its most celebrated marksman. He later drove a car with the license plate 'SNIPER'.

Gunnery Sergeant Carlos Norman Hathcock III was from a poor family that scratched a living near Little Rock in Arkansas. He lived with his grandmother after the divorce of his parents but his great love was the outdoors and he taught himself to hunt and shoot with a .22 rifle while still young. By the age of ten, he was bringing home meat for the table on a regular basis. He claims he knew where to find the rabbits and the squirrels he hunted. 'As a young'n,' he once said, 'I'd go sit in the woods and wait a spell. I'd just wait for the rabbits and squirrels 'cause sooner or later a squirrel would be in that very tree or a rabbit would be coming by that very log. I just knew it. Don't know why, just did.'

When he enlisted, he qualified from boot camp as an Expert marksman, a rare accolade. He began to win competitive shooting events, specialising in service rifle shooting. In 1965, he won the Wimbledon Cup, the most prestigious American 1,000 yard shooting championship.

Not long after, he was shipped to Vietnam but it was some time before his skills as a marksman were put to good use. The military had not quite realised the value of snipers in a war such as the one in which they were engaged. He started out as a military policeman but, desirous of more action, he volunteered for regular reconnaissance patrols. He felt uneasy, however, with the inexperienced soldiers he was working with, men who did not possess the particular skills that he did. He wanted to work on his own.

His fellow marines initially failed to see the point of a lone sniper but six months and fourteen kills later, they accepted his value. Hathcock responded to the responsibility by dedicating every waking minute to the war. He took no leave and never took a day off. So hard did he work, in fact, that towards the end of his first tour of duty, he was ordered to remain confined to quarters to prevent him going out on any more missions.

He attributed his prowess as a sniper to his ability to, as he put it, 'get in the bubble'. He was able to drop himself into an almost trance-like state of extreme concentration. He also had an innate understanding of the impact of everything around him on his work, every blade of grass and every breath of wind.

Although the five foot ten inch Hathcock weighed only 120 pounds, he also had to be extremely fit, of course. Once, when in hot, but careful pursuit of an enemy general, he had to crawl across more than a thousand metres of open countryside an inch at a time. It took him three days and nights. His superb grass and vegetation camouflage hid him from enemy troops who patrolled within twenty feet of him on a number of occasions. He was afraid, of course – 'Everybody was scared and those that weren't are liars,' he later said – but he used that fear to make himself more alert to everything going on around him. It helped him survive.

His career as a sniper was brought to a sudden end outside Khe San in 1969. Hathcock was riding on an amphibious tractor when it drove over a 500-pound box mine. With vicious flames engulfing the vehicle, he pulled seven marines off the vehicle before jumping to safety. Characteristically, he rejected the offer of a commendation for his extraordinary bravery.

But he received second- and third-degree burns that covered more than forty per cent of his body and was evacuated to the Brooke Army Medical

Center in Texas where he underwent thirteen skin graft operations. Saddest of all, he would never be able to shoot a rifle again in the way that he had before the incident.

He returned to active duty and helped set up a sniper school at the marine base at Quantico, but there was more bad news in 1975 when he was diagnosed as having the incurable degenerative nerve disorder, multiple sclerosis. He remained in the marines until just fifty-five days short of the twenty years' service that would have made him eligible for full retirement pay and left the service embittered. He went on to work with police departments, lecturing on the art of sniping.

Carlos Hathcock finally succumbed to his illness, aged fifty-six, in 1999. A plaque he was given when he retired demonstrates how he will be remembered as one of the greatest marine snipers. It reads: 'There have been many Marines. And there have been many Marine marksmen. But there is only one Marine Sniper-Gunnery Sgt. Carlos N. Hathcock II. One Shot – One Kill.'

Lon Horiuchi and the Siege of Ruby Ridge

Lon Horiuchi testified that he could hit a quarter from more than 200 yards. A third-generation Japanese-American who grew up in Hawaii, he was a politically conservative Catholic who home-schooled his six children and had worked for the FBI as a marksman for fifteen years. He was leader of an FBI Hostage Rescue Team sniper crew and to his bosses he was 'dedicated, hard working, aggressive. He was trying to do the right thing, trying to serve his country in a stressful environment.' To his critics, however, he was nothing less than a 'paid FBI assassin'.

Snipers are not the type of people to court publicity. The job itself requires a cool distance from the rest of us and a disengagement from the everyday. Lon Horiuchi exploded into the public eye in connection with two seminal moments in modern American history, moments when the fragility of our social infrastructure was exposed and we were shown how close to chaos we all are.

The sieges of Ruby Ridge and Waco both involved Horiuchi and there was controversy around his role in both instances. In the case of Ruby Ridge, however, the two shots that the sniper fired from his position in the rocks above Randy Weaver's cabin in Idaho, ricocheted around the United States and did not come to rest until 168 people lost their lives in the Oklahoma City bombing perpetrated by right-wing extremist Timothy McVeigh in 1995.

Former Green Beret Randy Weaver and his wife Vicky moved their family to the wilderness of northern Idaho during the 1980s to escape the evils of what they perceived to be a corrupt world. They also believed that Armageddon was approaching, a notion bolstered by the Arab-Israeli War of 1973 and the ensuing oil embargo both of which increased tensions around the world.

Vicky had been having visions and in one of them she saw a beautiful mountaintop retreat where she knew her family would be safe from evil and where they could survive the coming apocalypse.

The Weavers had long since become disenchanted with organised religions and treated the Bible as the literal word of God. They began referring to the government as ZOG – Zionist Organised Government.

Randy began assembling an arsenal of guns that he felt would be needed to protect his family while Vicky studied self-sufficiency. In 1982, they sold their house and with their children, Sara, Samuel and Rachel, headed for Montana. When they found property there to be too expensive, they moved on to Idaho. Shortly after, they found the place they were looking for, a glorious spot southwest of Bonners Ferry in the Selkirk Mountains, overlooking Ruby Creek and with a stunning view of Montana and Washington in the distance.

Randy constructed a cabin and they began their life there without running water or electricity, but for them it was paradise on earth.

A new member of the family arrived when Randy befriended a fifteen-year-old boy named Kevin Harris. Kevin had gone off the rails and when he encountered Randy was living on the streets and involved with drugs. The Weavers took the boy in and he became a member of the family.

It all began in 1984, when Randy became involved in a dispute over a $3,000 land deal with a neighbour, Terry Kinnison. Weaver won the subsequent lawsuit and Kinnison took revenge by informing the FBI, the Secret Service and the county sheriff that his neighbour had stated that he wanted to kill the

Pope, the President and the Governor of Idaho. This prompted an investigation by the FBI and a couple of agents visited the cabin to talk to the Weavers. Meanwhile, the Secret Service was told that Randy Weaver was a member of the white supremacist group, Aryan Nations and that at his cabin they would find a huge arms cache. But Weaver denied all the allegations and no charges were brought.

Although he did not agree with all of their views, however, Randy did attend several Aryan Nations meetings, in the process making the acquaintance of a member, Guss Magisono. Magisono was actually a Bureau of Alcohol, Tobacco and Firearms (ATF) informant whose real name was Kenneth Fadeley. Fadeley attempted to entrap Weaver by suggesting that if he could supply him with sawn-off shotguns he could earn good money. A few weeks later Weaver delivered the shotguns but shortly after, two ATF agents approached him and told him that he would be indicted on firearms charges unless he agreed to become an informant, passing information to them about Aryan Nations. Weaver refused and was indicted.

Agents decided that it would be too dangerous to confront Randy at home. Consequently, they waited until he and Vicky came down off the mountain to fetch supplies. As the Weavers drove down, they saw a camper van parked on a bridge with the bonnet up and a man and a woman looking at the engine. They stopped and offered to help but as Randy looked at the engine, the man pulled a pistol and held it to his neck. Several armed agents who had been waiting inside the truck emerged and Vicky, running back to their vehicle to get a gun, was tackled to the ground.

He pleaded guilty and later received a letter stating that his court date was set for 20 March 1991. The letter contained a mistake, however. The date given for the hearing in the letter was wrong and the actual date was a month earlier on 20 February.

When Randy failed to show on 20 February, he was declared a federal fugitive and an arrest warrant was issued, despite the mistake that had been made. It is hardly surprising that the Weavers began to believe there was a government conspiracy against them.

Vicky wrote apocalyptic letters to government agencies containing phrases such as: 'The tyrant's blood shall flow' and 'Whether we live or die we will not obey you … war is upon our land.' For sixteen months, the Weavers and their children did not leave the mountain. Meanwhile, Vicky gave birth to Elisheba Anne Weaver.

The US Marshals did not give up, however. They organised a Special Operations Group (SOG) to gather intelligence on the Weavers' cabin. At around 2.30 am on 21 August 1992, a heavily armed team, consisting of Larry Cooper, William Degan, Arthur Roderick, David Hunt, Larry Thomas, and Frank Norris set off up the mountain towards the Weaver cabin.

As they took up positions around the cabin, the Weavers' dogs began to bark and the Weavers, all armed, ran from the cabin. They jogged off down the track from the cabin towards positions where Cooper and Degan were hiding.

It is unclear what happened next, but Degan was shot by Kevin Harris who was in turn shot by Cooper. Roderick appeared on the scene and shot one of the dogs that had run down with the Weavers. Fourteen-year-old Samuel Weaver was then shot and killed as he ran back towards the cabin. Degan died at the scene and help was summoned.

Within a short time agents from the Boundary County Sheriff's Office, the U.S. Border Patrol, and the Idaho State Police had reached the scene, and the Idaho State Police Critical Response Team (CRT), the Idaho National Guard Armory, the FBI Hostage Rescue Team (HRT), a specialised full-time tactical team, based at the FBI Academy in Quantico, Virginia, and another group of the Marshals Service SOG units were en route.

The FBI's standard rules of engagement state that deadly force should only be used when an agent or another is in imminent danger of death or serious bodily harm. A proposal from the law enforcement officers on the mountain that these should be amended to deal with this situation and that basically deadly force could be used when an adult was seen at the cabin with a weapon was rejected by FBI headquarters but for some reason the rejection was never passed on to the officers in the field.

The media had by now converged on the scene at the foot of the mountain where a large crowd had also begun to assemble. Police cars, armoured vehicles and military vehicles arrived and made their way through the roadblock and up the mountain.

Later that day, the Weavers decided to go to an outhouse next to the cabin where they had laid Samuel's body. They wanted to pray over their dead son and sibling. They were unaware, however, that HRT 'Blue' sniper/observer team leader Lon Horiuchi was positioned on the mountainside looking down on the cabin. The sniper teams had been deployed in order to cover the approach of an armoured personnel carrier that would be bringing negotiators to the cabin. Horiuchi was about 646 feet from the front door, situated at a slight angle.

At 5.57 pm, he watched as Randy, Sara and Kevin left the cabin, carrying rifles, and made their way cautiously to the shed where Samuel's body lay. As Randy reached out to unlock the shed door, Horiuchi took his chance and fired a shot, without issuing a warning of any kind. Randy was hit in the upper right arm and screamed out, 'Mama, I been shot!' The three ran back towards the cabin and scrambled inside.

As the last of them, Kevin Harris, ran inside, Horiuchi aimed at the edge of the cabin door and squeezed the trigger of his rifle. The bullet smashed the glass panel on the door and hit Vicky Weaver in the head, exiting and striking Kevin Harris in the left arm and chest. The baby Elisheba that Vicky had been holding was miraculously unharmed. Still clutching the baby, Vicky fell to the floor. She was already dead. When Randy turned her over, he was horrified to see that her skull had been shattered and her face was unrecognisable.

Horiuchi would later testify that he had put the crosshairs of his gun-sight on Randy Weaver's spine but he had moved at the last moment and the bullet had hit Vicky.

On 31 August, after a siege lasting ten days and many hours of negotiations, Randy finally decided to surrender. By this time, Kevin Harris had already been allowed out of the cabin to be treated for his wounds in hospital and Randy was left there with his daughters.

At the 1993 trial of Randy Weaver and Kevin Harris, Harris was found not guilty of murder or any related charges, while Randy was acquitted of all federal charges. The only things he was convicted for were failing to appear in court and the violation of his bail conditions. He was sentenced to eighteen months, fourteen of which he had already served. From his prison cell, he said, 'I'm not a white supremacist. I'm a white separatist. I was born white. I can't help that. If I was black I'd probably be affiliated with Louis Farrakhan's group, but as it is, I don't belong to anything. I don't believe I'm superior to anyone, but I do believe I have the right to be with my own kind of people if I choose to.'

The police and other agencies were heavily criticised for their actions in the Weaver case and in 1997, sniper Lon Horiuchi was charged with involuntary manslaughter. The charges were dismissed in 2001, however, because, it was claimed, the state would be unable to prove the charge.

By then, however, Horiuchi had been involved in another controversy. He was present at the 1993 siege at the Branch Davidian compound in Waco when seventy-six members of the Branch Davidians, a fringe religious group led by David Koresh died after a siege lasting fifty days. Although the FBI denied that its officers fired any shots at Waco, there is a great deal of evidence that they did and there were shell casings found at the position occupied by Horiuchi and others.

The Ruby Ridge and Waco incidents fuelled anti-government sentiments and Timothy McVeigh targeted Lon Horiuchi in particular for the part he played in both incidents, issuing fliers about him and sending threatening letters to the sniper. Eventually, however, McVeigh decided, instead, to take out his anger with the government on the workers at the Alfred P. Murragh building in Oklahoma City on 19 April 1995.

The Shooting of Mark Saunders

It was a normal day for thirty-two-year-old Mark Saunders and Elizabeth, his wife of two years. Both solicitors, they rose at 6 am as usual and drove off from their house in Markham Square in Chelsea at about quarter to seven to Temple, London's legal district, where they both worked as solicitors. Life was good. They had spent the previous evening booking hotels for a holiday they planned to have in India later in the year and this morning Mark was looking forward to a client dinner he was going to have that evening.

He was a family lawyer, described by colleagues as 'popular, gutsy and polished.' He was good at what he did and had the trappings to prove it – he was very well-off and he and Elizabeth lived in a £2.2 million home in fashionable Chelsea.

He had grown up in the upmarket village of Alderley Edge in Cheshire, northwest England. Privately educated and with a degree in law from

Oxford University, his future looked very bright and many thought it inevitable that he would become a Queen's Counsel.

Mark Saunders, however, was living a lie. For a number of years he had been an alcoholic. He had sought professional help on a number of occasions, but each time he relapsed and embarked once more on solitary drink binges after which he felt guilty and depressed.

He had started drinking when he was thirteen years old and by the time he was reading law at Christ Church College, Oxford, his consumption of alcohol was already prodigious.

When he joined QEB, a leading set of Barristers' chambers that dealt particularly with family law, in 1999, his drinking became even worse and by the time he reached his late twenties, it was out of control. He was drinking on his own at home, consuming the equivalent of four bottles of spirits a week.

He briefly tried Alcoholics Anonymous but decided that psychiatric help might be more effective. The counselling he received advocated total abstinence but he was unable to handle that, although he did manage to control it to some extent. Every three months or so, it would erupt again, however, in a massive binge.

His therapist became increasingly concerned that the deadly mixture of alcohol and depression, for which he was by this time taking Prozac, would make him suicidal. Just five weeks before Saunders' death, he wrote: 'If he is depressed and is binge drinking during that period he is at greater risk of ending his life.'

The therapist worried too about the fact that Saunders became paranoid and belligerent when drunk and there was always a risk that he would become a victim of violence. A friend told how he often hurt himself when he had drunk to excess and he ended up in casualty on more than one occasion. 'You could not engage with him,' he said, going on to add that in this condition Saunders seemed to be in a fantasy world.

In 2005, he had been cautioned by police for being drunk and disorderly, but this did not prevent him obtaining a shotgun licence in 2006. He had found a new passion for shooting game and the day before his shooting, he was booking hotels for his next shoot.

It seemed that help might have been at hand when he fell in love with and married Elizabeth in August 2006. Eight years older than him, she had delivered an ultimatum – stop drinking or the relationship is over. She banned alcohol from their home and it seemed to work. In the two months before his death, he had, to his wife's knowledge drunk no more than one glass of red wine. She was unaware, however, that although he was staying away from alcohol, he had become a regular user of cocaine.

That morning, Saunders picked up some documents at work on which he was going to spend the remainder of the day working at home. He was preparing for a case the following day. He visited his wife in her office in order to pick up the car keys before driving back home to collect Elizabeth's mother who had been staying with them. It was the last time Elizabeth saw him.

He called her at 10.25 to let her know that her mother was on the train and joked about how she had talked non-stop all the way to the station. From the station, he went to a picture framer to collect a picture he had left there to be framed and then at 11.15 he made a call to a legal executive to discuss a forthcoming case. Everyone with whom he came into contact that morning confirmed that he seemed happy and relaxed, that there was nothing unusual about him.

Around 1.30pm, he and his wife exchanged a couple of text messages on their mobile phones but an hour later when Elizabeth Saunders tried to contact her husband, there was no reply. She immediately began to worry. Previous experience told her that all was not well.

At around 1.30, Saunders had visited a cash point in Chelsea. He then travelled to Kensington. His telephone records show that he telephoned escort agencies around this time, but no one has ever come forward to say whether or not he did actually meet an escort.

He started to send a series of odd text messages. One to a firm of solicitors that consisted simply of the message 'ha ha', repeated twenty-two times. Later in the afternoon, just after four o'clock, he sent one to a friend that quoted the lyrics of a song by rock band The Doors: 'This is the end, my only friend, the end.'

It seems evident from these that by this time, he was either drunk or high on drugs, a notion that was corroborated by witnesses. A taxi driver, David Hay, who picked him up at around ten past four on Cromwell Road, heard him say on the phone: 'make sure you've got ten ha has.' Hay said that when Saunders got out of the cab in Chelsea, he turned round and looking back up the King's Road said 'Ha ha ha.' When the driver gave him his change, Saunders looked him straight in the eyes and said, 'I'm going to die.' The driver added that 'his eyes were large and bulging. I could see the terror in his eyes. He looked like he was on drugs or something.'

Back home in Markham Square, Saunders loaded his two shotguns and at 4.40pm, while on the phone to Michael Bradley, a friend who was also a barrister, he fired his first shot out of the window of the kitchen of his and Elizabeth's second floor flat. Some of the shot smashed through the window of a neighbouring building.

Shortly after, he telephoned Ivor Treherne who was the senior clerk at QEB where he worked. Treherne realised immediately that Saunders had been drinking and warned him that he had better sober up as he had a dinner meeting later that evening. Saunders replied: 'I've got my gun and I've already shot it. He told Treherne to listen and fired the weapon again. Treherne urged him to put the gun down. Saunders told him that it was too late – the police were already there.

Ivor Treherne immediately called Elizabeth and she rushed out, grabbed a taxi and headed for Chelsea.

Meanwhile, police were converging on Markham Square. Some have said that the response was something of an over-reaction to the situation – 59 officers, 100 guns and twelve police marksmen with their weapons trained on the windows of the Saunders flat.

When Elizabeth arrived a little later, she found the square cordoned off. When she made it known who she was she was taken to a temporary operations base that had been set up in a nearby bank. There, she was quizzed about what weapons her husband had in the flat and she told them about his problem with alcohol, apologising profusely for what he was doing.

At this point, officers ordered Elizabeth to turn off her mobile phone, giving the reason that they wanted to control all communications with her husband. At the inquest into his killing, she claimed that this was an error, that if she could have talked to her husband, she could have talked him out of the flat and saved his life. In fact, it had only been after his death that she learned that he had asked repeatedly to talk to her. He had also sent her first a blank text message and then another saying, 'Call me now.'

At around 7 pm, Mark Saunders wrote his last message, scribbling on a piece of cardboard: 'I love my wife dearly, love Mark xxxx' and threw it out the window. A neighbour who found the message made efforts to get the police to allow Elizabeth to speak to him, interpreting the message, she later said, as 'a message from a young man in despair, not the message of a dangerous killer.'

Metropolitan Police marksmen were now in position in the street outside the flat. At 9.32 pm, as Saunders appeared at a window, seven of them opened fire, hitting him five times in the head and chest. CS canisters were fired into the flat and police stormed in to find Mark Saunders dead.

The inquest jury returned a verdict of lawful killing but there was a bizarre coda to the case when it emerged that one of the police firearms officers who gave evidence at the inquest had played a strange and insensitive game in court by inserting song titles into his oral evidence.

The man, identified only as AZ8 had been stationed on an adjoining conservatory roof and was one of two officers who had fired the shot, amongst the five that had hit him, that had probably killed Saunders.

Amongst the song titles it is believed he introduced into his testimony were *Enough is Enough* by Donna Summer, *Point of No Return* by Buzzcocks, *Line of Fire* by Journey, *Quiet Moments* by Chris de Burgh, *Kicking Myself* by As Tall As Lions and *Fuck My*

Old Boots by the Membranes. One example was the statement: 'I switched the light on, he turned towards me and I thought: "Fuck my old boots, I've got a gun trained on me"...'

The officer concerned was removed from operational firearms duty pending an investigation by the Metropolitan Police Directorate of Professional Standards.

JAMES HUBERTY

AND THE SAN YSIDRO MCDONALDS SIEGE

Chuck Foster was part of an elite group, men with special skills, able to kill with precision. It is legalised killing, though. They gun down the bad people who are intent on doing harm to others and sometimes – as in the case of James Huberty – by the time they get to them and are able to fire that shot that will bring it all to an end there has already been unimaginable carnage.

Foster was part of a SWAT (Special Weapons and Tactics) team, an elite paramilitary tactical unit that exists in most American police departments. Their task is to take over when a situation gets beyond the capabilities of regular police officers, situations such as hostage rescues or terrorist operations, situations that are high risk, violent and downright dangerous.

SWAT teams were created in response to such situations getting out of control, resulting in bloodbaths. They started to come to the fore after the Watts Riots of 1965 when gunmen fired on civilians and law enforcement officers from the rooftops of the Watts district of Los Angeles and the following year, when Charles Whitman created carnage from a tower at the University of Texas at Austin, police officers were armed only with outmoded hunting rifles that proved totally ineffective.

That year, the Los Angeles Police Department introduced one of the first SWAT teams. It was a counter-sniper team, according to one of its platoon leaders and, he added, most of its members were selected for it because they had their own high-power hunting rifles. During the years since, however, SWAT teams have evolved in line with the types of threats the modern world faces and the sniper is an intrinsic part of those teams, from the FBI's highly skilled specialist team to the smaller units working out of local city police departments.

Chuck Foster was one of those men. On a July afternoon in 1984, he was perched on the roof of a post office next to a McDonalds restaurant in the town of San Ysidro. He was ready to do his job.

Inside the restaurant he could see some movement despite the fact that the windows were steamed up. It was a man, carrying a Uzi submachine gun. The man walked around the restaurant and then stopped next to the body of one of his victims lying on the floor. 'I was trying to get a good bead on him,' Foster later said. As the man stopped, Foster caught him in his crosshairs and his finger began to squeeze the trigger of his rifle.

A moment later, the glass of the door shattered and the figure inside dropped to the floor with a bullet in his heart. It was over and James Oliver Huberty was dead. But so were twenty-one other people.

Huberty was born in Canton, Ohio in 1942. Abandoned by his mother when still young, he grew up sullen and withdrawn but succeeded in earning a degree in sociology. Later, he was granted a licence for embalming from the Pittsburgh Institute of Mortuary Science in Pittsburgh Pennsylvania. He met his wife Etna there and the couple went on to have two children.

While living in Canton, the Hubertys gained a reputation for violent behaviour. Huberty is remembered as an angry, lonely and paranoid man whose dogs would attack other people's dogs and who believed everyone was out to get him. Etna once filed a report with the Canton Department of Children and Family Services that her husband had 'messed up her jaw'. Allegedly, she was able to calm him down, however, with readings of Tarot cards.

But Etna also had a violent streak. On one

occasion, she ordered her daughter to physically assault a classmate and when the girl's mother objected, Etna is said to have threatened her with a 9mm pistol. She was arrested, but the pistol was not confiscated. Her husband later used it to shoot his German shepherd in the head after a neighbour complained that it had damaged his car.

Huberty was a survivalist who believed that society was on the brink of collapse. There was too much government interference and regulation, to his mind, and international bankers were bankrupting the nation. He dedicated himself to preparing for this event, stocking up with thousands of dollars of tinned food and assembling an arsenal of weapons with which he would protect his family.

Huberty worked as a welder but was unable to continue with his work when he developed an uncontrollable twitch in his right arm following a motorbike accident. In January 1984, the family left Canton, stopping briefly in Tijuana in Mexico before settling in San Ysidro in San Diego, California where he found work as a security guard. He was sacked, however, two weeks before the shooting.

As is often the case, it was a trivial event that triggered the massacre in San Ysidro.

On 17 July 1984, Huberty had made a phone call

to a mental health centre but had not said there was an emergency. Consequently, he was not called back and it seemed to make something snap inside him.

Next morning, he took his family to San Diego Zoo and, just a few hours before he would transform another branch of the fast food chain into a charnel house, he ate at the McDonalds in the Clairemont area of northern San Diego.

When they got home, he made ready to go out again, wearing jungle fatigues and a black T-shirt, but this time carrying a 9mm Uzi submachine gun, a 12-gauge shotgun and a Browning HP handgun. Etna asked him where he was going. 'Hunting humans,' was the chilling answer. He had told her earlier that day that society had had its chance. But Etna paid little attention to him, because, as she later said, he had been saying wild things for a long time.

A neighbour spotted him leaving his apartment block and walking down San Ysidro Boulevard with the guns and immediately phoned the police. Unfortunately, the dispatcher gave officers the wrong address.

The restaurant was just 200 yards from his apartment. He entered and finding a room filled with 'early dinner' customers, shouted 'Everybody down!' before opening fire. If anyone moved, he shot them and his victims, predominantly Mexican and Mexican-American, ranged in age from an eight-month-old baby girl to a woman of seventy-four.

It had begun at 3.40pm and by the time Chuck Foster squeezed his trigger, it had lasted seventy-seven minutes. Huberty expended 257 rounds of ammunition and walked around the restaurant telling the terrified people that he had killed thousands of people in Vietnam. He was lying, however. He had never served in any branch of the military.

To begin with, police and the emergency services went to the wrong McDonalds restaurant, converging on the branch located at the US International Border at Tijuana at 3.15 pm. Learning it was the wrong one, they turned round and made for the McDonalds next door to the post office, approximately two miles away.

San Diego Police Captain Miguel Rosario was the first police officer to arrive on the scene. What he found made him, he later said, sick to the pit of his stomach. Bodies were littered throughout the restaurant and outside. Two boys lay on the ground, tangled in their bicycles after being shot and people in the car park cowered behind parked vehicles. Rosario thought at first it was probably a robbery gone wrong.

Suddenly a side door of the restaurant opened and

there was Huberty, the Uzi hung across his chest. He stared at Rosario and then, as the policeman dived behind a pickup truck, opened fire on him.

Rosario realised that with his .38, he was seriously outgunned and he still did not know if he had accomplices inside the restaurant. He radioed in for a SWAT team to be sent.

A short while later, Chuck Foster took up his position and waited for a sighting of the killer in the restaurant.

PART THREE
ASSASSINATIONS

President James A. Garfield

On 2 July 1810, President James A. Garfield was due to leave Washington for his summer vacation. He was also due to deliver a speech that day at the university he had attended, Williams College, and had arrived at the Baltimore and Potomac Railroad passenger terminal that once stood on the southwest corner of modern-day Sixth Street and Constitution Avenue in northwest Washington DC.

It was a warm day and Garfield was feeling good, especially as he was about to get away from the travails of the presidency. It had been four months since he had narrowly defeated fellow Civil War General Winfield Hancock to win the presidential election. But he had inherited a nation still licking its wounds after the deeply divisive war between the North and the South and his first few months had been far from easy, every appointment and policy his administration tried to introduce being faced with stern opposition. Even his own party, the Republican, was deeply divided by factional fighting between the 'Stalwarts', who had wanted to re-elect General Ulysses S. Grant for another term, and the 'Half-Breeds', who had supported Garfield and had succeeded in getting him onto the ballot and subsequently into the White House.

His family had noted his good mood before he had left that morning – he had even performed handstands for his sons before getting dressed and checking the itinerary for his journey.

At nine that morning, he and his entourage, consisting of Secretary of State, James Blaine, and two of his sons, James and Harry, walked across the station concourse which was crowded with hordes of holidaymakers also making their way towards the trains. Secretary of War Robert Todd Lincoln, the son of the late President Abraham Lincoln, was waiting to see him off. All seemed normal as people went about their business and Garfield had no security detail. With the exception of President Lincoln during the Civil War, United States Presidents had never used bodyguards.

As the president entered the station's waiting room, a small man suddenly stepped forward, a pistol in his hand, and fired at the president from point-blank range. Garfield shouted, 'My God, what is that?' and threw up his arms. The man pulled the trigger again and the president's body crumpled to the floor. One bullet had grazed Garfield's upper arm, the other lodging in his spine but missing his spinal cord.

The gunman put his pistol back in his pocket, turned and walked away, heading for the exit where he had a taxi waiting. He was accosted, however, by police officer Patrick Kearney who was in such a state of nervous excitement to have captured the man who shot the president that he neglected to take the assassin's weapon from him until they arrived at the police station. Luckily, the gunman, whose name was Charles J. Guiteau, did not put up a fight.

Meanwhile, the president, in shock, but still conscious, was carried to an upper floor of the station, his youngest son Jim and Secretary of State Blaine accompanying him in tears. Robert Todd Lincoln was horrified to once again be living through the horror of the shooting of a president.

They conveyed him back to the White House where doctors informed him that he was unlikely to survive the night. But, he was still alive the following morning and even managed to remain conscious and fairly alert. They dared to hope that they might not lose him.

He somehow managed to live through the summer, his doctors issuing regular bulletins on his health. However, he often suffered from fevers and ate little.

It was hot that summer and to help keep the temperature in his room at an acceptable level, Navy engineers constructed around him an ingenious early version of the modern air conditioner. Large fans blew air over a container of ice into the room in which the president lay. It was effective, too, lowering the temperature by twenty degrees.

The bullet that had come so close to his spinal cord had proved impossible to find but doctors still probed, trying to locate it. It was a time before the merits of sterilisation had been discovered, however, and their hands, fingers and instruments were covered in germs. Still it could not be located even using a special metal detector invented by Alexander Graham Bell. Unfortunately, the metal frame of Garfield's bed rendered it ineffective.

As the weeks passed, the President began to weaken and his weight plummeted from two hundred down to one hundred and thirty-five pounds. Blood poisoning and infection began to set in causing him to suffer from frightening hallucinations for a time.

On 6 September, he was removed from the White

House to the Jersey Shore to get him away from the stifling city heat. It was hoped that the fresh air and peace and quiet might aid his recovery. But there was no improvement and, in fact, new infections set in. To make matters worse, he also began to suffer from angina.

At 10.35, on Monday, 19 September 1881, almost three months after the attempt on his life, and two months before his fiftieth birthday, President Garfield died of either a massive heart attack or a ruptured splenic artery aneurysm.

The following day, Vice-President Chester A. Arthur was sworn in as twenty-first President of the United States. Meanwhile, the man who was now his assassin, Charles J. Guiteau, went on trial.

Guiteau had been born in 1841, son of Luther and Anne Guiteau. The Guiteaus were considered an odd family and Charles's father held some strange views that were later shared by his son. He was an ardent follower of the utopian socialist John H. Noyes who advocated communal living, multiple sex partners and other views that were anathema to prim Victorians. It was Noyes, in fact, who invented the term 'free love'.

In 1860, the young Guiteau joined the Oneida Community which was the base for the Noyes cult, but, in spite of the free love espoused by the members of the community, he was singularly unsuccessful in attracting much interest from the opposite sex. Part of the problem was his inflated view of himself. The abuse – verbal and physical – that he had suffered at the hands of his father had made him feel worthless. His response was to become an arrogant and distinctly unpleasant person.

Frustrated, he left Oneida in 1865 and attempted to establish a newspaper to spread the Noyes philosophy. Unfortunately, like all his other business ventures, it failed to get off the ground and he increasingly found himself having to stay one step ahead of creditors.

He married in 1869 and, having just made it through the Illinois Bar Exam, set up a small legal practice. Again, he was unsuccessful and his wife sued for divorce in 1874 after Guiteau contracted syphilis from a prostitute.

He next tried his hand at being a travelling preacher, but his speaking appearances sorely disappointed his audiences.

In 1880, he was almost forty but, despite having been a failure at everything, Charles Guiteau was still convinced that he was destined for greatness. Perhaps politics was the arena in which he would finally achieve his dream. Election year was 1880 and Guiteau, a lifelong Republican, threw himself behind the Stalwarts who were trying to get Ulysses S. Grant re-elected. When that failed, he switched his allegiance to James Garfield. Guiteau campaigned for Garfield and sincerely believed that a speech he had delivered to almost no one in August 1880, had been the reason for Garfield's election. He moved to Washington to receive the rewards of political office that he believed he deserved.

He settled on becoming United States Ambassador to Austria and wrote to President Garfield accordingly: 'Next Spring I expect to marry the daughter of a deceased New York Republican millionaire and I think we can represent the United States government at Vienna with dignity and grace.' The fact that he had only seen the girl once and from a distance and that she had absolutely no idea who he was seemed irrelevant to him.

Needless to say, he received no reply from the President and wrote again, after visiting the White House and trying to see Garfield. 'I called to see you this morning, but you were engaged. I sent you a note touching on the Austrian mission. Mr Kasson of Iowa, I understand, wishes to remain at Vienna till fall. He is a good fellow (and) I do not wish to disturb him in any event. What do you think of me for Consul-General at Paris? I think I prefer Paris to Vienna … and I presume my appointment will be promptly confirmed.'

No response being forthcoming, he wrote to Secretary of State Blaine, amongst many others. Meanwhile, letter after letter arrived at the White House from him. Then, one day, Guiteau accosted Blaine, informing him that he was the writer of the letters. Blaine, in a fury, shouted at him, 'Never speak to me again on the Paris consulship as long as you live!' Guiteau was shocked but then became increasingly angry. He began to plan the assassination of Garfield, although he would later claim that he was commanded to do it by God.

On that warm July morning, after several aborted attempts, he ate breakfast and took a cab to the Baltimore and Potomac Railroad terminal and carried out the deed.

Throughout his subsequent imprisonment and trial, Guiteau believed that he had perpetrated a noble act. He described it as 'political necessity' and even had the gall to ask the American public to give money to his defense. After all, he reasoned, they had donated almost $200,000 to President Garfield's widow.

His trial was a circus, Guiteau interrupting testimony as the mood took him. But although many thought he was insane, he was found guilty and sentenced to death.

Charles Guiteau was hanged on 30 June 1882, regaling the watching crowd with a bizarre poem before the hangman placed the noose around his neck.

President Abraham Lincoln

Three days before he was assassinated, Abraham Lincoln, sixteenth President of the United States related a dream that he had had some days previously. He described a death-like stillness around him and the sound of sobbing. In the dream, he got out of bed and went downstairs where the sobbing continued, even though all the rooms he passed through were empty. Finally, he entered the East Room where, to his horror, he saw a catafalque on which lay a corpse wrapped in funeral vestments, its face covered. Soldiers were posted around the platform and a crowd of people were standing gazing at the corpse, weeping. 'Who is dead in the White House?' Lincoln asked one of the soldiers standing guard. 'The President,' he answered. 'He was killed by an assassin.' A loud exclamation of grief from the mourners woke him from his dream.

Matters had been proceeding well for the President in the American Civil War. On 3 April

Richmond in Virginia had been taken by his Union troops and six days later, the first army of the Confederacy also surrendered. The Confederates' days were numbered and a good many southerners had simply given up hope.

There were those, however, who maintained belief in the Confederate cause, amongst them John Wilkes Booth.

By the 1860s, Booth, a member of a prominent theatrical family, was a well-known actor, described by some theatre critics as 'the handsomest man in America'. In 1860, he was engaged on his first national tour as a leading actor, playing in cities such as New York, Boston, Chicago, Cleveland, St. Louis and New Orleans. At the outbreak of the Civil war, he was playing in Albany, New York and outraged theatre patrons by describing the South's struggle as 'heroic', for he was vehemently opposed to Lincoln's attempts to abolish slavery and his plans to extend voting rights to freed slaves. The South's defeat in the war was an outrage to him. His statements so enraged the citizens of Albany that some demanded that he be banned from the stage. He continued to perform, however, appearing in mostly Union and border states.

In early 1863, he was arrested in St. Louis when

he was overheard wishing that 'the President and the whole damned government would go to hell.' He was charged with making treasonous remarks against the government, but was released after swearing an oath of allegiance to the Union and handing over a sizable fine.

As President Lincoln's first term drew to a close, it seemed obvious that he was going to be re-elected, a fact that infuriated the Lincoln-hating Booth. At the start of the war, he had promised his mother that he would not enlist and he was now furious with himself for not playing his part in the fighting.

Deciding that he had to do something, he formulated a plan to kidnap Lincoln while he was at his summer residence at the Old Soldiers Home, a few miles from the White House. He planned to smuggle him across the Potomac River into Richmond where he would be used as a bargaining chip to secure the release of Confederate prisoners of war. He believed it would help to bring the war to a conclusion by bolstering support in the north for opposition to the war and by forcing the Union to recognise the government of the Confederacy.

He recruited a couple of friends – Samuel Arnold and Michael O'Laughlen – to help. Around this time, too, Booth travelled to Montreal in Canada where it is believed he met with representatives of the Confederate Secret Service, although it is not clear whether the Confederate leadership were aware of the plot to kidnap the President.

As expected, Lincoln won the 1864 election with a landslide, giving Booth fresh impetus to execute his plot. He and a group of sympathisers began to meet regularly at a house owned by Mary Surratt, mother of one of the conspirators. Meanwhile, his rants about Lincoln – 'making himself a king' – began to alienate Booth from his family, his brother Edwin telling him he was no longer welcome in his house in New York.

When it came to Booth's attention that Lincoln would be attending a performance of the play *Still Waters Run Deep* at a hospital close to the Old Soldier's Home, he decided they would kidnap him en route, but the President unwittingly foiled him by changing his plans at the last minute, attending a reception at the National Hotel in Washington, instead.

Something snapped inside John Wilkes Booth when he heard that Confederate General Robert E. Lee had surrendered on 12 April 1865. He told his friends that he was finished with the theatre, enigmatically saying that there was only one play that he wanted to stage – Thomas Otway's *Venice Preserv'd*, a play about an assassination. Booth had now abandoned kidnapping, coming to the conclusion that assassination was the only option. He had, in fact, been present outside the White House the previous day when Lincoln had delivered an impromptu speech from a window, stating that he was in favour of giving freed slaves the right to vote. Booth declared to his co-conspirators that it was the last speech that Abraham Lincoln would ever make.

On the morning of 14 April, Good Friday, Booth went to Ford's Theater to collect his mail and learned that the President and Mrs Lincoln would be present there that evening to see the play Our American Cousin. They would be accompanied by General Ulysses S. Grant and his wife. Booth realised that this was his opportunity and began to plan the assassination, arranging a horse on which to make his escape and informing his colleagues that he was going to kill the President. But, it was not just his intention to get rid of Lincoln. He wanted to completely destroy the Union government. He assigned Lewis Powell the task of assassinating Secretary of State William H. Seward and George Atzerodt that of killing Vice President Andrew

Johnson. Meanwhile, David Herold was given the role of helping them to escape into Virginia. He was anticipating the Union being thrown into utter confusion, allowing the Confederacy time to reorganise.

Booth was well known at Ford's Theater and had access to all areas. He used this freedom to bore a small hole in the door of the presidential box so that he would later be able to observe the President and his company.

The President, meanwhile, had his customarily busy day. He had called a cabinet meeting that had lasted from eleven in the morning until two in the afternoon. At the end of the meeting, however, General Grant informed him that he would be unable to come to the theatre that evening as he and his wife had decided instead to go and visit their children. In their place, Lincoln invited Major Henry Rathbone and his fiancée, Clara Harris to join them. This determination to go to the theatre, though, was frowned upon by some of Lincoln's staff. Secretary of War Edwin M. Stanton counselled against it, pleading with the President not to put himself in unnecessary danger. Lincoln would have none of it, however. He even declined the offer of extra security and when he and his party arrived at the theatre that evening shortly after eight, the only protection he had was John Parker, a policeman known to be fond of a drink, a fondness he indulged at the play's interval, abandoning his post and going to a tavern across the street from the theatre. By the beginning of the play's third act he had still not returned to his post at the door to the box.

At around 10.15, as actor Harry Hawk was uttering the line, 'Don't know the manners of good society, eh? Well, I guess I know enough to turn you inside out, old gal – you sockdologizing old mantrap!' the door to the box burst open and John Wilkes Booth leapt in, pointed a small derringer at the back of the President's head and fired. Mary Lincoln screamed and reached out to her husband as he slumped forward in his seat. The assailant pulled out a dagger and yelled the Latin words '*Sic Semper tyrannis*!' (Thus always to tyrants). Major Rathbone tried to intercept him and his arm was slashed to the bone by Booth who then leapt dramatically from the box on to the stage, breaking his left leg as he did so. Limping badly and in a great deal of pain, he made his way through the shocked theatre staff to the stage door.

Booth leapt on a horse being held by an innocent theatre employee and galloped off at speed in a southerly direction. Twelve days later, he was cornered and shot dead by Boston Corbett of the 16th New York Cavalry near Bowling Green, Virginia.

Meanwhile, Lincoln, shot behind the left ear, was carried to the house of a German tailor, William A. Peterson across the road from the theatre. A crowd gathered in the room and outside, but Lincoln, although still breathing, was, to all intents and purposes, dead.

At 7.22 the following morning, 15 April, his wife by his side and his son Robert sobbing at the head of the bed, President Abraham Lincoln breathed his last.

President William A. McKinley

The 1901 Pan American Exposition at Buffalo, New York, gave visitors a glimpse into the future with exhibitions on agriculture, transportation and especially science. Its highlight was the massive Electric Tower, an illuminated obelisk that astonished and delighted visitors. By the time the Expo closed in November 1901, an astonishing eleven million people had passed through its turnstiles.

The exposition would, however, mainly be remembered for one thing. It was the scene of the assassination of the 25th President of the United States.

In early September, a twenty-eight-year-old man, Leon Franz Czolgosz, could be found wandering around the exhibitions at the fair. Czolgosz, son of Polish immigrants and a man of slight build and a pale complexion, seethed with an anger that had been born of his frustration at the way the world worked. He was an anarchist, a disciple of the political radical, Emma Goldman, and his action on that early

September day would change American history. Anarchy in its most basic form is not a violent social philosophy. It is the belief that people should not be subject to governmental authority, that all government is oppressive and destructive. In the late nineteenth century, however, some anarchists began to espouse violent means to achieve their aims, especially in Europe. These people believed that it was only possible to bring down capitalism by violence and assassination. A number of assassinations gave voice to this creed. In 1881, Czar Alexander II of Russia and twenty-one others were killed by a bomb thrown by an anarchist. In Chicago, in 1886, an anarchist bomb killed seven police officers during the Haymarket Square Riot. French President Marie-Francois Sadi Carnot was stabbed to death by an anarchist in 1894 and Italian King Humbert I was assassinated in 1900 by an Italian-American anarchist.

Newspapers, therefore, were filled with scare-mongering about anarchists who were generally assumed to be violent killers.

Leon Czolgosz's family had immigrated to America in the eighteen-sixties and he was born in Detroit, Michigan, in 1865, into a life blighted by grinding poverty. The family moved to Cleveland where Leon and one of his brothers found work at the American Steel and Wire Company. For several years they earned good money but when workers went on strike, the company simply fired them and hired replacements. It was common practice in those times before unions and there was nothing the workers could do about it.

Czolgosz was outraged by such action by the bosses and was disgusted that the people who ran the country allowed such things to happen. He began to mix increasingly with anarchists who were sympathetic to his views.

In 1898, he is said to have suffered a breakdown, probably brought on by financial difficulties as well as mental problems. He returned home and withdrew from the world, spending his time reading radical literature and rarely leaving the house.

In 1900, when news arrived of the assassination of King Umberto I of Italy by the anarchist Gaetano Bresci, Czolgosz was delighted. He viewed the assassin as a hero and became increasingly of the opinion that murdering enemies of the people was a justified act.

On 31 August 1901, Czolgosz travelled to Buffalo where he found a cheap room to rent. He had decided that he was going to assassinate the

US President William McKinley but had not as yet formulated a plan of how he was going to do it. McKinley represented everything that he believed to be wrong with society, a man who had everything while people in his country had nothing, who were starving and suffering from terrible poverty. His room in Buffalo was located above a noisy saloon and the only time he left it was to visit the Pan American Exposition to which, he had heard, the President was going to pay a visit.

On 5 September, he took a major step towards achieving his goal when he purchased a .32-calibre Iver-Johnson revolver in Buffalo.

Born in 1843, President William McKinley was the last President of the United States to have fought in the American Civil War, having taken part in battles on the Union side at Cedar Creek, Opequon and Fishers' Hill. He had also fought at the Battle of Antietam in 1862 in which 22,000 men were killed or wounded. After the war, he became a teacher and then a lawyer. He entered Congress as a Republican in 1877 and went on to serve seven terms. In 1891, he left Congress and was elected Governor of Ohio. Leaving that office in 1896, he began campaigning for the presidency, eventually defeating William Jennings Bryan by a large margin.

When the Pan American Expo opened in May 1901, President McKinley was as eager as any other American to see its wonders. He arrived in Buffalo by special train on September 4 and was taken to the house of John Milburn, the director of the Expo, which would be his home for the next two days.

On 5 September, the Expo opened to even bigger crowds than usual, excited by the appearance later that day of the President to give a speech and at midday, a huge crowd of some 50,000 people cheered McKinley onto the dais from which he was to deliver the speech. As he and the First Lady stepped out of their carriage, a tumultuous roar greeted them. That day he spoke of America's great prosperity and his hopes for the future of the nation. The speech was greeted by applause and cheers.

McKinley was then taken on a tour of the site, passing at one moment, close to Czolgosz who wisely decided there were too many bodyguards around the President to attempt anything at that point. He later said that he was not afraid, but was concerned that he would be stopped before he could carry out the deed.

McKinley returned to Milburn's house late in the afternoon and spent a second night there.

The next day dawned in bright sunshine. The

President and First Lady went to Niagara Falls and then returned to the fairground at around three-thirty in the afternoon. He was due to give a speech and then host a reception in the Temple of Music which lay on the southwest side of the Expo. He was accompanied by his old friend and Cabinet Secretary, George Cortelyou as well as an attachment of Secret Service officers. The Secret Service was not officially responsible for the protection of US Presidents, but it had been providing informal security since 1894 when President Grover Cleveland had been in office. There were also a dozen Buffalo police officers present as well as eleven Army servicemen who were ordered to keep a watchful eye on the crowd and after his speech, the ever-cautious Cortelyou, always concerned that McKinley got too close to the crowds, suggested to the President that he skip the reception, but the President would have none of it.

Thousands had gathered outside the doors of the Temple of Music waiting for him. At the front of the crowd stood Leon Czolgosz, his .32 wrapped in a handkerchief in his jacket pocket.

When the doors were opened at four, there was a mad dash by members of the public to get in and when McKinley finally appeared, he was greeted with a roar and he began immediately to greet people. He stood in the centre of the hall and the public was allowed to approach him in single file, shaking hands as they passed him. The hall's organist played softly in the background as people silently passed the President, reaching out their hands.

Czolgosz was edgy as he waited in the line of people. He had wrapped his hand in a white handkerchief in order to hide the gun and kept himself close to the person in front so that it could not be seen. Secret Serviceman George Foster, who was nearby, would not have noticed him anyway as he was more concerned about the six-foot six inch black man who stood in line behind the anarchist.

At exactly seven minutes past four, Czolgosz stood in front of the President. As McKinley reached out his hand, Czolgosz suddenly brushed it to one side and fired the gun wrapped in the handkerchief twice. Realising what was happening, George Foster punched him in the face and Czolgosz fell, the gun dropping to the floor where it was grabbed by Private Francis O'Brien, one of the soldiers guarding the President.

Meanwhile, as Czolgosz was dragged away, McKinley remained on his feet, shouting after them, 'Don't let them hurt him!'

He was worried that the angry crowd would seize the gunman and lynch him. Eleven minutes later, an ambulance arrived to convey the wounded President to the Expo's hospital.

Two shots had been fired, one bullet deflecting off his ribs while the other had hit him in the abdomen, passing through his stomach, hitting a kidney, damaging his pancreas and becoming lodged somewhere in his back muscles. The doctors were unable to find it and decided to leave it in.

That night Czolgosz confessed to shooting the President and to acting alone.

McKinley, however, appeared to be recovering. He was able to receive visitors on Saturday, 7 September and on the following morning a bulletin stated that he had passed a good night.

The Cabinet and Vice President Theodore Roosevelt immediately travelled to Buffalo but by Tuesday 10 September, he had improved so much that the Vice President went off on a hiking vacation.

On the Thursday, however, McKinley seemed to take a turn for the worse and by the next day his condition was being described as serious. It deteriorated as the day wore on and at 2.15 am on the morning of Saturday, 14 September, he died.

Roosevelt was summoned back from his holiday and the same day was sworn in as the 26th and, aged forty-two, the youngest President of the United States.

The trial of Leon Czolgosz began amid high security on 23 September 1901, but the outcome was fairly inevitable and even his defence attorney held out no hope for him. His confession was read out as well as a written statement in which he explained why he had assassinated the President. 'I killed President McKinley because I done my duty,' he wrote. 'I don't believe one man should have so much service and another should have none.'

The trial took a mere eight hours and twenty-six minutes and it took the jury only thirty minutes to arrive at a guilty verdict. Czolgosz was sentenced to die in the electric chair.

The sentence was carried out at 7.12 am on the morning of 29 October 1901 just six weeks after the death of the President.

Archduke Franz Ferdinand

The announcement that Archduke Franz Ferdinand, heir to the throne of the Austro-Hungarian Empire, was going to visit Bosnia-Herzegovina in June 1914, created a great deal of disquiet amongst Serbs. The empire had been created in 1867 as a monarchic union that ruled huge swathes of Central Europe with twin capitals in Vienna and Budapest. Now the man next in line to its throne would be arriving on a significant date – the anniversary of the 1389 Battle of Kosovo in which the Ottoman Turks had defeated the Serbs. It would be almost five hundred years before Serbia was free of Turkish rule and the anniversary, consequently, represented a humiliating collective memory to all Serbs.

In the 1878 Treaty of Berlin, Austria-Hungary was given the mandate to occupy and govern Bosnia-Herzegovina, while Serbia was recognised as a kingdom. Initially, the monarchs who were put in place were content to rule within the borders set by the treaty, but a coup in 1903 installed a more nationalistic king whose allegiances lay more with Russia than Austria-Hungary. The result was a decade of disputes between Serbia and its neighbours as it sought to build its power and reclaim the lands that had formed the Serbian Empire before the Turks seized control in the fourteenth century. In the years prior to Franz Ferdinand's visit, two Balkan Wars had erupted during which Serbia conquered Macedonia and Kosovo from the Ottomans.

By 1914, feelings were running high. Nationalistic Serbs were outraged at Austro-Hungarian control of Bosnia-Herzegovina. There were numerous attempts on the lives of Austro-Hungarian officials in Croatia and Bosnia-Herzegovina, often with the support of Serbia.

Franz Ferdinand's views also irritated Serbians. He believed in combining the Austro-Hungarian Slavic lands into a buffer against Serb nationalism, a plan that his assassin later stated in court, fuelled his motivation to kill the archduke.

Franz Ferdinand was being sent to Bosnia primarily to observe military manoeuvres and on their completion, he was to open the new state museum in Sarajevo. His wife Sophie insisted on accompanying him because, in the prevailing political situation, she feared for his safety. Interestingly, it was one of the only opportunities that she would have to sit in a carriage with him. Sophie was a Czech countess but was treated by the Austrian court as a commoner. She could not, therefore, share the splendour of his rank; her children would not be allowed to ascend the throne and she was not even allowed to sit beside him on state occasions. The only occasion on which she could enjoy the recognition of his rank was when he was on military duty. The trip to Bosnia was just such an occasion and Sophie was determined to enjoy it, seated side by side, for once, with her husband.

When the visit was announced, Colonel Dragutin Dimitrijevíc, chief of the Intelligence Department in the Serbian Army and head of the secret Serbian nationalist society, the Black Hand, ordered that Archduke Franz Ferdinand was to be assassinated. Serbian youths Vaso Ubrilovi and Cvjetko Popovíc were recruited for the operation, as were three other young Austro-Hungarian Bosnian Serbs, Gavrilo Princip, Trifun Grabež, and Nedjelko Cabrinovíc who had volunteered to carry out an assassination.

The weapons for their assault were delivered to Tuzla in Austria-Hungary on 26 May – six hand grenades, four Browning automatic pistols and ammunition. Money, suicide pills and training were also provided. A special map that told them where the police would be located was given to them and a small card that authorised the use of a secret tunnel that was used to get agents and weapons into Austria–Hungary.

Princip, Grabež, and Cabrinovič left Belgrade by boat on 28 May. At Sabec, they were given train tickets to the border town of Loznica. On 30 May, they were taken to an island in the middle of the Drina River where they were handed over to the agents of the Serbian nationalist group Narodna Odbrana. They were then moved through a number of safe houses, crossing the border into Austria-Hungary on 1 June. On 4 June, they arrived in Sarajevo, where other conspirators awaited them and where they temporarily separated, Princip visiting his family in Hadžici, before returning to Sarajevo on June 6 and moving into the house of the mother of Black Hand member, Danilo Ili. Grabež, meanwhile, visited his family in Pale and Cabrinovič went to his father's house in Sarajevo.

The weapons were brought to Sarajevo on 18 June and handed out to the conspirators on 27 June, the eve of the assassination.

On the morning of 28 June, Franz Ferdinand and his party travelled by train from Ilidža Spa to Sarajevo where they were greeted at the station by Austro-Hungarian Governor, Oskar Potiorek. Six cars waited for them, but the first serious security lapse occurred at this point. Three local police officers climbed into the first vehicle with the chief security officer, leaving behind the specialist security officers who were supposed to ride with the chief. In the second car were the Sarajevo Mayor and Chief of Police. The third car was a magnificent Gräf & Stift sports car with its top down to allow the crowds a view of Franz Ferdinand, Sophie, Governor Potiorek and Lieutenant Colonel Count Franz von Harrach who would be travelling in it.

The first stop on the busy itinerary was at a military barracks where the archduke was to carry out an inspection. At ten o'clock, the royal convoy was to leave the barracks and drive along the Appel Quay that ran alongside the River Mljacka to Sarajevo's town hall.

The first assassin, Mehmed Mehmedbašić, was stationed in front of the garden of the Mostar Café with a bomb, but as the procession passed in front of him, he failed to act. Next to him stood Nedjelko Cabrinović, armed with a pistol and a bomb who also froze. The royal convoy proceeded along the quay.

At 10.10, Nedjelko Cabrinović threw his bomb as the car containing Franz Ferdinand approached. It bounced off the vehicle onto the street, exploding under the car following, blasting a large crater in the road and injuring around twenty people. Cabrinović swallowed his cyanide pill and jumped over the parapet into the river. But, the cyanide failed to work and the river was shallow at this point. He was dragged from the water and arrested.

The convoy sped towards the town hall, three other assassins failing to act as it passed.

At the town hall, the reception for the archduke proceeded as planned although Franz Ferdinand was visibly stressed, interrupting the mayor's speech to express his outrage at the events of the morning.

It was decided to visit the wounded in hospital and the car left the town hall with Count von Harrach occupying a protective position on the car's running board.

Meanwhile, Gavrilo Princip had gone into a delicatessen to buy something to eat, but, as luck would have it, as he exited the shop, he saw the archduke's car reversing, having taken a wrong turn.

Oskar Potiorek had devised a route straight along the Appel Quay to the hospital but had neglected to tell the archduke's driver, Franz Urban. Princip was about two metres from the vehicle as he pulled out the Belgian-made 9 x 17mm (.380 ACP) Fabrique National semi-automatic pistol with which he had been issued. He fired two shots at the vehicle, the first of which wounded the archduke in the jugular vein, the second of which struck his wife in the abdomen.

Bystanders leapt on Princip while in the car von Harrach tried to wipe away the blood pulsing from Franz Ferdinand's neck. The car sped in the direction of the Governor's residence at Konak with the wounded royals still seated upright, but dying. Franz Ferdinand's last words were, 'Sophie, Sophie! Don't die! Live for our children!'

He then said a number of times, 'It is nothing,' when von Harrach asked him about his injury. Sophie was already dead when the cars skidded to a halt outside the Governor's residence and Franz Ferdinand died ten minutes after her.

Immediately following the shots, Princip had tried to turn the gun on himself but a man standing nearby realised what he was doing and seized his arm. Others joined in and Princip was soon under arrest.

Princip and Nedjelko Cabrinović were both interrogated by the police, eventually providing the names of their fellow conspirators. Mehmedbašić escaped to Serbia but the others were arrested and found guilty of treason and murder.

As under Austro-Hungarian law capital punishment could not be imposed on anyone under the age of twenty, Princip, nineteen years and eleven months at the time of the assassination, was given the maximum penalty of twenty years' imprisonment. During the trial, his only sign of regret was in a statement that he was sorry to have killed the wife of the Archduke. He had aimed only at her husband and would have preferred that the other bullet should have struck General Potiorek.

Austrian reaction to the assassination was swift, the Austrian foreign minister Count Leopold von Berchtold deciding to make use of the incident to crush once and for all the Serbian nationalist movement. He sent an envoy to Berlin, who was assured by Emperor William II that Germany would fully support any action the Dual Monarchy might take against Serbia.

On 23 July 1914, Austria-Hungary presented Serbia with a lengthy list of demands, and gave a forty-eight-hour period in which to comply with them. They included abolishing all Pan-Serb propaganda, expelling from office any persons thought to have nationalist sympathies, taking legal action against officials designated by Austria-Hungary, and allowing agents of the Dual Monarchy to control all investigations and proceedings concerning the Sarajevo assassinations.

A few minutes before the deadline on 25 July, Serbia issued a conciliatory reply to von Berchtold's demands, suggesting that the dispute be submitted to the International Tribunal at The Hague. Von Berchtold rejected this and on 28 July 1914, Austria-Hungary declared war on Serbia.

A few days later, on 30 July, Germany began to mobilise. France responded by mobilising her troops a day later, as Germany declared war on Russia. Finally on 4 August, following an 'unsatisfactory reply' to a demand that Belgium be kept neutral, Great Britain declared war on Germany. The First World War had begun.

Meanwhile, the man whose bullets had started it – Gavrilo Princip – remained in prison until he succumbed, on 28 April 1918, to the tuberculosis from which he had suffered since childhood.

MICHAEL COLLINS

On his deathbed, Michael Collins's father, seventh son of a seventh son, is said to have predicted that his daughter Helena would become a nun, which she did. He also instructed his family to take care of the youngest child in the family because, as he said, 'One day he'll be a great man. He'll do great work for Ireland.'

Indeed, he did. He became an active force in the Irish independence movement, took part in the Easter Rising of 1916, suffering imprisonment in England as a result, and was subsequently responsible, with Arthur Griffith, for negotiating the 1921 treaty that created the Irish Free State. Ironically, however, he would be killed not by the British, as might have been expected, but by Irishmen working on behalf of the rival faction in the Irish Civil War.

He was born into a family of eight children in Sam's Cross, West Cork in 1890. His father had been a member of the republican Fenian movement, but had left it to settle down and take up farming. But Michael inherited his father's nationalist passion, and was encouraged in it by the local blacksmith, James Santry and later by Denis Lyons, a member of the Irish Republican Brotherhood who taught at the Lisavaird National School that Michael attended.

Aged fifteen, he left school and took the British Civil Service examination in Cork. He was given a job with the Royal Mail.

1910 saw him moving to London where he was employed as a messenger by Horne and Company, a firm of stockbrokers. He lived with an older sister, studied at King's College, London and became a member of the Irish Republican Brotherhood. In 1915, he returned to Ireland.

Now a person of standing within the IRB, and known as a skilful organiser, he was appointed financial adviser to Count Plunkett, the father of one of the organisers of the Easter Rising, Joseph Mary Plunkett. He would later become the younger Plunkett's aide-de-camp.

During the Rising, Collins fought alongside Patrick Pearse and others in the General Post Office on Dublin's O'Connell Street, although in principle he was opposed to the action. Pearse had promoted a theory of 'blood sacrifice', suggesting that the deaths of the leaders of the Easter Rising would inspire others but Collins believed that the seizure of indefensible positions in Dublin such as St. Stephen's Green was foolhardy. As he would later demonstrate in the War of Independence, guerrilla warfare was a much more effective strategy. Collins was arrested after the Rising, but narrowly avoided execution, being imprisoned instead at Frongoch internment camp in Wales.

After the failure of the Rising, he became a prominent figure in the nationalist party, Sinn Féin, serving on the executive and becoming director of the military organisation, the Irish Volunteers, founded in 1913 as a response to the founding of the loyalist Ulster Volunteers.

In 1918, he was one of the senior Sinn Féin members who were elected in the general election to the British House of Commons. He became MP for Cork South, but like his Sinn Féin colleagues, he refused to take his seat. Instead, they set up an Irish Parliament – the Dáil Éireann (Assembly of Ireland) – in Dublin. It met in January 1919 for the first time, although by that time the Dáil Éireann president, Eamon de Valera and many other senior nationalists, had been arrested. Collins, having learned in advance from his intelligence network that the arrests were going to happen, had warned his colleagues but they chose to ignore him. Some believed, in fact, that it would be positive publicity for the movement if they were arrested.

In 1919, Collins was elected president of the Irish Republican Brotherhood and was appointed Director of Intelligence of the Irish Republican Army, the new name for the Irish Volunteers.

On 21 January 1919, the Irish War of Independence began when a platoon of Royal Irish Constabulary men were ambushed by a party of IRA volunteers in County Tipperary, two police officers being killed.

Collins by this time had added another responsibility to his already long list – that of Minister for Finance. Whereas, in the prevailing situation, such government titles were little more than honorary, Collins did actually create a Finance Ministry that even organised a large bond issue to fund the new Irish Republic.

He also created a hit squad, an assassination group known as The Squad, the aim of which was to kill British agents. Meanwhile, with Richard Mulcahy, he ran the Irish Republican Army, helping to create the famous 'flying columns', the guerrilla units that did so much damage to British troops. In 1920, a reward of £10,000, a considerable sum in those days, was offered for information leading to his capture or death.

When a truce was called in 1921, a conference was organised between the British government and nationalist leaders. Collins attended the conference in a delegation led by Arthur Griffith.

Negotiations resulted in the Anglo-Irish Treaty, a document to which Collins said he put his name feeling as if 'I have signed my own death warrant'. It envisaged a new Irish state, the Irish Free State which was established in December 1922. It was to enjoy the status of a dominion with a bicameral parliament, executive authority vested in the king but exercised by an Irish government.

The treaty proved hugely controversial in Ireland. The purists believed it to be a sell-out, particularly as an Oath of Allegiance had to be sworn to the king. Britain also retained control over Ireland's southern ports, threatening Ireland's right to direct its own foreign policy. De Valera was furious that Collins had signed off any agreement without his or his cabinet's prior approval and most of the Irish Republican Army were against it. Civil war loomed.

In the new government that followed the failure of de Valera to secure re-election as president, Arthur Griffith took over the leadership, although this regime had no legal standing in British constitutional law. Collins formed a Provisional Government, as Prime Minister.

The six counties of Northern Ireland were partitioned but Collins was planning a secret guerrilla war against them and had been preparing his troops for it, sending money and arms north. Under pressure from the British, however, the offensive was called off on 3 June, although there were still some small attacks.

Civil war in the south was inevitable, although Collins made efforts to prevent it. On 14 April 1922, 200 anti-treaty IRA men occupied the Four Courts in Dublin. Collins finally attacked on 22 June and the civil war had begun.

In July 1922, with the war raging, and against the advice of his colleagues, Collins decided to travel to his native Cork, laughing off their concerns and saying, 'They wouldn't shoot me in my own country'.

In Cork City he met with some neutral IRA men, with the intention of organising a truce. He was dead, however, before that came to fruition.

As Collins was travelling towards Bandon in County Cork in the back of an army truck, his column stopped to ask directions. They had the misfortune, however, to ask directions from a man called Dinny Long, a member of the local anti-Treaty IRA. Long immediately informed his IRA colleagues and an ambush was set up for the column on its return journey to Cork City. They would have to take the same road as the other two routes that they could have taken had both been made impassable by Republicans.

Most of the ambush party was in the pub when the column approached Beal na Blath near Clonakilty on its return journey. The five men who had been left behind immediately opened fire from a hillside when they saw it advance towards them.

Collins grabbed a rifle, jumped out of the truck and began to return their fire, while rashly standing up in full view. He was shot in the head and fatally wounded, the only casualty in the twenty-minute gun battle. He had chosen to stop and return fire and not to escape in the car that accompanied the convoy or by climbing into the safety of the armoured car in the column. Instead, he returned fire on the ambushers until he was fatally wounded.

No one is entirely certain who fired the shot that killed Michael Collins. One authoritative account suggests a former British Army sniper, Denis 'Sonny' O'Neill as his killer. O'Neill was using dum-dum bullets that disintegrate on impact and do huge damage and indeed, Collins was left with a gaping wound in his skull. O'Neill threw away the remainder of his bullets, terrified of reprisals by Free State supporters.

The body of Michael Collins was brought back to Cork and then shipped to Dublin due to the fear that it would be kidnapped if conveyed by road. He lay in state for three days in Dublin City Hall where thousands of mourners filed respectfully past his coffin. Five hundred thousand people lined the streets of Dublin for his funeral, a staggering one-fifth of the population of Ireland at the time.

Doubts and questions remain about Collins' shooting. Some Republicans maintain that he was, in fact, a British spy. Others insist that de Valera was behind the assassination. One of his own men, Jock McPeak, is even blamed, especially as he defected to the Republican side a few months later. However, the commander of the ambush, Liam Deasy, demonstrated he had no time for such theories when he said, 'We all knew it was Sonny O'Neill's bullet'.

Mahatma Gandhi

Mohandas Karamchand Gandhi was not only one of the greatest men of his time, but one of the greatest men of any time. The political and ideological leader of India during its long struggle for independence from the British, he was the pioneer of a new kind of protest – *satyagraha*. This was resistance to tyranny and oppression through mass civil disobedience and non-violence. It was a style of protest that not only helped India to cast off imperial shackles but also inspired civil rights and freedom movements around the world during the twentieth century, from the African-American struggle in the United States to Nelson Mandela and the anti-apartheid movements of South Africa.

Gandhi is known in India as the 'Father of the Nation' and his birthday is celebrated as a national holiday and across the world as the International Day of Non-Violence. Tragically, however, the life of this man who was so vehemently opposed to violence, ended in a dreadful, violent act.

He was born in the coastal town of Porbander in modern-day Gujurat in Western India in 1869 and politics was part of his life from an early age, his father holding the office of Prime Minister of the state. He was brought up in the Jainist religion which imbued him with many of the principles that would become significant features of his life – vegetarianism, the practice of fasting to achieve a purity of the soul, compassion to all sentient beings and an abiding tolerance of different people no matter their colour, creed or religion.

Married early, as was the custom, he travelled to London at the age of nineteen to study law at University College. Returning to India on the completion of his studies, he found it difficult to establish himself as a lawyer in Mumbai. He returned, therefore, to Gujurat, but was forced to close his practice after a disagreement with a British army officer. It was 1893 and a legal career in India was beginning to look unlikely. He decided to take up a year's contract to work on behalf of an Indian legal firm in Natal in South Africa.

Gandhi immediately experienced the racial discrimination that characterised South Africa even at the end of the nineteenth century. On his arrival in the country, he was not allowed to travel in a first class compartment of a railway train and was beaten when he refused to travel on the footboard of a stagecoach in order to make room inside for white passengers. When he arrived at his destination, he had great difficulty finding a hotel that would let him in.

He decided to remain in South Africa longer than his contract in order to help the many Indians resident there to fight new legislation that would deprive them of the right to vote. He also founded the Natal Indian Congress in order to provide a voice for South Africa's Indians. It was dangerous, however, and on one occasion he narrowly avoided being lynched by a mob of white racists.

He invented *satyagraha* during a demonstration in the Transvaal against a new law that required the Indian population to register. In the next seven years thousands of Indians were imprisoned, flogged or shot for engaging in peaceful resistance. The government was eventually forced to negotiate a settlement.

Returning to India in 1915, he threw himself into politics, championing poverty-stricken and oppressed Indians in Champaran. He established an ashram and helped villages rid themselves of the scourges of alcoholism, famine and dire poverty. He was arrested and ordered to leave the province but a protest by hundreds of thousands of people led to the charges being dropped.

The little man's fame was spreading and people named him 'Bapu' (Father) or addressed him as 'Mahatma' (Great Soul). But his greatest campaign – the struggle for Indian independence was just beginning.

It was an incident that took place on 13 April 1919 that became the catalyst for his decision that India should be in control of its own destiny. In Amritsar that day, around 20,000 Indians gathered to peacefully protest against the passing in Britain of the Rowlatt Act which extended emergency measures that had been enacted during the recently-ended First World War. Without reason, the British army opened fire on the unarmed crowd and, to the horror and outrage of the nation, 379 people were killed and more than 1,000 wounded in just ten minutes of firing.

In 1921, Gandhi was elected leader of the Indian National Congress and began an extraordinary campaign with the ultimate goal of complete independence. He introduced a policy of boycotting all foreign-made products, particularly those made in Britain. British institutions such as schools, colleges and law courts should be boycotted and those in government jobs were asked to resign their positions.

Non-cooperation was embraced wholeheartedly by Indians, but another violent incident brought the danger of the situation into sharp focus and made Gandhi doubt whether he could ever control his people. In 1922 an angry mob set a police station on fire in Chauri Chara, killing twenty-two policemen trapped inside. Even though in response Gandhi called off the campaign of non-cooperation, he was arrested, charged with sedition and sent to prison for six years, of which he served two.

Released from prison, he withdrew from active politics, concentrating on social issues such as poverty, ignorance and the inequalities of India's caste system. But in December 1928, he returned to front-line politics with a demand that India be granted the same dominion status as that enjoyed by Canada and Australia. The alternative, he declared, was another campaign of civil disobedience.

In March that year, he led a 248-mile march in protest against the tax on salt that resulted in some 60,000 Indians being imprisoned. At last, however, the British government seemed to be listening and asked for a meeting with Gandhi. The result was the Gandhi-Irwin Pact, signed in March 1931 by which the British agreed to release all prisoners and Gandhi promised an end to civil disobedience.

Its lack of focus on independence was, however, disappointing to Indians.

Gandhi's activities – such as fasts on behalf of Dalits, or Untouchables – made many enemies and in 1934 there were the first of a number of attempts on his life.

By 1938, the Congress Party was under new leadership and had begun to move away from Gandhi's policies of non-violence and non-cooperation. When Britain unilaterally took India into the Second World War, Gandhi remarked that it would be difficult for India to fight for the cause of democracy when she did not enjoy it. However, a defining moment arrived in July 1942 when the Indian National Congress passed a resolution demanding complete independence. If the demand was not met, they continued, there would be a massive campaign of civil disobedience. On 8 August, the Quit India Resolution was passed by a meeting of the All-India Congress and Gandhi launched the Quit India movement, urging followers to act as an independent nation and to ignore the orders of the British.

Gandhi and all the other political leaders were arrested and imprisoned and the Congress Party was outlawed. Nonetheless, even without leadership, Indians took part in the greatest show of civil disobedience yet. They failed to turn up for work, and went on strike. However, there were also outbreaks of violence – bombs went off and power lines were cut.

Gandhi was in prison for three years and during that time his wife, also imprisoned, died. The little man was by this time very frail. Frequent fasts had taken their toll on him and the authorities, terrified that he would die in custody, released him.

It was becoming clear to the British that it was only a matter of time before India would have to be given independence and it finally arrived in 1947.

There was a great deal of antagonism towards Gandhi and there had been five attempts on his life since 1934.

On Friday, 30 January, the seventy-eight-year-old woke as always at three-thirty in the morning. Life had been turbulent of late. Twelve days earlier, he had ended a successful fast to bring an end to violence between Hindus and Muslims in Delhi. Ten days earlier, a bomb had exploded a short distance from him as he addressed a prayer meeting.

He was still weak from his fasting and had to be helped from his bed and into another room by his grand-nieces. He started his last day by working on the draft of a new constitution for the Congress Party.

Then, at around 9.30, he had breakfast. He met with Muslim leaders and gave a series of interviews in the afternoon, the last of them ending at 4 pm.

Five in the afternoon was the customary time for prayers but on this day Gandhi was already running ten minutes late. He slipped on his sandals and walked out into the garden of the Birla House in New Delhi where he had been staying, his grand-nieces walking on either side of him, carrying his prayer book, glasses case and rosary.

Gandhi was usually surrounded by security guards and around thirty had been stationed at Birla House. On that particular day, however, his personal security officer, A.N. Bhatia was absent, having been re-assigned elsewhere.

Running late, he took a shortcut across the lawn to the steps that led to the terrace where prayers were held. He was happy and laughed and joked with the two girls who walked either side of him.

At the top of the steps, he brought his palms together in greeting and the crowd that had gathered parted in order to allow him to make his way to the wooden platform.

He had walked only a few steps when a man pushed his way through the crowd and approached the little man with his hands together in front of his face. He was Nathuram Godse, a member of the right-wing organisation, the Hindu Mahasabha which hated Gandhi for what they regarded as his appeasement of the Muslims. Hidden in Godse's hands was a small black Italian Beretta pistol. It had been easy to smuggle in as Gandhi had forbidden police officers from searching people as they came into the grounds of the house.

Godse bowed low and said, 'Namaste Gandhiji'. Gandhi returned his greeting, putting his palms together. One of his grand-nieces tried to motion Godse away so that Gandhi could get on with prayers but Godse pushed her hand aside and the gun appeared in his right hand. Pointing it at Gandhi, he pulled the trigger, pumping three bullets into the little man's abdomen and chest at almost point-blank range.

Gandhi did not fall immediately. His palms still together, he gasped, 'He Ram, He Ram', (Oh God, Oh God) and slowly sank to the ground. Panic ensued but during it he lay on the ground, his head resting on the lap of one of his grand-nieces, her white, Australian wool shawl turning red with the little man's blood. He died at seventeen minutes past five.

PRESIDENT JOHN F. KENNEDY

Everyone remembers where he or she was when the news came through that the 35th President of the United States had been assassinated in Dallas. It was a moment when the world seemed to come to a standstill – the most powerful man on earth having been felled by shots from a book depository as he drove in a motorcade of open-topped vehicles through the city. It is an event that still grips the consciousness of America and conspiracy theories abound. Was Lee Harvey Oswald really the assassin and was he working alone? Were other bullets fired from other locations? Did the Mafia order the killing? They are tantalising questions to which we will probably never know the answers.

The 22 November 1963 dawned warm and sunny in Dallas and the city was looking forward to celebrating the visit of the young President John F. Kennedy and his glamorous wife, Jacquie. Kennedy had travelled to Texas to prepare for the 1964 presidential election. The Governor of the state, John Connally and Senator Ralph Yarborough were at odds and Kennedy needed them to work together to help him secure re-election. The visit was intended to give Kennedy the opportunity to use his famous charm to bring the two men together in the common cause of re-election of the president.

Preparations for the visit had been going on for some time and as usual, the FBI had arrived well in advance. On 8 November, Agent Winston Lawson had been briefed about the trip and had been given a tentative itinerary by Agent Roy H. Kellerman, the man responsible for the motorcade's route through Dallas. Around this time, Governor Connally confirmed that he would be joining the president in Dallas on 22 November.

On 14 November, Agent Lawson was joined by another agent on a drive along the planned route that would take the president from Lovefield Airport to the Trade Mart where Kennedy would be giving a speech to civic and business leaders. The precise route was published by a Dallas newspaper five days later, a dreadful lapse in security.

Airforce One, the President's plane, stopped briefly in Fort Worth, leaving Carswell Air Force Base at ten minutes past eleven to make the short hop to Dallas. At 11.39 it touched down and within ten minutes the Kennedys were pulling out of the airport in their midnight blue 1961 Lincoln Presidential Limousine. The plastic bubble top of the car had been removed and its bullet-proof side windows were rolled down because of the clement weather. It was also the way that the President liked to travel. Behind it was the Secret Service's 1955 Cadillac convertible, carrying eight agents with four standing on the car's running boards ready to jump off and provide protection for the president if required.

It was a journey of eleven miles from the airport to the Trade Mart, a winding route that led through downtown Dallas and the president and his wife sat in the back while Governor Connally and his wife Nelly sat in the front seats behind the driver. They drove through streets lined by enthusiastic crowds who were keen to see the young president and his wife.

The motorcade arrived in Dealey Plaza before swinging slowly right from Main Street into Houston Street. Seconds later, it turned one hundred and twenty degrees into Elm Street. As they approached the Texas School Book Depository, a large, seven-storied, redbrick building, Nelly Connally turned round to the president and said, 'Mr. President, you can't say Dallas doesn't love you'. Kennedy acknowledged the remark, but a few moments later a shot rang out. Kennedy was hit in his upper back, the bullet penetrating his neck and slightly damaging a spinal vertebra and the top of his right lung. It exited through his throat just beneath his Adam's apple. He clenched his fists in front of his face and slumped forward and slightly to the left, Jacquie Kennedy, reacting instinctively, putting her arms around him. Meanwhile, the same bullet struck Governor Connally in the back, exiting just below his right nipple. It then hit him on the wrist, breaking the bone, before exiting through his palm and entering his left inner thigh.

Moments later, a second shot was fired which blew a gaping hole in the back right side of the President's head. Blood and brain and bone fragments were spread across the interior of the vehicle as well as onto the Secret Service agents behind and the motorcycle outriders. Mrs. Kennedy reached out onto the rear of the car, possibly to retrieve a piece of her husband's skull, crawling over the boot as Agent Clint Hill leaned forward from the rear bumper in a futile effort to protect the car's occupants. Jacquie was heard by Governor and Mrs. Connally to say, 'They have killed my husband. I have his brains in my hand'. The car then gathered speed and raced off to Parkland Memorial Hospital, Agent Hill clinging precariously to the back.

On arrival at the hospital, it was obvious that there was no chance of the President surviving. He was given the Last Rites and at 1 pm was pronounced dead. On the way back to Washington from Dallas, Vice President Lyndon B. Johnson was sworn in as 36th President of the United States.

Meanwhile, back in Dallas, the hunt for the assassin was under way. In the Book Depository, a police officer and a supervisor encountered a man named Lee Harvey Oswald. Oswald was identified as an employee and allowed to pass, nonchalantly drinking a soda. He left the building shortly before it was sealed off by police, the only employee to do so.

At 12.40, he got on a bus, dismounting two blocks later because of the slow progress the bus was making through the traffic and taking a taxi to his rooming house. He put on a jacket in his room and then left again.

A short distance from the rooming house, a police cruiser pulled up alongside him and patrolman J. D. Tippit rolled down his window and spoke to Oswald. The officer then got out of the car but was gunned down by Oswald who pumped four shots into him and ran off.

Minutes later, Oswald was seen ducking into the entrance of a shoe shop to avoid passing police cars. He then went into the nearby Texas Theater, without paying. The shoe shop's manager spotted this and immediately alerted the ticket clerk who telephoned the police. Shortly after, the house lights were switched on and the store manager pointed out Oswald who was sitting close to the rear of the cinema. Oswald more or less surrendered, saying, 'Well, it's all over now'. Suddenly, however, he struck an officer and a struggle broke out, during which he was disarmed. He shouted out that he was a victim of police brutality as he was hustled out of the building.

He arrived at the Police Department building at two o'clock and was immediately recognised as the only Book Depository employee who had not been accounted for. Shortly after, he was charged with the murders of President Kennedy and Officer Tippit.

Later that afternoon, as he walked down a corridor surrounded by police officers, he said to the reporters who lined the corridor, 'I didn't shoot anyone' and 'They're taking me in because of the fact I lived in the Soviet Union. I'm just a patsy!'

He continued to deny the murders in several interrogations during the next two days and denied even owning a rifle. He further denied bringing a long, heavy package to work on the morning of the assassination and claimed that photographs of him holding a pistol and a rifle were fakes. He had been having lunch in the Depository's lunchroom, he claimed, at the time the President was shot. Later, however, he said that he had been working on an upper floor when the shots had been fired.

On Sunday, 24 November, at 11.21 am, Oswald was being led through the basement of the Dallas Police Headquarters to be transferred to the county jail when a Dallas nightclub owner, Jack Ruby, distraught, he later claimed, at Kennedy's death, stepped out of the assembled crowd and fired a bullet into Oswald's abdomen. It was all captured live on television and transmitted to an audience of millions. Oswald was rushed to the same hospital in which the president had died two days earlier but was pronounced dead at 1.07 pm. It was the end of an extraordinary life.

He had been born in New Orleans in 1939 and raised by his mother after the death of his father before his birth. A withdrawn and temperamental child, he was diagnosed as having 'schizoid features and passive-aggressive tendencies'. He was an avid reader and by the age of fifteen had declared in his diary that he was a Marxist. He joined the Marines in 1956, by which time he had lived in twenty-two different places and had attended twelve schools. In 1959, he obtained a hardship discharge from the Marines, claiming he had to care for his mother, but instead travelled to the Soviet Union, using $1,500 he had saved from his Marine pay. He attempted to obtain Soviet citizenship, but his application was rejected. He then went to the United States embassy in Moscow and announced that he wished to renounce his American citizenship.

He was sent to Minsk where he worked as a lathe operator and was given an apartment in a prestigious building although he was still under constant surveillance by the Soviet authorities. Soon, he was bored, however, and began to re-consider his decision to remain in Russia. He wrote to the US embassy, requesting the return of his passport.

In March, he met Marina Nikolayevna Prusakova, a nineteen-year-old student and the two were married less than six weeks later. A daughter June was born in February 1962. They obtained the appropriate documentation for Marina to emigrate to the United States and left the Soviet Union in June of that year.

Back in the States, he found work but his rudeness,

arrogance and inefficiency always let him down.

On 10 April 1963, he is said to have made an attempt on the life of retired Major General Edwin Walker, an outspoken, Communist-hating, segregationist conservative. Having bought a 6.5 mm calibre Carcano rifle, Oswald fired at Walker through the window of his study. He missed and Walker's only injury was some bullet fragments in his arm.

He returned to New Orleans where he worked at the Reilly Coffee Company but was fired, as usual. He next announced plans to travel to Cuba via Mexico and was granted a visa, but never used it. Instead, he returned to Dallas where on 16 October 1963, he was taken on by the Book Depository. During the week, he stayed at the rooming house while weekends were spent with Marina in Irving where she was staying with friends. On 20 October, the couple's second daughter was born.

Meanwhile, FBI agents twice visited the house where Marina was staying, suspecting her of being a Soviet agent. Oswald was furious and tried to speak to someone about it. When no one would see him, he left a note saying, 'Let this be a warning. I will blow up the FBI and the Dallas Police Department if you don't stop bothering my wife. Signed – Lee Harvey Oswald.'

On 21 November, Oswald unexpectedly visited his wife in Irving in the middle of the week under the pretext of picking up some curtain rods. He returned to Dallas the next morning leaving behind $170 and his wedding ring. He carried a long paper bag and thirty minutes prior to the assassination was seen on the sixth floor of the Book Depository.

Lee Harvey Oswald

It is one of the most sensational pieces of live television ever broadcast. A corridor crowded with people, cameras, film crews, reporters, all jostling for a look at, and possibly a chance to throw a question at, President John F. Kennedy's assassin, Lee Harvey Oswald. It was 24 November and Oswald, who had been apprehended shortly after the President had been shot in Dealey Plaza two days earlier, was being transferred from Dallas Police Headquarters to the county jail.

Oswald had denied shooting Kennedy, on one occasion, replying to a reporter's question as he walked down the corridor, 'I didn't shoot anybody. I'm a patsy'. He complained about his lack of legal representation. Asked to account for his whereabouts when the president was shot, he said he ate lunch in the Texas Book Depository's first-floor lunchroom and then went to the second floor for a Coke and that it was at that point that he encountered a policeman. On 24 November, he provided a different version, claiming to have been on an upper floor when the assassination took place and to have then gone downstairs where he bumped into the policeman.

That Sunday, as the crowds swarmed the corridor, Oswald emerged, as he had done several times in the last two days, handcuffed to officer James Leavelle and surrounded by tall, white-hatted Texas Rangers who pushed through the throng. His left eye was swollen and bruised and he had told a reporter that a policeman had hit him. Behind him in this bizarre procession came a man holding aloft the 6.5 mm Mannlicher-Carcano rifle that he had allegedly used to kill the president.

On television, Oswald and the officers disappeared through a doorway, heading for the underground car park from where he was to be whisked away in an armoured prison transfer van that had earlier reversed into the garage.

The garage was just as crowded as the corridor had been and Oswald and his minders walked through a path in the middle of the crowd.

At 11.21, in full view of the watching millions, a figure, wearing a dark suit and a trilby hat, suddenly dashed out of the crowd of onlookers with a .38-calibre Colt Cobra in his hand. He pointed it at Oswald's abdomen and fired, shouting, 'You killed the President, you rat!' Oswald put his hands up and spun his body slightly to the right as if he could somehow stop the bullet, and pandemonium broke out. Horrified police officers immediately leapt upon the gunman and wrestled him to the ground, seizing his weapon.

Oswald, meanwhile, had collapsed to the floor of the garage. An ambulance was summoned and he was rushed to parkland Memorial Hospital, ironically the same one to which President Kennedy had been rushed two days earlier and where he had died. Another media scrum was already waiting for him as the ambulance arrived and again on television he was seen being carried on a trolley into the hospital. He died at seven minutes past one.

Oswald's killer was Jack Leon Ruby, a Dallas strip-club owner who had been born in Chicago in 1911with the Jewish name Rubenstein but had legally changed it in 1947 to Ruby. He was the fifth of eight children of Polish Jews who had emigrated to America in the early nineteen-hundreds.

At school, Jack was trouble and at the age of eleven underwent psychiatric treatment. His home life was difficult, his father a violent man who was often arrested for assault and his mother a dangerously unstable woman who was eventually diagnosed as suffering from psychoneurosis and sent to Elgin State Hospital. Jack was brought up by foster parents,

Leaving school at sixteen, he worked at a variety of odd jobs and even, it was rumoured, worked for gangster Al Capone at one point. He spent time in Los Angeles and San Francisco but returned to Chicago to work for the Scrap Iron and Junk Handlers Union. But when, in 1939, the man who had found him the job was shot dead by the president of the union, Ruby left the job to become a salesman.

He was called up in 1943, serving in the Army Air Force at various places in the United States before being honourably discharged in 1946.

Back in Chicago, he worked for his brother for a while before moving to Dallas in 1947 to run the Singapore nightclub for his sister, Eva Grant. He borrowed money from a friend to purchase the Silver Spur Club and the Bob Wills Ranch House, a western-style club. In 1954, he added part-ownership of the Vegas Club to his responsibilities. Finally, in 1960, he opened the Carousel Club where he employed a master of ceremonies and four strippers.

By that November of 1963, Ruby was a paunchy, slightly balding fifty-two-year-old. His hair was dark and oily and smoothed back on his head. He had a cleft chin and always looked like he needed a shave. He wore cuff-links and diamond pinkie rings but was obsessed with being 'classy', although he never came within a million miles of achieving it. He believed his second-rate strip joint, the Carousel, had class and had a gold-framed oil painting of a horse above the bar to prove it. It cost $2 to get into the square room with its dark red carpet and black plastic booths and the stage on which his girls would bump and grind was about the size of a boxing ring.

The world in which Ruby operated immediately brought claims that he had links with organised crime, leading some to suggest that he was part of a wider conspiracy to kill the president and then cover up the names of those behind it. In fact, Ruby had close connections with both the police and the mob. It was probably his familiarity with Dallas police officers that enabled him to mingle with reporters at Dallas Police Headquarters during the weekend of Kennedy's assassination. He had attended the press conference that had been held on the Friday night after the assassination and had even been amongst those who had corrected District Attorney Henry Wade when he described an organisation of which

Oswald was a member as the 'anti-Castro Free Cuba Committee'. As Ruby and others pointed out to him, he should have called it 'the pro-Castro Fair Play for Cuba Committee'.

The House Committee on Assassinations later noted Ruby's friendship with restaurateurs Sam and Joseph Campisi who had connections with other shady underworld figures such as Joseph Civitello, head of organised crime in Dallas. The Campisis were said to be lieutenants of Mafia boss, Carlos Marcello who had been known to have talked about assassinating Kennedy. A day before Kennedy was shot, Ruby was seen visiting Joe Campisi's restaurant.

The Mafia had an interest because of their long-standing ties with anti-Castro Cubans, ties that had been formed before the revolution when they ran lucrative casinos in Havana. These Cubans hated Kennedy for his lack of support for the failed Bay of Pigs invasion. Furthermore, his Attorney General and brother, Robert, had been waging an unprecedented attack on organised crime.

It was this world in which Jack Ruby operated.

Or was it? There are just as many sources that suggest that Ruby was simply too small-time to be involved in the assassination of a president. In fact, some think it is downright laughable. His brother Earl has denied allegations that his brother was involved in racketeering of any kind

Many say that Ruby, in fact, just killed Oswald on the spur of the moment. He later claimed that he did it in order to save the reputation of Dallas in the eyes of the world, to make Jews look good and to save the President's wife, Jacquie, the anguish of having to testify at the trial of Lee Harvey Oswald.

In the six months following that eventful weekend, Ruby repeatedly asked to speak to the Warren Commission that was investigating the circumstances surrounding the assassination. The commission, however, showed no interest in him. It was only after his sister wrote to them and their refusal to talk to Ruby became public that they eventually agreed to talk to him.

In June 1964, Chief Justice Earl Warren, Representative, and later President, Gerald R. Ford and other members travelled to Dallas to meet him. Ruby told Warren that he feared for his life in Dallas and informed him that if Warren did not have him transferred to Washington, he would refuse to cooperate. Warren refused to comply – the legal complications would be too great.

Some observers believed Ruby would be found

guilty of murder without malice and would get off with a possible five-year prison sentence. However, his lawyer, Melvin Belli, put up a defence of insanity, bolstered by his mother's condition and a history of mental illness in the family. This strategy proved disastrous and Ruby was instead found guilty of murder with malice in March 1964 and sentenced to death.

He appealed, his lawyers claiming that he could not have had a fair trial in Dallas due to the extraordinary publicity surrounding the case. Around that time, he spoke to reporters, saying somewhat enigmatically, 'Everything pertaining to what's happening has never come to the surface. The world will never know the true facts of what occurred, my motives. The people who had so much to gain, and had such an ulterior motive for putting me in the position I'm in, will never let the true facts come above board to the world.' A reporter then asked him, 'Are these people in very high positions Jack?'

Ruby answered, 'Yes.'

He was granted a re-trial and his conviction and death sentence were overturned. The new trial was set for February 1967, in Wichita Falls, Texas, but on 9 December 1966, Ruby was admitted to Parkland

Hospital suffering from what doctors believed to be pneumonia. It turned out to be cancer.

Ten days later, Jack Ruby made a final statement from his hospital bed saying that he had acted alone in shooting Lee Harvey Oswald. 'There is nothing to hide,' he said. 'There was no one else.'

He died fifteen days later, on 3 January 1967.

Malcolm X

It is hardly surprising that Malcolm X was a victim of assassination on 21 February 1965 because by that time, he had enemies everywhere. Members of the African-American religious movement Nation of Islam in which he was once a leading figure resented what they saw as efforts to supplant their leader, Elijah Muhammad. The United States Government was wary of his increasing international focus that seemed destined to turn the country's racial problems into an international human rights issue and he had gained the support of civil rights leader, Dr. Martin Luther King, to present a petition of human rights violations to the International Court of Justice conference at the Hague in the Netherlands. They were also concerned about the fact that politically, he was leaning increasingly to the left. Moreover, he had gained the ire of organised crime figures by campaigning in Harlem against narcotics, alcohol and crime, championing the ethics of black pride, the doctrines of Islam and the establishment of independent black businesses. Meanwhile, US law enforcement agencies viewed him and his activities as radical, criminal and dangerously anti-social.

He was born Malcolm Little in 1925 in Omaha, Nebraska, his father, Earl, an outspoken Baptist lay preacher who was a proponent of the Pan-African views of Marcus Garvey and a prominent figure in his local Universal Negro Improvement Association (UNIA). In 1926 the family fled the threat of the Ku Klux Klan, re-locating to Milwaukee, Wisconsin and then to Lansing, Michigan.

In 1931, Earl Little was killed, apparently by a streetcar, but the local black community disputed the cause of death, believing that he had been assaulted by white supremacists before being thrown onto the tracks.

The family struggled on with very little money and eventually Malcolm's mother Louise had a nervous breakdown, was declared insane and committed to the state mental hospital. She would remain there for twenty-six years before Malcolm and his brothers and sisters were able to secure her release.

Malcolm, meanwhile, proved to be a good student, one of the best in his junior high school. However, when he was told by a white eighth-grade teacher that his ambition to be a lawyer was 'no realistic goal for a nigger', he felt humiliated and dropped out of school. He moved to Boston where he was looked after by an aunt and worked on the New Haven Railroad.

By 1943, Malcolm was living in Harlem in New York, living off what he earned from drug-dealing, gambling, racketeering and robbery. Declared 'mentally unfit for military service' after telling an examining officer that he could not wait to 'steal us some guns and kill us some crackers', he launched a burglary career, breaking into the houses of wealthy white New Yorkers. In 1946, he was arrested as he tried to collect a stolen watch he had left at a jewellery shop to be repaired. He was carrying a gun and was sent to prison for eight to ten years for possession of an illegal firearm, larceny and breaking and entering.

In Charlestown State Prison, he began to educate himself, and it was while incarcerated there that he first heard about the Nation of Islam, in a letter written to him by his brother Philbert.

The Nation of Islam was like the UNIA of which his father had been a member. It preached black self-reliance and had the ultimate aim of uniting all peoples of the African diaspora and achieving freedom from white European and American domination. Initially contemptuous of all religions when he had arrived at the prison, to the extent that he had become known as 'Satan', he became fascinated by the Nation of Islam, stopping smoking and refusing to eat pork.

In 1948, now in an experimental prison in Norfolk, Virginia that had a much larger library, he wrote a letter to the leader of the NOI, Elijah Muhammad. Muhammad replied, telling him to atone for his crimes by accepting Allah and renouncing the kind of life he had lived until that point. Malcolm became a member of the Nation of Islam.

Released on Parole in August 1952, he travelled to Chicago to meet Elijah Muhammad where he changed his name to Malcolm X, the 'X' representing the real African name that he would never know.

He soon came to the attention of the FBI, initially after describing himself as a Communist, but then as he rapidly began to rise to prominence in the Nation of Islam. In June 1953, he was appointed assistant minister of the NOI's Temple Number One in Detroit and by the end of that year, he had established Temple Number Eleven in Boston. After more work in Philadelphia, he was selected in mid-1954 to lead Temple Number Seven in Harlem, growing its membership rapidly.

A television documentary about the NOI in 1959 brought Malcolm X to a national audience and he was beginning to appear regularly in the media.

Meanwhile, he continued to deliver powerful speeches, audiences mesmerised by the brilliant, handsome, six feet three inch black man in front of them. He talked of black people being the original people on earth and how they were superior to white people, predicting the imminent demise of the white race. It was the opposite message to that being preached by the civil rights movement. They fought segregation; he demanded separation. He also rejected non-violence as a means to achieve his goals, believing that black people were entitled to use any means possible to defend themselves and their objectives. For many black people, tired of waiting for the equality promised by the civil rights movement, it was a powerful message and they flocked to the Nation of Islam.

The two sides of the argument railed at each other, civil rights activists considering Malcolm X and the NOI as dangerous extremists, while Malcolm X considered Martin Luther King to be 'a chump', describing the march on Washington as 'the farce in Washington'.

Following the assassination of President Kennedy in 1963, Elijah Muhammad ordered the leaders of the NOI to make no comment. Malcolm X, however, characteristically ignored the edict, saying that the assassination was a case of 'chickens coming home to roost'. The resulting media storm did not please leaders of the NOI and in March the following year, Malcolm X announced that, although he would remain a Muslim, he was no longer a member of the organisation. His unhappiness had been confounded by rumours that Elijah Muhammad had been enjoying extramarital liaisons with young women.

He set about creating his own black nationalist organisation – Muslim Mosque Inc. – and expressed a desire to work with other civil rights leaders. In April 1964 he delivered a famous speech called 'The Ballot or the Bullet' in which he warned African Americans to use their vote wisely. He further cautioned the American government that if African-Americans did not soon attain full equality, it would be necessary to take up arms.

Early on the morning of 14 February 1965, Malcolm X and his family were awakened by explosions at their home in Elmhurst, New York, the result of Molotov cocktails being tossed through the windows of the house. They managed to get out but narrowly escaped being burnt alive. The perpetrators were never captured, although Malcolm told investigating officers that he suspected it had been the NOI.

A week later, he was due to speak at the Audubon Ballroom in the Washington Heights neighbourhood of Upper Manhattan, in New York City. Four hundred people turned up to hear him, but there was a nervous anticipation in the air and not just because Malcolm X was going to speak. There had been rumours that there was going to be an attempt on his life. The police had turned out but according to some, Malcolm, worried that their presence would inflame the situation, asked them to station themselves in the hospital across the street from the ballroom.

At approximately 3.08 pm, Malcolm X walked on to the stage, shaking hands with the man who had introduced him. He strolled to the podium and greeted the audience. At that moment, however, there was a commotion at the back of the ballroom, two men leaping to their feet and knocking over their chairs. One shouted, 'Get your hand out of my pocket!' Malcolm X attempted to calm them, shouting, 'Cool it there, brothers,' but as he said it, a loud explosion rocked the back of the room which rapidly filled with acrid smoke.

It was a clever ruse, because with everyone's attention diverted to the back of the room, a man stood up in the front row, pulled out a sawn-off shotgun from beneath his coat and fired twice at Malcolm X, hitting him in the chest. He fell backwards to the floor of the stage as two other men rushed up and fired more bullets into his body. They ran off, firing more bullets as Malcolm's followers rushed onstage to help him. Meanwhile, panic reigned in the auditorium as people tried to flee the smoke and the gunshots.

Malcolm's wife, Betty Shabazz, ran to her fallen husband but by the time she reached him he was already dead. The shotgun blasts had ripped through his heart and aorta and he had ten bullet wounds in his chest plus wounds elsewhere on his body.

Two of the assassins, trying to escape down a stairway, were attacked by the angry crowd, wielding chairs and whatever else they could find. Twenty-two-year-old Talmadge Hayer – also known as Thomas Hagan – was shot in the leg and almost beaten to death, although his accomplice escaped.

As well as Hayer, Norman 3X Butler and Thomas 15X Johnson, both members of the Nation, were arrested and charged with the murder of Malcolm X. All three were convicted and sent to prison, although they have all now been released on parole, Butler and Johnson still maintaining their innocence.

MARTIN LUTHER KING

At one minute past six on the evening of 4 April 1968, a single shot rang out at the Lorraine Motel in Memphis, Tennessee. Dr Martin Luther King, leader of African Americans in their struggle for civil rights and a fervent advocate of non-violence, had himself fallen victim to that very violence. As he lay on the balcony of room 306, blood flowed from a gaping wound, the result of a bullet fired from a sniper's gun.

Just a couple of minutes before, Dr King had walked onto the balcony accompanied by Jesse Jackson and Ben Branch, a musician who was scheduled to perform that night at an event that King was attending. They talked briefly and Dr King turned to walk back into his room, saying to Ben Branch, 'Ben, make sure you play Take My Hand, Precious Lord in the meeting tonight. Play it real pretty.' As he did so, a sound that was described as being like a firecracker, was heard and he collapsed to the ground. The Reverend Ralph Abernathy who had heard the shot from inside the room came running out onto the balcony.

King was rushed to hospital, but it was futile; he was already dead. The bullet had struck him on his right cheek, travelling down his spinal cord before lodging in his shoulder. His jugular vein was severed and several other arteries had also been damaged. He was rushed into the operating theatre where, at 7.05 pm, despite desperate efforts to save him, he was pronounced dead at the age of thirty-nine.

The shooter, meanwhile, had been seen by witnesses fleeing the building that overlooked the Lorraine hotel and from one of whose windows he had fired the fatal shot. As he ran, he dropped an object wrapped in a blue blanket. Inside the blanket was a box containing the rifle, a radio, some clothing in a blue zippered bag, a couple of beer cans, an advert for the New York Arms Company and a receipt. The man ran to a Mustang parked nearby, jumped in and drove off at speed.

Fingerprints found on the rifle were run against a list of fugitives from the law and the name of an escaped convict emerged – James Earl Ray.

Ray was a career criminal. Born into a poor Illinois family in 1928, he left school aged fifteen and when he was old enough enlisted in the army. When he returned to civilian life, he had no qualifications and few prospects. As a result, he drifted into petty crime, serving eight months in prison for burglary in 1949. In 1952, he started a two-year sentence for armed robbery. In 1955, convicted of stealing postal money orders, he was sent to the Federal Penitentiary at Leavenworth.

Released from prison in 1958, he stayed out of trouble for a year, but was once again arrested for armed robbery. On this occasion, being a repeat offender whose crimes seemed to be escalating in seriousness, he was sentenced to twenty years to be served in Missouri State Prison in Jefferson City. Ray, however, was determined to escape. Twice he failed but six years into his sentence he came up with what he believed to be a foolproof plan.

Every day a truck left the prison to deliver bread baked by prisoners to the institution's external facilities and farms. Ray talked himself into a job in the bakery and then, with the help of another prisoner, made a false bottom in one of the large containers in which the bread was transported. He clambered in, covered himself with the false bottom and his accomplice poured loaves in on top. The truck drove out through the gates and at a safe distance from the prison, Ray clambered out and escaped.

He started to travel slowly in the direction of Canada from where he planned to get a job on a boat and make a fresh start in another country. He deliberately kept a low profile, working menial jobs and staying out of trouble as he headed north, but he need not have worried. His escape had not even warranted a mention on the news and a reward of only $50 was offered.

In July 1967, he crossed into Canada, heading for Montreal and calling himself Eric S. Galt. His main problem when he got there, however, was getting a job on a ship. To do that, he needed a union card and in order to obtain one of those, he needed a passport. In the waterfront bars of Montreal, he let it be known that he was looking for work and hinted that it need not be entirely legal. One afternoon, as Ray later told the officers interrogating him about the murder of Martin Luther King, a man called Raoul got talking to him, asking Ray if he would like a job smuggling for him. He explained that he wanted a package to be carried over the Canada-United States border and then driven south and across the Mexican border. In return for this, Raoul promised he would provide Ray with the Canadian passport he needed so badly. Ray agreed to do it.

He drove over the border into the United States and met Raoul in Detroit but was furious when Raoul told him he did not yet have the passport for him. He calmed down, however, when Raoul handed him a substantial pile of cash. They separated and Ray drove to Birmingham, Alabama, where, as instructed by Raoul, he picked up a letter in a post office. It instructed him to buy a car and he purchased a pale yellow 1966 Mustang on 20 August 1967.

The letter also told him to buy some film equipment by mail order. He bought a Super 8mm movie camera, projector, editing machine and a twenty-foot remote control cable. He also purchased an expensive Polaroid camera. Sources are a little vague as to why he was told to buy this equipment – some say it was intended for a move into the porn business.

In autumn 1967, Ray did some more smuggling for Raoul, conveying packages across the Mexican border hidden in the spare tyre of his car. After a month's holiday, he drove to Los Angeles where he stayed for five months, keeping himself occupied by attending bar-tending school and taking dance classes.

He met Raoul again in New Orleans where he was promised a Canadian passport plus $10,000 in return for another smuggling job, this time involving guns. After this, he returned to Los Angeles, picking up his life again and having some plastic surgery done on his nose in February 1968 in order to make it more difficult for anyone to identify him – not that they were looking for him.

Raoul now informed him that he had clients in Memphis who wanted rifles. He instructed Ray to buy a rifle and once the clients had approved it, a quantity would be purchased and sold to these men. Ray bought a Remington Gamemaster Model 760 .30-06 calibre rifle and, as instructed by Raoul, drove to Memphis at the beginning of April. On 4 April, he moved to a boarding house some of whose rooms overlooked the Lorraine Hotel where Martin Luther King and his entourage were staying.

The Raoul story has never been confirmed and the man himself was never found. It may just have been a red herring introduced by Ray to muddy the water. James Earl Ray may just have been a black-hating sociopath who suffered from delusions of grandeur and it was for these reasons he assassinated Martin Luther King.

King had travelled to Memphis to support black sanitary public work employees who had been on strike for higher wages and better working conditions since 12 March. On 3 April, he had addressed a rally at Mason Temple, delivering his 'I have been to the mountaintop' speech. It would be his last public utterance.

After the assassination, investigators pieced together James Earl Ray's life since his escape from prison. Learning from inmates of the jail that Ray had talked about getting a Canadian passport, they searched through 175,000 recent passport applications, checking the photographs that had been submitted. Eventually, at the beginning of June 1968 they found it, in the name of George Ramon Sneyd. His passport application had been processed on 24 April, almost three weeks after the assassination. Checking with airlines, they discovered that Ray had booked a return ticket from Toronto to London on 6 May.

From Scotland Yard in London, it was found out that Sneyd had exchanged the return section of his journey for one to Lisbon in Portugal and had flown there on 7 May, before returning to London on 17 May. He was sensationally arrested on 8 June, as he tried to board a plane from London to Brussels.

He was extradited to the United States where, although he claimed that the mysterious Raoul was the man behind the assassination, he faced a watertight case that led his lawyers to advise him to plead guilty. It was the only way, they told him, that he could avoid the death penalty. At his trial, he pled guilty and was sentenced to ninety-nine years in prison.

Shortly after, however, Ray withdrew his guilty plea, deciding, instead, to appeal the decision. On 10 June 1977, however, he was free again, having escaped from Brushy Mountain State Penitentiary in Petros, Tennessee with six other inmates. They were all recaptured three days later and a year was added to Ray's sentence, making it a round one hundred years.

He persisted in his claims that he was not responsible for the shooting and he and his attorney, Jack Kershaw, met the United States House Select Committee on Assassinations, convincing them to run ballistics tests to prove that Ray had not fired the shot. These, however, proved inconclusive.

As part of an interview with *Playboy* magazine, Ray took a polygraph test. The magazine said later that the test proved that Ray had in fact killed Martin Luther King and, in doing so, he had acted alone.

James Earl Ray died in prison on 23 April 1998, aged seventy, from complications related to kidney disease and liver failure caused by hepatitis C, probably contracted through a blood transfusion he had been given after being stabbed at Brushy Mountain Penitentiary.

He had expressed a desire not to be buried in the

United States because of 'the way the government had treated him' and his ashes were flown to Ireland, from where his family had emigrated.

Meanwhile, the identity of the mysterious Raoul was never discovered.

ALDO MORO

Like much of Italian politics, the assassination of Italian Prime Minister Aldo Moro by the revolutionary Marxist group, the Brigati Rossi (Red Brigades) is shrouded in mystery, accusation and suspicion. There is evidence of machinations and manoeuvring at the highest level of Italian politics and the murky involvement of some very powerful people.

Moro was born in Puglia in southern Italy in 1916, moving to Milan with his family four years later. He studied law and became Professor of Law and Colonial Policy and Criminal Law at the University of Bari in the early nineteen-forties. After teaching there for twenty years, he moved to the Sapienza University in Rome.

While in Bari, Moro's interest in politics had developed, initially as a socialist but then as a Christian Democrat because of his Catholic faith. In 1946, he was elected to the Italian Constitutional Assembly, helping to re-write the Italian Constitution after the war and in 1948, he was elected to the Italian Parliament. In the next fifteen years, he held various ministerial posts, in 1963, becoming Prime

Minister of Italy for the first of five times, his party being supported in a coalition by the Italian Socialist party, and other minor political alignments. In 1968, Moro stepped down in the face of internal opposition, turning his considerable skills to guiding Italy's foreign policy. In 1974, however, he once again became Prime Minister of Italy.

Aldo Moro was an immensely popular politician, a diplomatic genius with the uncanny knack of being able to say things that could be interpreted either way, something of a necessary skill in the volatile world of Italian politics. He was a soft-spoken man who carried with him an air of calm, even during steamy debates in the Italian parliament. Although somewhat stiff and aloof and very conservative in dress and manners, he was said to possess astonishing stamina, presiding over ten-hour cabinet meetings without so much as a glass of water or a cup of coffee.

Moro had always advocated the establishment of an alliance between the Christian Democrats and the Italian Socialist Party in order to unite the Italian left in one grouping. To that end, he succeeded in negotiating what became known as the Compromesso Storico (Historic Compromise) between his party and the Italian Communist

Party which would bring the Communists into government for the first time in more than thirty years. It was an idea vehemently opposed, however, by the Red Brigades because it interfered with their declared aim of an armed Marxist revolution in Italy, led by a 'revolutionary proletariat'.

Moro believed the coalition with the Communists to be necessary because they had been gaining in the polls, winning 34.4 percent of the vote in the recent elections. Only with this coalition, Moro believed, could he finally bring real stability to Italy.

Little did he know, however, the problems he was about to create. It was a political act that would cost him his life and plunge Italy into one of its biggest crises since the war.

The 16 March 1978, was a special day, the day that the Compromesso Storico was going to be enacted and Moro was being driven from mass at a church near his house to the House of Representatives in Rome, to oversee the process. He was a devout Catholic and attended mass, without fail, every morning.

Suddenly, as his car drove along Via Mario Fani, northwest of the centre of the city, a white Fiat drove in front of Moro's car along with a motorcycle. The Fiat braked suddenly and Moro's vehicle crashed into it. Gunmen piled out of the Fiat and others who had been waiting nearby, dressed in airline uniforms and wearing false moustaches and wigs, produced pistols and submachine guns. A gun battle ensued and five of Moro's bodyguards were shot dead. Moro, meanwhile, was bundled into another vehicle that sped off taking him to a safe house in the centre of Rome.

Police later made safe a time bomb that had been placed in a vehicle at the scene. It was timed to detonate as investigators examined the scene and if it had gone off, would have caused a massacre.

A short while later, a phone call was received from a Red Brigade spokesperson who made the grim announcement: 'We kidnapped Aldo Moro. He is only our first victim. We shall hit at the heart of the state.'

The man demanded that the trial in Turin of Renato Curcio, the leader of the Red Brigades and twelve other members of the organisation be suspended and that the accused should be freed in exchange for Moro's release.

The Red Brigades had been responsible for death and destruction across Italy for eight years prior to Moro's kidnapping, launching 2,080 terrorist attacks in 1977 alone. It had first signalled its existence in 1970, by firebombing an electronics company in Milan but had really come to prominence in April 1974 when its members kidnapped Genoa magistrate, Mario Sossi, threatening to kill him unless eight of their members were released from prison. Genoa District Attorney Francesco Coco ordered the prisoners to be released but a court in Rome immediately cancelled Coco's order after Sossi had been released. Coco and two of his bodyguards were subsequently assassinated.

Since then, the organisation had proved elusive and it had been difficult to prosecute its members after they had been arrested – on one occasion, a terrified jury deserted en masse and on another a lawyer was murdered.

Five thousand police officers launched a nationwide manhunt. Police closed ports and airports, set up road blocks and checked everyone leaving the capital. Trade unions called a twenty-four hour general strike in reaction to the abduction.

The Italian government immediately refused to negotiate with the kidnappers, Giulio Andreotti saying that the terrorists were 'destroying the fabric of the nation and threatening to make it ungovernable.'

Two days after the kidnapping, the Red Brigades issued a photograph of Aldo Moro in captivity, an accompanying communiqué announcing that he would be standing trial before what they described as a 'People's Tribunal'.

On 25 March, Andreotti, heading the Christian Democrat government, introduced the harshest police powers since the days of fascism. Meanwhile, another message from the Red Brigades announced that Moro's trial was still taking place.

On 29 March, a letter arrived from Moro himself pleading with Andreotti and the Christian Democrats to begin negotiations with the terrorists. The following day, following a meeting of all the parties who made up the ruling coalition, it was announced that there would be no negotiations.

The fourth communiqué arrived from the Red Brigades on 4 April as well as an angry letter from Moro, again demanding that the government should enter into negotiations.

On 15 April, a month after Moro had been abducted, a communiqué from the Red Brigades grimly declared that he had been sentenced to death and three days later they announced that he had been executed and that his body could be found in a lake, fifty-five miles east of Rome. A massive search was launched.

On Thursday 20 April, the Red Brigades described the last communiqué saying that Moro was dead as a 'government fake'. They were adamant that he could still be saved by the release of the jailed terrorists. The message was accompanied by a photograph of Moro holding the previous day's newspaper, an iconic image that would become famous. Chillingly, however, the terrorists added that the government had forty-eight hours left in which to negotiate and save his life. As the deadline approached, Pope Paul VI and United Nations Secretary General, Kurt Waldheim, appealed for Moro's release. The Pope even offered to take Moro's place as a captive.

After fresh demands by the Red Brigades for the release of the terrorists, on 26 April, Giulio Andreotti called their demands 'absurd', receiving backing in this from most other Italian political parties, although there was some criticism of the government's intransigence.

On Saturday 29 April, eight leading Italian statesmen each received a handwritten letter from Aldo Moro pleading with them to persuade the government to negotiate and the Moro family openly criticised the government. There was a growing suspicion that, although the refusal to negotiate was seen as courageous by many around the world, there could actually be more to the government's resolute stance than was being articulated, that government ministers had slightly less honourable intentions. The authorities speculated in the meantime that Moro had been forced to write his letters by being tortured or being forced to take mind-altering drugs.

On 5 May, the Red Brigades finally announced that the sentence was going to be carried out – 'We are concluding the battle begun March 16 by executing the sentence'. A farewell latter from Moro was received by his wife in which he wrote, 'I kiss you for the last time.' He told her that he did not want anyone from his party at his funeral.

Moro had been kept in what the Red Brigades described as the 'people's prison', a makeshift partition in a middle-class apartment in Rome. He was told to get ready to come out of his hiding place and knew at that moment that he was about to die. Led out to the building's garage, he was ordered to climb into the boot of the car and cover himself with a blanket. Eleven bullets were then pumped into his body by a person or persons unknown.

On 9 May, his bullet-riddled body was discovered in the boot of the car that had been abandoned in Rome near to the Communist and Christian Democrat headquarters.

For Italians, hearing the news of Aldo Moro's death was reminiscent of the feelings of Americans on the day that President John F. Kennedy was assassinated. The radio announcer informing the nation broke down before he could finish his announcement and people froze in their tracks as they went about their business, shocked and saddened.

Conspiracy theories about the death of Aldo Moro have flourished in the decades since. Did he, as some have suggested, provide the Red Brigades with secrets about those in power that compromised them and if made public would expose corruption at the highest levels? Was that perhaps why they refused to negotiate?

Some have suggested that the United States was against the Compromesso Storico, believing that the increase in Communist influence on the Italian government would inevitably weaken American influence in the country. Therefore, according to this theory, a shadowy organisation called Gladio that was under the control of NATO had been responsible for Aldo Moro's death. It may be no coincidence that the journalist who was investigating this theory, Mino Pecorelli, was assassinated a year after Moro. Giulio Andreotti was investigated for the murder of Pecorelli who had also accused him of being connected with the Aldo abduction and murder through his connections with the Mafia.

He was acquitted in 1999, but, aged eighty-three, was convicted on appeal in 2002 and sentenced to twenty-four years in prison. In 2003, the conviction was overturned by an appeals court and he was also cleared of having ties to the Mafia, but only because of the expiry of statutory terms and the court had indeed established that he did have close links with the Mafia and had used them to further his political career.

The CIA and the Italian Masonic lodge known as P2 have also been implicated in Aldo Moro's murder.

The Red Brigades were effectively finished after Moro's death. In 1980, 10,000 far-left activists were arrested and many fled the country.

At last the time that had become known as the 'Anni di Piombo' (Years of Lead) were at an end and so too were the bombings, abductions and assassinations.

Indira Gandhi

The autumn morning of 31 October 1984 was bright and sunny with just a gentle breeze blowing through the trees in the sprawling compound at 1 Safdarjang Road in New Delhi, India's capital city. Indira Gandhi, Prime Minister of India, lived there in one of the two bungalows situated within the compound, sharing her living quarters with her son, Rajiv, his wife, Sonia and their two children, Rahul and Priyanka. The other bungalow contained offices and public rooms.

Forty-year-old Rajiv, Mrs. Gandhi's sole surviving son, after the death of her other son, Sanjay in an air crash in 1980, was away on political business that day. There were going to be elections in mid-January of 1985 and he had journeyed to West Bengal to make sure that preparations for the elections were proceeding satisfactorily. He was heir apparent to the Nehru dynasty as well as to the leadership of his country. His grandfather, Pandit Jawaharlal Nehru, had been a prominent activist who had become the first Prime Minister of an independent India in 1947 and his great grandfather, Motilal Nehru, had been a leading light in the early days of the Indian National Congress, the political movement that would become India's principal political party.

But Rajiv's elevation to the leadership of the Gandhi dynasty seemed to be some way off that autumn morning because at sixty-six years of age, Indira Gandhi did not look like letting up and was enthusiastically looking forward to a fifth term as Prime Minister.

Storm clouds had been gathering over the world's most populous democracy, however, and the sectarian violence that had blighted India's first forty years of independence had once again risen to the surface. Rebellious Sikhs had been agitating for greater autonomy for their homeland Punjab. In July 1982, an armed Sikh group, led by the controversial Jarnail Singh Bhindranwale, had taken up residence in the Guru Nanak Niwas, a guest house that lay within the precincts of Sikhdom's holiest place, the Golden Temple at Amritsar. Six months later, fearing arrest, the Sikhs moved to the sacred Akal Takhat, one of the five seats of Sikh temporal religious authority. Bhindranwale fortified the temple with light machine guns and rifles and other weapons were brought in. For a while, the authorities seemed to pay them no attention.

On 6 June 1984, however – one of the Sikhs'

holiest days – in an initiative called Operation Bluestar, Indira Gandhi ordered the army to surround the Golden Temple and then to remove the armed militants from the complex. The army opened fire and around six hundred people – including Bhindranwale – were killed in the ensuing gun battle. No one knew at the time but it would also cost Indira Gandhi her life.

At eight minutes past nine that morning, Mrs. Gandhi, in a buoyant mood, stepped through the door of her bungalow, descended a few steps and walked along the winding gravel path towards the larger administrative building. Five security men followed her at a discreet distance.

Her first appointment that morning was with the famous British actor-director, Peter Ustinov, who had arrived earlier with a film crew to conduct an hour-long interview with her. Ustinov and his crew had been travelling with her for the last few days as she campaigned in the eastern Indian state of Orissa. The two got on well and she appreciated Ustinov's wit and intelligence.

About halfway along the path stood two uniformed security men, their heavy beards and turbans identifying them as Sikhs. They were Beant Singh and Satwant Singh, the former a particular favourite of Mrs. Gandhi who had been with her for ten years. When asked about the possible dangers of having Sikh security guards, given the strength of Sikh feeling after the siege at the Golden Temple, she had replied that with men like Beant Singh, she had little to fear and when the director of India's central intelligence agency had recommended to the Prime Minister that she remove all Sikhs from her security staff, she had stubbornly refused. Her note back to him had asked that if such a policy was adopted, 'How can we claim to be secular?'

As she approached the two men, she placed her hands together in front of her face and uttered the traditional Indian greeting, 'Namaste'. It was the last word Indira Gandhi ever spoke.

Beant Singh suddenly drew a .38 revolver and fired three shots into the Prime Minister's abdomen. As she crumpled to the ground, Satwant Singh emptied his Sten automatic submachine gun – about thirty rounds – into her body. At least seven bullets entered her abdomen, three hit her chest and one penetrated her heart. She died immediately.

The two Sikhs calmly let their weapons fall to the ground as the five deeply shocked security men who had been following Mrs. Gandhi, rushed towards them. As they seized the two men, Beant Singh said stoically, 'I've done what I had to do. You do what you want to do.'

They were dragged to a guardhouse as shocked people began to gather around the blood-soaked body of the Prime Minister. Once in the guardhouse, however, Beant Singh made a lunge for a Sten gun being carried by one of the guards. At the same time, Satwant Singh pulled a dagger that he had secreted inside his turban. Without hesitation, the guards shot them both, Beant dying instantly and Satwant being critically wounded. He would later claim to be part of a conspiracy that included within its ranks a high-ranking military officer. He told investigators that Rajiv Gandhi was another target of the conspirators.

Satwant survived his injuries and was sentenced to death along with co-conspirator, Kehar Singh. He was hanged in Tihar jail in Delhi on 6 January 1989.

Hearing the shots in the garden, Mrs. Gandhi's daughter-in-law, Sonia rushed out of the bungalow, stumbling down the steps screaming, 'Mummy! Oh, my God, Mummy!' When she arrived at the scene, guards were already picking up Mrs. Gandhi's lifeless body, her orange sari now soaked in blood. They carried her to her white, Indian-made Ambassador car where Sonia cradled her head in her lap as the vehicle sped through the streets of New Delhi to the nearest hospital, the All-India Institute of Medical Sciences.

Peter Ustinov and his film crew had witnessed the entire incident and now rushed to the bungalow where chaos had broken out. 'The security men were still running around, shaken and unbelieving,' he said. 'One minute there was gunfire, and afterward the birds in the trees were singing. The security men kept us there for five hours, polite all the time, but they wanted to be sure we didn't have something on film that they could use as evidence. Sadly, we did not.'

Meanwhile, the Ambassador containing Mrs. Gandhi had arrived at the hospital where it was rushed to an operating theatre on the eighth floor. The twelve doctors there realised she had lost a huge amount of blood and was already dead, but a desperate effort was launched to try to revive her. She was connected to an artificial heart and lung machine and they began to remove the bullets. Eighty-eight bottles of blood were pumped into her while cabinet ministers paced the hospital conference room awaiting news. There was an eerie silence interrupted by weeping. At 1.45, however, more than four hours after the two Sikhs had opened fire, a bulletin was released by an Indian news service. It stated that Indira Gandhi was dead.

In West Bengal, the car in which Rajiv Gandhi had been driving to the last meeting of his campaign tour was stopped by a police jeep. He was informed that there had been an accident in the house and that he should return immediately to Delhi. Rajiv immediately ordered his aides to get him to the nearest airport. At 12:30 pm, he was waiting for a helicopter to take him to Calcutta, when he heard on the BBC news that his mother was in a critical condition. A few of the Congressmen in his party burst into tears, but Rajiv reassured them. 'Don't worry,' he said. 'She's tough.'

He arrived from Calcutta around two o'clock on board a special airliner that had been sent to fly him to New Delhi. It was at that point that he was informed that his mother was dead. He set off for the hospital amidst unprecedented levels of security with sharpshooters lining every inch of his route. At the hospital, he was greeted by his mother's distraught cabinet members.

On hearing the news, many recalled the words of the speech Indira Gandhi had delivered to a large crowd in Bhubaneswar, capital of Orissa, the previous evening. 'I am not interested in a long life,' she had said. 'I am not afraid of these things. I don't mind if my life goes in the service of this nation. If I die today, every drop of my blood will invigorate the nation.' It was a fatalism that was characteristic of her, a fatalism that led to her refusing to wear the bulletproof vest that might have saved her.

Her body lay in state for two days at Teen Murti House, the mansion that had formerly been the residence of her father when he was Prime Minister, and hundreds of thousands of Indians filed past her in tribute. On Saturday afternoon, her body was carried on a gun carriage the seven miles to the banks of the Yamuna River. Her father and younger son, Sanjay, had both been cremated there. The streets were lined by close to one million Indians while a huge audience of many millions more watched on television. She was placed on a flower-bedecked sandalwood and brick pyre and her son Rajiv lit the flame.

VERONICA GUERIN

'The only place to get good information is from the crims,' she once said, and to do so, it meant that she had to descend into Dublin's seedy underworld, a world she described as a 'culture of violence, money and evil.' It was a strategy that would result in her being beaten, shot in the leg and, ultimately, it resulted in her death at the hands of a gunman.

By the 1990s, parts of Dublin had become virtual no-go areas, places where drugs were dealt with impunity and the gangs dealing them seemed to be untouchable. It was against those gangs that Veronica Guerin went to war, waging a one-woman crusade to expose the drug barons and their deadly trade.

Veronica had been born in Dublin in 1959, one of five children. She attended a Roman Catholic school and from an early age displayed a talent for sport. She played basketball, football, and camogie – the women's version of the Irish sport of hurling.

Her father was an accountant and she followed in his footsteps, studying accountancy at Trinity College, Dublin, working for his company after she graduated.

She was well connected in the world of Irish politics, working in 1983 during the New Ireland Forum as secretary to the leader of the Fianna Fail political party, Charles Haughey, a family friend. Haughey had already served as Taoiseach – Prime Minister – of Ireland and would be again towards the end of the decade and into the nineteen-nineties. She enjoyed Mediterranean holidays with the younger members of the Haughey family and in 1987, she would act as election agent and party treasurer in Dublin North for Haughey's son, Sean, who would later take over his father's parliamentary seat.

Following her father's death, she changed careers, launching a public relations business that she ran for seven years.

In 1990, Veronica made another career change, switching to journalism and working with the *Sunday Business Post* and the *Sunday Tribune*. In 1994, she began to write fearlessly about Dublin's underworld for the *Sunday Independent*, bringing the eye for detail she had honed as an accountant to her reporting. Always carrying two phones with her, she is said to have made around sixty calls a day in pursuit of her subject. Her editor at the *Sunday Business Post* said, 'I have never met a reporter so unrelenting in pursuit of a story.'

She began to focus on the figures that ran crime in Ireland, from Tipperary farmers who were reputed to be involved in dubious financial transactions to the heads of families who made fortunes from armed robbery. She was especially exercised about the major drug dealers who were flooding Ireland with heroin and cocaine.

The Celtic Tiger, the economic miracle that brought Ireland and its people incredible economic growth, was beginning to roar and for those who were beginning to benefit from its effects, cocaine was the drug of choice, a lifestyle accessory that no dinner party or event could be without. The drug gangs did a roaring trade to these people as well as to the people for whom the Tiger had no meaning. The only difference was the type of drug; their drug of choice was heroin.

She was forced by Ireland's stringent libel laws to disguise the subjects of her investigations with nicknames but even so Veronica began to rattle the purveyors of death.

The first instance of violence against her occurred in October 1994 when two shots were fired into her home. Then, on 29 January, she published a story about the three million pound Brinks-Allied bank robbery in Dublin. No arrests had been made and

Veronica questioned the fact that the robbery's chief suspect, Gerald Hutch, known as 'The Monk', had been the beneficiary of a tax amnesty. He was also the biggest cocaine dealer in Ireland.

The day after the story hit the newsstands, she answered her doorbell to be confronted by a man wearing a motorcycle helmet and holding a pistol in his hand. He pointed it threateningly at her head before lowering it and shooting her at close range in the leg. She was undaunted, however, and was soon filing reports from her hospital bed. When she was released from hospital and while still on crutches, she demonstrated that she could not be intimidated by having her husband drive her around the criminal hotspots of Dublin. *Independent Newspapers* installed a state-of-the-art security system to give her added protection.

In September 1995, she succeeded in gaining access to the £5 million equestrian centre in County Kildare owned by a man called John Gilligan. She wanted to interrogate Gilligan, about how, having just been released from prison, he could afford to live such an affluent lifestyle with no visible source of income. Gilligan was a career criminal whose earliest conviction was at the age of fifteen. After a spell in prison, in 1993, he launched a smuggling operation that initially dealt only in cigarettes but had soon moved on to the importation of large quantities of drugs into Ireland.

When she tried to interview Gilligan, he attacked her, ripping her blouse and viciously beating her. The following day, he telephoned her at home and told her, 'If you do one thing to me or if you write about me I will kidnap your fucking son and ride him. I will shoot you.'

She alerted the police and charges of assault were brought against Gilligan. The police offered her round-the-clock protection, but she was unhappy with this, believing it hampered her in her work. Criminals were not going to talk to her if they knew that she had a police escort. She dispensed with it soon after.

Just before lunchtime, on 26 June 1996, Veronica was driving her red Opel Calibra on the busy Naas dual carriageway near Newlands Cross on the outskirts of Dublin. As usual, she was busy talking on each of the two mobile phones she took everywhere with her. She had just been to court to answer charges of having ignored countless parking tickets and speeding fines and was leaving a light-hearted message with a police contact, laughing about having escaped with a nominal fine of just one hundred euros, when a motorcycle pulled up alongside her stationery car at a red light. The pillion passenger pulled out a Magnum .357 revolver, leaned across towards her window and fired six bullets into her body. He sped away leaving the lifeless body of the journalist sprawled across the front seats of her car in a pool of blood.

There was unparalleled shock and outrage at Veronica Guerin's murder. John Bruton, the Irish Taoiseach decribed it as 'an attack on democracy.' A massive investigation was launched immediately. The Gardai, the Irish police force, at one point deployed over one hundred officers on the case, their investigations leading to 214 arrests, 39 convictions, and 100 illegal guns being confiscated. Several thousand people were questioned and hundreds of premises were searched. As a result, drugs worth £5 million were seized and property worth £6.5 million was confiscated.

The Irish parliament introduced legislation dealing with the proceeds of crime and criminal assets in 1996. This meant that assets purchased with money that had been obtained through criminal activity could be seized by the government through a body called the Criminal Assets Bureau.

Soon, the police were making some headway in their investigation. Two associates of John Gilligan –

Charles Bowden and Russell Warren – were arrested in connection with the murder in October 1996 and Gilligan, who had flown to London the day before Veronica was shot, was arrested at Heathrow Airport.

Two other men, Brian Meehan, who had driven the motorbike and Paul Ward, who had disposed of the bike in the River Liffey afterwards, were arrested and jailed for life for murder.

Bowden and Warren agreed to testify against Gilligan, in return for immunity from prosecution for the murder. In order to provide ongoing protection for them and their families, Ireland introduced its first-ever witness protection initiative.

Bowden showed police officers the lock-up garage where Gilligan stored his cannabis and led them to a Jewish cemetery in Dublin where guns were dug up that were alleged to belong to Gilligan.

Patrick 'Dutchy' Holland was named by the witnesses as the man riding pillion who shot Veronica that fateful day. Although born in Dublin, Holland was a former United States Marine and following the murder, he had fled to Amsterdam. Arrested in April 1997 as he arrived at Dún Laoghaire ferry port, on suspicion of having a firearm at the junction of Naas Road and Boot Road on 26 June 1996, he was convicted of drug offences relating to the activities of John Gilligan's gang, but was never convicted of Veronica's murder. Indeed, he denied having anything to do with it until his death in a British prison in 2009, aged seventy. 'I haven't killed anybody ever. There is no blood on my hands,' he insisted.

For three and a half years, Gilligan fought extradition from England to Ireland where he would face murder charges. He was finally extradited on 3 February 2000, but, to the horror of the Guerin family, was acquitted of her murder, the judge describing Warren and Bowden as self-seeking liars and saying that there was not enough corroborating evidence to convict him.

Gilligan was instead convicted of importing 22,000 kilos of cannabis worth £32 million and sentenced to twenty-eight years in jail, a sentence reduced to twenty on appeal. 'Never in the history of the state,' said the judge, 'has one person been responsible for so much wretchedness to so many.'

In 2002, the courts ordered his seventy-seven-acre equestrian ranch to be confiscated and sold but he contested the order and won the case. Nonetheless, his assets were frozen by the Criminal Assets Bureau.

In January 2008, Gilligan appeared in court in

an attempt to stop the State from selling off his assets. During the proceedings, he cited a botched Gardaí investigation and planted evidence as the reason for his current imprisonment and accused another Dublin criminal, John Traynor, of having ordered Veronica Guerin's murder. Traynor, one of Veronica's confidential contacts in the criminal world, was at the time of her murder, pursuing a high court order to prevent her from publishing a book about his involvement in organised crime. It has been claimed that Traynor tipped off Gilligan about Veronica's whereabouts on the day of her murder but Gilligan claims that Traynor went ahead with the hit without his permission.

Traynor was arrested along with Brian Meehan but was subsequently released without charge. He was arrested in Amstelveen by Dutch police in August 2010 and is awaiting extradition to the United Kingdom where, in 1992, he absconded while serving a seven-year sentence.

PART FOUR
CELEBRITY SHOOTINGS

ALEXANDER HAMILTON

The famous duel between two US political rivals, Alexander Hamilton and Aaron Burr, on 11 July 1804 was the culmination of one of the most notable personal conflicts in American political history. It had tremendous ramifications for not just the two men involved but also for American political history.

The two were born just under a year apart, Burr in February 1756, Hamilton on 11 January, the following year. From an early age, Burr, an orphan from three, showed signs of having a brilliant mind.

Hamilton was born in Nevis in the British West Indies, son of an itinerant Scottish trader and a French woman, and had been illegitimate, something that was still frowned upon at the time.

At the age of eleven, Burr started work as a clerk in a counting house, showing such potential that he was sent to America to further his education. Burr by thirteen, was a sophomore at the College of New Jersey that would later become Princeton, graduating in 1772 and inheriting around that time the modest sum of £10,000 left by his father. He launched a legal career.

Hamilton, meanwhile, having been rejected by the College of New Jersey, entered New York's King's College in 1773, at the age of sixteen. A year later, he showed his interest in politics in the publication of his pamphlet, 'A full Vindication of the Measures of Congress' which defended the First Continental Congress's proposal to impose a trade embargo on British goods.

On the outbreak of war between Britain and her thirteen American colonies in 1775, Burr asked George Washington, Commander-in-Chief of the Continental Army for a commission, but was disappointed to learn that there were no more available. Therefore, he joined Benedict Arnold's expedition that marched north to attack British strongholds in Canada. He finally gained his commission after acts of conspicuous bravery, rising to the rank of lieutenant colonel.

Alexander Hamilton, meanwhile, raised a company of men and received a commission in the Continental Army. Like Burr, he distinguished himself in battle.

But Burr was rising fast. In June 1776, he was appointed to General Washington's staff as military secretary but failed to get along with Washington and the following year he was given command of a regiment instead. Eventually, exhausted and unwell following tough years of military command, he retired.

Hamilton was promoted to the rank of lieutenant colonel and appointed to Washington's staff in 1777. Unlike Burr, he got on with Washington and began a lifelong friendship with him.

By 1783, both men had been admitted to the New York Bar. Burr was a skilful lawyer who commanded substantial legal fees and became known for the lavishness of his lifestyle – handsome carriages, beautiful houses, fashionable clothes and generous entertaining. He was living beyond his means, however.

Both men begin to build their political credentials, Hamilton being appointed by Washington as Secretary of the Treasury in 1789 and in 1791 Burr winning a seat in the Senate as a Republican, defeating Federalist Philip Schuyler, Alexander Hamilton's father-in-law.

The real trouble between the two political rivals began in 1800 when Aaron Burr published a document written by Hamilton entitled 'The Public Conduct and Character of John Adams Esq., President of the United States'. In it he attacked Adams and his presidency, but the document had been intended for private circulation only. Its publication caused a seismic rift in the Federalist Party and Hamilton and Burr became mortal enemies.

Burr's star was in the ascendant, however, and in 1801 he narrowly missed out on being elected President, losing out in the 36th ballot by Congress to Thomas Jefferson after the two had deadlocked in the election. Burr became Vice President and his defeat was to a large extent the result of furious campaigning by Alexander Hamilton in Congress.

By 1804, it had become clear that Jefferson was about to dispense with the services of Aaron Burr as Vice President. He, decided, therefore, to run in the race for the Governorship of New York, a powerful political position and one that Hamilton was determined he would not achieve. He campaigned vigorously against his rival and Burr, standing as an independent, was beaten by Republican Morgan Lewis in a landslide.

Now the antipathy felt by the two men began to reach new heights.

On 24 April, a letter appeared in the Albany Register newspaper that had originally been sent from American politician Charles D. Cooper to Hamilton's father-in-law, Philip Schuyler. It spoke of 'a still more despicable opinion which Mr.

Hamilton expressed of Mr. Burr at a political dinner'. Burr immediately wrote to Hamilton, demanding 'prompt and unqualified acknowledgment or denial of the use of any expression which would warrant the assertion of Dr Cooper'.

On 20 May, Hamilton wrote to Burr that he could not be held responsible for what Cooper had thought he had said. The following day, Burr wrote back to him, 'political opposition can never absolve gentlemen from the necessity of a rigid adherence to the laws of honor and the rules of decorum'. Hamilton's reply was that he had 'no other answer to give than that which had already been given'. This letter was delayed for three days while friends of each man – William P. Van Ness for Burr and Nathaniel Pendleton for Hamilton – tried to negotiate a settlement of the matter between the two men.

Following their negotiation, Pendleton delivered the following: 'General Hamilton says he cannot imagine to what Dr Cooper may have alluded, unless it were to a conversation at Mr. Taylor's, in Albany, last winter (at which he and General Hamilton were present). General Hamilton cannot recollect distinctly the particulars of that conversation, so as to undertake to repeat them, without running the risk of varying or omitting what might be deemed important circumstances. The expressions are entirely forgotten, and the specific ideas imperfectly remembered; but to the best of his recollection it consisted of comments on the political principles and views of Colonel Burr, and the results that might be expected from them in the event of his election as Governor, without reference to any particular instance of past conduct or private character.'

Pendleton further offered: 'In relation to any other language or conversation or language of General Hamilton which Colonel Burr will specify, a prompt or frank avowal or denial will be given'. The offer was rejected, however and Burr felt he had little option but to formally challenge Alexander Hamilton to a duel.

Early on the morning of 11 July 1804, the two men crossed the Hudson River from Manhattan to the Heights of Weehawken in New Jersey. Duelling had been made illegal in New York and this spot had become a popular one for such activity.

Burr, accompanied by his second, Van Ness, Matthew L. Davis and politician, Samuel Swartwout, arrived at six o'clock that morning while Hamilton, accompanied by his second, Pendleton, and Dr David Hosack, arrived shortly before seven. They picked lots for choice of position and to decide which of the two seconds should start the duel. Pendleton won both for Hamilton and chose the upper edge of the ledge for his man.

The rules of duelling stipulated that, when each party was in position, the second should ask whether they were ready. If both answered in the affirmative, the second said 'Present!' The participants then raised their guns and fired when they wanted. If one fired before the other, the opposite second counted 'One, two, three, fire,' and if his man did not fire then, he lost his chance.

Often, duelists fired into the ground and this would swiftly, and bloodlessly, bring the matter to an end and it seemed that morning as if Hamilton fired into the air, although it is not known whether this was intentional. Burr immediately returned fire, hitting Hamilton in the lower abdomen, above the right hip, the musket ball causing substantial damage to his internal organs before becoming lodged in his back. He fell to the ground, dropping his pistol and Burr moved towards him, looking as if he regretted his action. He was quickly hustled away, however, hidden behind an umbrella, by Van Ness because the doctor and the others were approaching and they could not tell anyone who had shot Hamilton if they had not seen his face.

Dr Hosack began to attend to the wounded man, but immediately feared he would not survive, finding no pulse or heartbeat. Hamilton was carried to the boat and the doctor rubbed his face, lips and temples with spirits of hartshorn. After a few minutes, Hamilton seemed to revive and even spoke, warning them that his pistol was still cocked. After a while he complained that he had no feeling in his legs and soon after that, he was conveyed back across the river. He lingered for a while, but finally died the following day.

Burr was charged with murder in New York and New Jersey, but the case never came to trial. He fled to South Carolina but returned after a short while to complete what was left of his term as Vice President, delivering an emotional farewell speech when he left office in 1805.

His political life over, Burr travelled west where, it was alleged, he intended to establish a new independent empire in the Louisiana Territory. When his plans fell through, he was accused of treason, although he was later acquitted.

He returned to his legal practice and died in 1836 without ever apologising to the family of Alexander Hamilton.

JOSEPH SMITH

The shooting dead of its founder and leader, Joseph Smith, by an angry mob on 27 June 1844, changed the Church of Jesus Christ of Latter Day Saints forever.

At the time of his death, Smith was mayor of the town of Nauvoo, Illinois and was thinking of running for President of the United States, a long way from his early life in a fairly unremarkable New England farming family into which he was born in 1805. Not long after his birth, a series of crop failures forced the family to move to Palmyra, New York.

When he was fourteen, Smith was confused about which church he should attend. Until that age he had remained home with his father while his mother went to Presbyterian Church meetings. He later claimed to have prayed for help and as a result was visited by God and Jesus Christ who told him that all the existing churches were wrong. Despite the scepticism of a local minister about his vision, Smith insisted it had happened.

Four years later he was the recipient of another revelation. While praying in his bedroom, he was visited by an angel named Moroni who told him about a buried book of golden plates that contained a record of the ancient inhabitants of America. The angel led Smith to find the plates in a stone box close to his father's farm. Moroni did not permit him to remove the plates for the next four years, however, during which time Smith had a job searching for precious metals. He claimed to possess an ability to find lost items and buried treasure using seer stones or 'interpreters', special stones that also helped him to receive his divine revelations.

At the end of four years, the angel permitted him to remove the plates and used the stones to translate the characters inscribed on them. He took ninety days to complete the translation and published it in March 1830 as the 588-page *Book of Mormon.* It told the 1,000-year history of the Israelites as recorded by a prophet named Mormon.

On 6 April 1830, Smith, with a few dozen believers, created the Mormon Church and began to gather his people into settlements, known as 'Cities of Zion'. In these places, he claimed, they would be protected from the turmoil and chaos of the last days, the end of the world. A missionary programme was initiated, resulting in tens of thousands of converts by the time of Joseph Smith's death.

The members of the church, known as Saints, gathered at Independence, Missouri, but were forced to move on by other settlers. Smith moved his family to Kirtland, Ohio.

By the summer of 1835, there were around two thousand Mormons in the area of Kirtland. Again, however, the locals resented the presence of this fast-growing sect that looked like it was going to take over their town and mobs began to attack Mormons in their homes and settlements. Smith cautioned his followers to exercise patience in the face of the first three assaults, but following a fourth onslaught, ordered them to begin to defend themselves.

The church itself began to be torn apart by internal disputes, especially over the issue of polygamy. Smith had, according to some, been preaching the doctrine of polygamy since around 1831 and had entered a polygamous relationship with a servant girl in his household. He may even have married her in 1833. Members of the Kirtland community disagreed with this practice. At the same time, creditors were pursuing Smith following the building of a large temple in Kirtland. The church was deeply in debt and schemes to raise much-needed cash failed, leading to many defections.

Following the issue of a warrant for his arrest on a charge of banking fraud, he fled Kirtland for Missouri on 12 January 1838, settling in the town of Far West. Construction of a new temple began in this new Mormon 'Zion' as the hundreds of Saints who had followed him, began to arrive in the town. Intolerance by locals once again led to violence but Smith declared that the Mormons would defend themselves, leading to what is known as the Mormon War of 1838.

Eventually, Governor Boggs ordered that the Mormons be 'exterminated or driven from the state'. On November 1, Smith and his people surrendered to state troops and agreed to leave the state. Smith was court-martialled and came close to being executed for treason, but he was saved by his attorney's defence that he was a civilian. Instead, he was imprisoned but escaped on 6 April 1839 by bribing the sheriff transporting him and other prisoners to another jail.

The Mormons re-grouped at the abandoned town of Commerce in Illinois, re-naming the place Nauvoo which was Hebrew for 'Beautiful Place'. Much of the country was against the expulsion of the Mormons from Missouri, leading Smith to begin to promote the Saints as an oppressed minority.

The construction of a temple was begun, being completed only after Smith's death, while the town rapidly expanded, attracting converts from the United States and even Europe. By 1844, with a population of 12,000, it rivalled Chicago as the state's largest city. By that year, it is speculated that Smith may have married more than thirty women, while publicly denying that he was in favour of polygamy.

In 1844, several of Smith's disaffected rivals launched a newspaper, the Nauvoo Expositor, the only issue of which was published on 7 June 1844. Some of those involved claimed that Smith had tried to marry their wives – about eight of his wives were plural wives, in that they were also married to other men. The paper attacked Smith on three counts. Firstly, it called him a fallen prophet due to his advocacy of polygamy. Secondly, as mayor of the town and President of the church, they claimed that too much power was vested in him. And thirdly, he had corrupted women by coercing them into plural marriages.

The paper was declared a public nuisance by the city council which ordered the paper's printing press to be destroyed. Smith's critics accused him of violating the notion of a free press and some started to bring charges against him, including riot which allegedly took place when the printing press was destroyed, and treason. Violent threats were made against both him and the Mormon community.

When warrants against Smith were brought in from outside Nauvoo, they were dismissed by the city's court, and Smith declared martial law, calling out the 5,000-strong city militia, the Nauvoo Legion.

To calm things down, the Governor of Illinois proposed a trial of Joseph Smith by a non-Mormon jury in Carthage and guaranteed his safety. Smith reluctantly agreed and allowed himself to be arrested. On 25 June, he and Hyrum, his older brother, who was also a church leader, and fifteen city council members and friends surrendered to a Carthage constable on the charge of riot. Joseph and Hyrum were additionally charged with treason against the state of Illinois for the declaration of martial law, treason being a capital offence.

Following a preliminary hearing, the city council members were released on bonds of $500, pending a later trial. Joseph and Hyrum, however, were ordered to be kept in Carthage jail where they were joined by two other Mormons, Willard Richards and John Taylor.

Late on the afternoon of 27 June 1844 a mob of around two hundred men, armed and with their faces painted black with wet gunpowder stormed Carthage jail. Seeing them approaching, the frightened jailer informed Joseph Smith who was later reported to have said that there was nothing to worry about as the men were coming to rescue him. He wrongly believed that Jonathan Durham, major general of the Nauvoo Legion, had dispatched a unit to free him from prison as he had ordered him to.

The Carthage Greys, the city's militia force, which had already made threats to Smith, merely put up a pretence of defending the jail, firing blanks or aiming over the heads of the attackers. Some of them even joined them when they invaded the building and rushed up the stairs towards the room in which the men were being held.

The mob fired shots through the wooden door before trying to get the door open. In this fusillade, Hyrum Smith was hit in the face and screamed, 'I am a dead man!' as he fell to the floor. The attackers pumped another five bullets into his prone body to make sure he was dead.

Meanwhile, Joseph Smith, Taylor and Richards did what they could to defend themselves, Taylor and Richards using walking sticks to push the guns away as they were pushed into the cell from behind the door.

Earlier that day, during a visit, church leader, Cyrus Wheelock, had surreptitiously slipped a small pepperbox pistol to Joseph Smith that he now tried to fire at their attackers. But although he succeeded in wounding three of the attackers, three of the six barrels of the revolver misfired.

John Taylor was brought down, seriously wounded by four or five bullets while Richards was pushed behind the door as it was finally pushed open and remained unharmed.

Smith, meanwhile, ran to the window with the intention of escaping by jumping down to the ground outside. Just as he was about to jump, he was shot twice in the back while a third bullet, fired from a musket on the ground outside, struck him in the chest. As he plummeted from the window, he cried out, 'Oh Lord, my God,' alleged by some to be a Masonic distress signal.

Reports differ on what happened next. Taylor and Richards reported that Smith was dead when he hit the ground. One eyewitness, however, wrote in an 1845 account that Smith was, in fact, alive when the mob got to him. He claimed that they propped his seriously wounded body up against a well, gathered together a firing squad and shot him dead before fleeing the scene.

The bodies of Joseph and Hyrum Smith were initially buried under the unfinished Nauvoo House, the boarding house that was being built by Joseph but were then re-interred under an old out-building on the Smith homestead.

There was a great deal of speculation about who was actually responsible for the raid on Carthage jail. Governor Ford was suspected but denied it, although he later described Joseph Smith as 'the most successful impostor in modern times.' Eventually five men were tried for the murder of the Smith brothers but the non-Mormon jury acquitted them.

Meanwhile, following a schism in the Church of Jesus Christ of Latter Day Saints over the question of who should succeed Smith, most Mormons followed Brigham Young into the Utah Territory where they founded Salt Lake City which remains the headquarters of the church to this day.

WILD BILL HICKOK

He was arguably the most famous of all western gunfighters, a man of undoubted courage and phenomenal skill with six-shooters who, in his day, thanks to dime novels and newspaper reports, was possibly more famous than the President of the United States.

He was a man of striking appearance. General George Armstrong Custer's wife, Libby, with whom it was rumoured he had an affair, wrote admiringly of him: 'Physically, he was a delight to look upon. Tall, lithe, and free in every motion, he rode and walked as if every muscle was perfection, and the careless swing of his body as he moved seemed perfectly in keeping with the man, the country, the time in which he lived … He was rather fantastically clad, of course, but all seemed perfectly in keeping with the time and place. He did not make an armory of his waist, but carried two pistols. He wore top-boots, riding breeches, and dark blue flannel shirt, with scarlet set in front. A loose neck handkerchief left his fine firm throat free. I do not remember all his features, but the frank, manly expression of his fearless eyes and his courteous manner gave one a feeling of confidence in his word and in his undaunted courage.'

Of particular note, however, were the two Navy Colts that he wore tucked into a red sash around his waist, the ivory handles turned forward so that he could execute the underhand 'twist' draw for which he became famous.

James Butler Hickok was born in 1837 in Illinois where his father owned a farm that became a station on the 'Underground Railroad', the network through which slaves escaped to freedom. The young James Hickok helped in this work. During his free time, however, he would roam the nearby woods, hunting wolves and improving his skills with the gun.

At eighteen, he left home and headed west, joining General Jim Lane's vigilante 'Free State Army', also known as the Red Legs, and meeting twelve-year-old William Cody who later became famous as Buffalo Bill.

By 1858, Hickok was a constable of Monticello Township in Kansas and two years later, he joined the Russell, Waddell and Majors freight Company, working a year later at the Rock Creek Station in Nebraska that had recently been bought from David McCanles. Unfortunately, McCanles had not been fully paid and he and some family members arrived one day, intent on reclaiming the station. A gunfight ensued and the three McCanles men were shot dead by Hickok, J. W. Brink and Horace Wellman.

In the Civil War, he fought on the Union side as a spy, scout, detective, military policeman and sniper. At the Battle of Pea Ridge in Arkansas, in 1862, he utilised to the full his facility with a gun, taking out a number of Confederates from a position high above Cross Timber Hollow.

He had first been called 'Wild Bill' in the 1850s, possibly when he and his brother helped stop a lynch mob and a woman onlooker called one or both of them 'wild'. Another story has the name originating from an incident in Independence when he stopped an angry mob from doing further damage and a woman said 'Good for you, Wild Bill.'

His legend was really launched in 1865, after the conclusion of the Civil War, when he shot and killed gunman Davis Tutt. Hickok had borrowed money from Tutt while they were both gambling in Springfield and they argued over it. The rancour between the two was exacerbated by a falling out over a woman, Susannah Moore.

Hickok was arrested for murder but the charge was reduced to manslaughter before the jury decided it had been a 'fair fight' and acquitted him.

Harper's New Monthly Magazine journalist Colonel George Ward Nichols arrived in Springfield to write a story about Hickok that appeared in the February 1867 issue. It seriously exaggerated his exploits, telling of the hundreds of men that 'Wild Bill' had supposedly killed. Eventually, it would become difficult to separate fact from fiction.

Suddenly, Wild Bill was a hero and for the remainder of his life he would be pursued by a relentless press eager to hear about his exploits, whether fictional or true. Re-telling the same stories over and over to reporters and writers, the notoriety quickly became wearing to Wild Bill. It also made him a target for every gunslinger in the West who wanted to achieve instant fame by being the man to outshoot Wild Bill Hickok.

Wild Bill tried to obtain the post of City Marshal of Springfield, but having lost the election, took the job of Deputy United States Marshal at Ford Riley in Kansas. There, he also often served as a scout for General Custer's Seventh Cavalry. Custer thought highly of him, writing in his book, *My Life on the Plains*: 'Whether on foot or on horseback he was one of the most perfect types of physical manhood I ever saw. Of his courage there could be no question. His skill in the use of the rifle and the pistol was unerring. His deportment was entirely free from all bluster and bravado. He never spoke of himself unless requested to do so. His conversation never bordered on the vulgar or blasphemous. His influence among the frontiersmen was unbounded; his word was law; and many are the personal quarrels and disturbances which he had checked among his comrades by the single announcement that "this has gone far enough," if need be, followed by the ominous warning that, if persisted in, the quarreller "must settle with me . . .". I have a personal knowledge of at least half a dozen men whom he has at various times killed, others have been seriously wounded – yet he always escaped unhurt in every encounter.'

Hickok continued to work in law enforcement, burnishing his legend while based in Hays City, Kansas as Sheriff of Ellis County. He was victorious in famous gunfights against Bill Mulvey and then a month later when he outgunned Samuel Strawhun.

In 1871, he was Marshal of Abilene, one of the most lawless towns in the west. He brought it under control with the threat to troublemakers: 'Leave town on the eastbound train, the westbound train or go north in the morning', north meaning boot hill.

He encountered legendary gunman John Wesley Hardin there. Hardin, one of the deadliest shots in the West fled when he heard that Hickok was after him.

While in Abilene, Wild Bill came up against Phil Coe, owner of the Bull's Head saloon. The two had a dispute about a woman and then Hickok challenged Coe on the street after the saloon owner had been on a drunken shooting spree through town. When both men drew their guns, Coe missed but Wild Bill did not, pumping two bullets into Coe who died two days later.

A tragic accident followed, however. Immediately after shooting Coe, out of the corner of his eye, Wild Bill saw someone rush towards him. He turned instinctively and fired, killing the man who turned out to be his deputy and close friend, Mike Williams, who had been rushing to help him. Williams would be the last man Hickok killed and he would never quite get over the circumstances of his death.

Wild Bill could be found in Niagara Falls in 1874, taking part in a Wild West stage show, but he soon realised that the life of the performer was not for him. He headed back west and in 1875, met and married internationally renowned circus owner and performer – horsewoman, tightrope walker, dancer and lion-tamer – Agnes Lake. Shortly after, Hickok left for the Black Hills in order to make some money through gambling and prospecting. He would never see his wife again.

In Deadwood, he set up camp with his old friends, the brothers Charlie and Steve Utter and Joe Anderson. His arrival in town had caused consternation for the town's lawless elements who feared that he might start to clean things up and stop them preying on the earnings of honest gold prospectors.

Two men, Tim Brady and Johnny Varnes, lynch-pins of the Deadwood underworld, offered Jim Levy and Charlie Storms the job of assassinating Wild Bill but they rejected the offer. What they did not know was that Hickok's eyesight was deteriorating, partly due to the brightness of the stage lights from his time as a performer. He was only a shadow of the gunman he once was.

There have since been stories of a relationship with Martha Jane Cannary, otherwise known as Calamity Jane, at this time but any relationship was mostly in her mind and, as evidenced by the heartfelt letter he wrote to his wife on 1 August 1875, the day before he died, Wild Bill was still very much in love with her: 'Agnes Darling. If such should be we never meet again, while firing my last shot, I will gently breathe the name of my wife – Agnes – and with wishes even for my enemies I will make the plunge and try to swim to the other shore. J. B. Hickok. Wild Bill.'

The following day at around four in the afternoon, Wild Bill walked into Carl Mann's Saloon No. 10 and joined a poker game in which the other players were gunman Charles Rich, Con Stapleton, Captain Willie Massie, a Missouri steamboat pilot and the saloon owner, Carl Mann. Hickok was the last to sit down and, although he always made sure he sat with his back to the wall, as a precaution against being taken unawares, this time the only seat left put his back to the rear entrance to the bar. He tried to change seats with Rich but Rich merely laughed about it.

At this point, Jack McCall, who was also known as 'Crooked Nose Jack' and who did odd jobs about the place, entered the saloon. He casually walked around before walking towards the back door, behind Wild Bill's chair. He watched the game for a few minutes, listening as Hickok and Massie joked about Massie's alleged spying on other players' hands.

Suddenly there was the loud retort of a gun. McCall had pulled his .45 revolver from his coat pocket and shot Hickok in the back of the head from a range of only three feet.

Wild Bill seemed to freeze for several moments before tumbling over backwards and falling dead to the floor, the cards he had been holding fluttering to the floor. It was the hand that would famously become known as the 'Dead Man's Hand' – a pair of aces and a pair of eights.

McCall's motive for killing Hickok has been much debated. Some say he was humiliated by Wild Bill who offered him the money to buy breakfast after he had been cleaned out at the poker table the previous day. Another story has it that Wild Bill had killed McCall's brother in Abilene. McCall was tried in Deadwood and acquitted, but later was again tried in Yankton – Deadwood was not recognised – and found guilty and hung.

Almost the entire town attended the funeral of the Wild West's greatest gunfighter. He was buried by his friend Charlie Utter in Ingleside cemetery, Deadwood's original graveyard, his wooden grave marker reading: 'Wild Bill, J. B. Hickock (sic) killed by the assassin Jack McCall in Deadwood, Black Hills, 2 August 1876. Pard, we will meet again in the happy hunting ground to part no more. Good bye, Colorado Charlie, C. H. Utter.'

JESSE JAMES

Jesse James never realised that there was a traitor in his gang, a traitor who would shoot him dead in his own house as he reached up to straighten a picture. The traitor has been characterised in song and on film as 'the dirty little coward Robert Ford'.

Robert Newton Ford was born in Ray County, Missouri, in 1861. While still a boy, he came to admire the outlaw Jesse James both for his war record and for his daring bank and train robberies. He finally got a chance to meet the famous outlaw in 1880 after his older brother Charlie took part in the James Gang's Blue Cut train robbery on 7 September 1881 in Jackson County near Glendale, Missouri. Robert began to hang around the fringes of the gang which by this time had diminished in numbers due to shooting deaths, the capture of its members and some just moving on. Therefore, when the Ford brothers expressed their interest in joining his gang, Jesse let them. Neither, however, played a very big role and there is no record that Robert Ford ever participated in any robberies carried out by the James Gang. It seems more likely that he performed menial tasks for the gang such as holding the horses.

Jesse James is seen by some as a dashing folk-hero who upheld the pioneering values of the Old West against the rapid industrialisation of the late nineteenth century. Others see him as championing the remains of the Confederate South that had just lost the American Civil War. The other view, of course, was one that described him as a ruthless killer, a train and bank robber who would gun down anyone who got in his way during the sixteen years in which he cut a bloody swathe across what remained of the Wild West. The reaction of the public to Jesse James was extraordinary for the time. Crowds would often turn up to watch his robberies and cheered him like a modern-day movie or rock star.

He was born in Clay County, Missouri in 1847 and was fourteen by the outbreak of the Civil War. His family was caught up in it, his eighteen-year-old brother Frank riding with the Confederate soldiers of Quantrill's Raiders. Union soldiers burned down the James family farm in revenge for Frank fighting on the Confederate side and when Jesse protested at their actions, he received a severe beating.

As soon as he was seventeen, he enlisted, riding with the notorious guerrilla unit led by 'Bloody Bill'

Anderson, a man feared by the Union side for the brutality he showed to both Union soldiers and pro-Union civilians in Kansas and Missouri. On one occasion, on 21 August 1863, in Lawrence, Kansas, he and his men killed as many as two hundred men and boys.

As the war came to a bitter and disappointing conclusion for the Confederacy, Jesse was seriously wounded as he tried to surrender after running into a Union cavalry patrol near Lexington, Missouri. It was his second serious chest wound, having already been wounded in the summer of 1864. He was nursed back to health by his cousin Zerelda who, after a nine-year courtship, he would eventually marry.

Following the end of the war, Missouri was in chaos and many former soldiers found it impossible to re-adjust to civilian life. A number inevitably drifted into criminality, including Jesse and Frank who began to ride with a group of former guerrillas led by Archie Clement. They carried out the first post-war bank robbery, robbing the Clay County Savings Association in Liberty, Missouri. Jesse shot and killed an innocent bystander during the robbery but later claimed that he had taken part only in order to get back the deeds to his family's land. Nonetheless, it was the first of many robberies in which he participated.

His legend began to grow following the robbery of the Davies County Savings Association in Gallatin, Missouri. Believing him to be the man who had killed Bill Anderson, Jesse shot and killed Captain John Sheets, a cashier at the bank. Even though he killed the wrong man, his self-proclaimed act of honourable revenge and his and Frank's bold escape through a posse, brought him to the attention of the media. The editor of the Kansas City Times, John Newman Edwards, a Confederate sympathiser, began to publish letters written by Jesse in his newspaper, backing them up with editorials that supported the bank robber's controversial political views.

Frank and Jesse joined forces with the Younger brothers – Cole, Bob and Jim – and with some other former Confederate soldiers, formed what became known as the James-Younger Gang. They robbed their way across the West, graduating to robbing trains in 1873, hamming it up for the increasingly large crowds that gathered to watch.

Eventually, with the new Pinkerton National Detective Agency devoting manpower to finding them, the Governor of Missouri, Sam Woodson, offered a $2,000 reward for their capture and the state legislature budgeted $10,000 to fund the hunt. The gang, meanwhile, carried out their most profitable heist to date, stealing $30,000 from a train near Muncie in Kansas.

Increasingly desperate, Alan Pinkerton, Scottish-born founder of the eponymous detective agency, staged a raid on the James farm. An incendiary device was thrown into the house, Frank and Jesse's nine-year-old half-brother dying in the ensuing explosion and Jesse's wife Zerelda losing an arm.

Jesse moved everyone to Nashville and from there he began to write numerous letters to the press, defending his actions and stating his antipathy to the way the country was going.

Eventually, the James-Younger Gang met its end following a disastrous raid on a bank in Northfield, Minnesota. Although Jesse and Frank escaped, the Younger brothers were captured.

For the next three years the James boys kept a low profile in Nashville but by 1879 were on the road again with a new gang, staging robberies in Alabama, Kentucky and Missouri. In October 1879, they held up the Chicago and Alton Railroad, stealing $40,000. In September 1880, they robbed a Wells Fargo Stagecoach in Kentucky and, shortly afterwards, a paymaster's office in Muscle Shoals, Alabama. The Seton Bank in Riverton, Iowa, brought them a $5,000 haul. Jesse's fame increased and dime novels told fantastic stories about him while newspapers raved about him. He grew a dashing beard to enhance his image.

He struck the Chicago and Alton train for the second time in 1881, but the safe yielded disappointingly slim pickings. So, for only the second time in his career, he ordered his men to rob the passengers of their valuables. He walked through the train, the only member of the gang not wearing a mask, introducing himself to the astonished passengers. This one, however, would be his last robbery.

In November 1881, Jesse moved his family to St. Joseph, Missouri where he rented a house in the name of J. D. Howard, playing the part of an ordinary law-abiding citizen and appearing to want to quit the harsh realities of the outlaw life – death by gunshot or hanging seemed to be the inevitable way it would end. He became a model citizen but to make his retirement work, he needed one more big payday. He was targeting a bank in Platte County, Missouri.

But, Missouri's new Governor, Thomas T. Crittendon, was determined to end Frank and Jesse's careers. He persuaded the state's railroad executives to put up a huge reward – $10,000 – for the capture, dead or alive, of the James brothers. It was just too much money for new gang member Robert Ford to ignore. He arranged a meeting with the governor and made a deal to kill Jesse and claim the reward.

By this time, the gang membership was dwindling. A number of the men had surrendered to the authorities and eventually Jesse was left with only Bob and Charlie Ford. He instinctively distrusted Bob, but on 3 April 1882, he had breakfast with them at his house. They then went through to the parlour where they began to discuss plans for the Platte County heist. Bob was especially relieved to notice that a relaxed Jesse was not wearing his gun-belt.

Distracted for a moment in the middle of their conversation, Jesse stood up. He had noticed that a framed needlepoint picture that had been done by his mother was not hanging straight. He walked over to it, pulled up a small footstool in front of the picture and stepped up onto it. As he reached out to straighten it, Bob Ford realised that his moment had arrived – Jesse was unarmed and had his back to him. Ford leapt out of his seat, pulled his revolver out from under his coat, pointed it at Jesse and fired from a distance of around four feet. The outlaw was hit just below the right ear and he immediately grabbed at the wound, but another three bullets echoed around the room and the stool fell over, Jesse's body crashing to the floor, already dead. He was thirty-four years old.

Bob Ford was originally charged with murder but Governor Crittendon was true to his word and pardoned him. To Ford's eternal disappointment, however, he only ever received a fraction of the reward money. Furthermore, when he and his brother returned to their hometown of Richmond, Missouri, they found themselves to be unpopular because of the killing of Jesse James.

On hearing that Frank James was searching for them in order to exact revenge for his brother's murder, Charlie fled, moving from town to town for the next two years and using an alias. He finally committed suicide in 1884.

Bob, on the other hand, exploited his notoriety, appearing onstage in an act called Outlaws of Missouri. He recounted his story every night, always omitting the part about shooting Jesse James from behind. The act proved unpopular, however, and he was often booed off the stage by an audience that had loved the exploits of the famous outlaw.

He eventually ran a saloon in Las Vegas, New Mexico before moving to Creede, Colorado. On 8 June 1892, a man named Edward O'Kelley walked into the makeshift tented saloon that Ford had opened carrying a sawn-off shotgun. O'Kelley shouted to Ford who had his back to the door, 'Hello, Bob!' and as Ford turned, O'Kelley blasted him with both barrels, killing him instantly.

O'Kelley became the man who shot the man who shot Jesse James.

WILLIAM DESMOND TAYLOR

In his day, William Desmond Taylor was one of the greatest and most respected Hollywood directors, making around fifty films featuring the great stars of the silent era – including Mary Pickford, Wallace Reid and Dustin Farnum. His murder on 1 February 1922, created a scandal in the film colony of which he was a leading figure and although his killer was never found, there was no shortage of suspects.

He was born William Cunninghame Deane-Tanner in 1872 in Carlow, Ireland, one of four children of a retired British army officer but in 1890, when he was eighteen, he quarrelled with his father and left for England. He started to act and obtained a small role in a production of *The Private Secretary* staged by the famous actor and producer, Sir Charles Hawtrey. When his father heard about his son's thespian ambitions, he was disgusted and decided to send him to the Runnymede institution in Kansas, an organisation dedicated to turning wayward boys into gentlemen farmers.

He left after eighteen months and worked in a variety of jobs but eventually arrived in New York City where for a while he pursued an acting career before marrying Ethel May Hamilton in 1901. Her father, a wealthy broker, loaned him the money to open the English Antiques Shop and he and his wife established themselves as fixtures in New York society. Suddenly, however, in 1908 Deane-Tanner vanished after an affair with a married woman, leaving behind his wife and a daughter. He had experienced odd mental lapses in the past and his family wondered if perhaps he had suffered another. Really, however, he was just bored. It seemed to run in the family because his brother did exactly the same thing in 1912.

For the next four years, he once again worked in a variety of jobs, even panning for gold in Alaska at one point but four years after his vanishing act he was working as an actor in Hollywood where silent movies were at their popular peak. By this time he was going by the name of William Desmond Taylor.

He played small roles in westerns, gradually beginning to build a reputation as a handsome actor who always did a good job. As he grew older, however, he decided that he wanted to be behind the camera directing rather than acting in front of it.

He was given a chance as a director by the Balboa studio, his first film, *The Awakening*, being released in October 1914. The movie brought him romance in the shape of its lead actress, Neva Gerber. It was a relationship that would last until 1919.

After the demise of Balboa, Taylor moved to the American Film Company with whom he enjoyed his first real box-office smash with *Diamond From the Sky*. In the coming years, he worked with many different studios, directing hits for all of them.

In 1918, however, with the war in Europe raging, and at the age of forty-six he suddenly spurned the glamorous Hollywood life to enlist in the British Army and fight in the war. Starting out as a private, he was a lieutenant by the time he was honourably discharged in 1919, although he never saw any action.

Back in Los Angeles, he was elected to the prestigious post of President of the Motion Picture Directors Association and picked up where he had left off, directing the great stars of the time in films such as *Anne of Green Gables* and *The Green Temptation*.

By 1 February 1922, Taylor was at his most successful. He lived in the fashionable Hollywood area of West Lake Park, in one of a collection of

Spanish-style bungalows that were laid out in a U-shape around a beautifully manicured landscaped garden in the exclusive compound of Alvarado Court. Around him lived people like him, movie people like Edna Purviance, Agnes Ayres and Douglas MacLean.

His life was not without its upheavals, however. Just a month earlier, while Taylor was out of the country, Edward Sands who worked as his valet, cook and secretary, had crashed the director's car and defrauded him of more than $5,000. He had stolen jewels and clothes and vanished.

The replacement for Sands, Henry Peavey, brought him further trouble when he was arrested for vagrancy and indecent exposure which were the charges usually brought against homosexuals out looking for partners. Taylor stood bail for his servant and promised that he would appear as a character witness on Peavey's behalf on 2 February, when the case came to trial. By then, however, he would be dead.

That day, 1 February, Taylor was visited by the film star, Mabel Normand. Normand was a popular star of Mack Sennett's Keystone Studios and had starred in films with Fatty Arbuckle and Charlie Chaplin. Like many in Hollywood at the time, however, she had experimented with drugs and had become addicted. Taylor, a close friend, was helping her to kick her addiction. She visited that day to borrow a book on German philosophy from him, leaving his house at around 7.45 pm.

She was the last person to see him alive. At around 8 pm, he was shot in the back and killed in the living room of his house by a killer who, many people later surmised, had probably sneaked in through the door he had left open when he went out to wave goodbye to Normand.

Actor Douglas MacLean and his wife Faith lived in the bungalow next door to Taylor's and Faith, eating her evening meal, was surprised by a loud bang. Getting up from the table, she went outside, looking in the direction from which the noise came, towards Taylor's bungalow. At that moment, a man, a stranger to her, who she estimated later to have been in his mid-twenties, appeared in the lit doorway of Taylor's bungalow. The man looked in her direction and then calmly turned and went back into the house. A short while later, he came out again, strolling through the courtyard that separated the MacLean and Taylor bungalows. He seemed unconcerned and Faith put the noise down to a car backfiring and returned to her dinner.

At 7.30 the following morning, Taylor's valet, Henry Peavey turned up for work, unlocking the front door and walking into the living room. There, to his horror, he found the body of William Desmond Taylor lying in a pool of blood on the floor. He had not been robbed. His wallet contained $78 and he had been left with his silver cigarette case and an ivory toothpick. His expensive pocket watch and wristwatch also remained untouched.

As has happened in Hollywood since they started making pictures, a clean-up operation was immediately launched, probably by the head of Paramount for whom Taylor was working at the time. Anything that could be used to denigrate Taylor's reputation was removed. Letters and bootleg booze were spirited away and documents were burned. The reputation of Hollywood was also at stake. Recent scandals involving famous names such as Fatty Arbuckle had besmirched the movie world and the studio heads wanted no more. It was bad for business.

The disappearing valet, Edward Sands, was immediately suspected. He claimed to be British and certainly spoke with a cockney accent. Taylor declared him to be 'the most marvellous servant in the world'. But Sands was not all that he seemed.

For a start, he was not English and had certainly never been within hearing distance of Bow Bells – so he was no cockney. Records showed, that he had, in fact, been born in Ohio in 1894 as Edward Snyder. Having joined the Navy, he had been court-martialled for embezzlement and served a year in a naval prison before receiving a dishonourable discharge. Amazingly, he re-enlisted at the outbreak of the First World War but had deserted in 1919.

For a third time, he enlisted in the Navy, under a false name this time, but after three months he once again deserted, immediately enlisting in the Army from which he deserted six months later. After that, as Edward Sands, he became Taylor's valet. In June 1921, he robbed Taylor and disappeared.

He was never found by the police, but there actually was never any evidence to suggest that he had been involved, anyway.

His valet at the time of the murder, Henry Peavey was cleared early in the investigation but some persisted in believing he was the murderer. They suggested that he and Taylor were lovers and that Peavey had become jealous of his employer-lover and shot him. None of it was ever proved.

Another suspect was a woman that Taylor was involved with, the actress, Mary Miles Minter.

Thrust onto the stage at an early age by her ambitious mother, Minter had never really wanted to be an actress. She met Taylor in 1919 when she was just sixteen and he was fifty. Although it has never been proved, some think he had an affair with her, despite her youth. Did her strong-willed mother find out and, outraged at Taylor's seduction of her daughter, shoot him dead, or hire someone else to do it? Or could she have been dressed as a man that night. Was she the person that Faith MacLean saw? She had an alibi for the night, however, and in 1937 demanded a grand jury investigation into Taylor's death which was hardly the action of someone who had committed the murder she wanted investigated.

There were those who suggested that Mabel Normand's drug habit got Taylor killed, that he had antagonised the dealers supplying her. Or perhaps she was in love with him and was jealous of his affairs with other women?

Other suggestions have been made through the decades since the murder – he was killed by someone from his past who bore a grudge or someone from his time in the army, but it has all come to nothing.

It is unlikely that we will ever know who killed William Desmond Taylor, but it is equally unlikely that the speculation over his murder will ever stop.

JOHN DILLINGER

From September 1933 until July 1934 a period of just eleven months – John Dillinger and the gang of ruthless criminals he led established an unparalleled reputation for robbery and outrage and Dillinger himself became the consummate public enemy, perhaps the most notorious of all the gangsters who took advantage of difficult times to make a name, and often a fortune, for themselves.

During that short space of time, the Dillinger gang robbed up to twenty banks, pillaged three police arsenals, stealing enough weaponry to supply a small army, engineered three extraordinary prison breaks and shot their way out of traps set by the police, gun battles in which ten men died and many others were wounded.

In the midst of it all was the handsome, stylish and daring figure of John Dillinger displaying an insouciant contempt for authority. Dillinger simply did not give a damn. He was dramatic, often leaping acrobatically across the counter and on one occasion perching cross-legged on a seven-foot-high barrier in a bank, automatic in hand and hat set at a jaunty angle, smiling down at the surprised manager. In the midst of a robbery, he would think nothing of flirting cheekily with blushing older female bystanders. On one occasion, Dillinger saw a farmer in the queue clutching a wad of cash. 'Is that your money, or the bank's?' he asked the man. The farmer replied that it was his and Dillinger told him to keep it, adding, 'We just rob banks'.

Of course, the standing of the institutions he was robbing was at an all-time low. The Depression had led to banks foreclosing on mortgages and going bust, swallowing up people's life savings. Therefore, anyone giving them a hard time was looked upon as a kind of hero.

Dillinger's contempt for authority emerged at an early age. Born in 1903, he was the leader of a teenage gang, the Dirty Dozen, in his hometown of Indianapolis, Indiana. He was frequently in trouble for petty crime and a move to Moorsville to try to straighten him out, made little difference. At the age of seventeen, he was arrested for stealing cars.

He enlisted in the US Navy, but deserted within months and was given a dishonourable discharge. Returning to Moorsville, he made an effort to settle down, marrying a sixteen-year-old local girl in April 1924. A few months later, Dillinger was launching his criminal career with the armed robbery of a grocery store. During the heist, however, the gun he was carrying went off and Dillinger fled, believing he had shot the store-owner. He had not, but after his father persuaded him to give himself up, the court showed no leniency. He was sentenced to ten to twenty years in prison.

Three times he escaped and three times he was recaptured. These escapes, plus his flagrant and regular violation of prison rules, led to him spending a large amount of his jail time in solitary confinement.

In Michigan City Prison, he still managed to forge some useful friendships, however. Men such as bank robber, Harry Pierpont, and train robber and car thief, Homer Van Meter, would become stalwarts of Dillinger's gang and they were able to teach him everything there was to know about robbing banks.

The three planned meticulously for an escape. Dillinger was about to be released and it was arranged for him to carry out bank robberies in order to quickly raise the money needed to bribe the prison guards. Therefore, when he walked through the prison gates on 22 May 1933, his first task was to contact potential gang-members whose names had been provided by Pierpont and within weeks the White Cap Gang, as they became known, were hitting stores and banks.

The bribes began to be paid and the escape date was set. There was a problem, however, when a package containing guns was thrown over the wall and found by a prisoner who handed them over to the guards. Weapons finally made it into the jail hidden in a box of thread. Nine prisoners broke out on 25 September 1933 but Dillinger was not waiting to greet them. He had been targeted by Captain Matt Leach of the Indiana State Police and was arrested while visiting the sister of one of his cellmates in Dayton, Ohio.

It was not a great problem, however. The men who had broken free merely walked up to the gates of the jail where Dillinger was being held, shot the sheriff, found the keys and Dillinger was freed. The next eleven months would be spent running rings round the forces of law and order and making John Dillinger the most famous and most audacious gangster who ever lived.

They made their way to Chicago, en route breaking into the police arsenal at Peru, Indiana. They were now armed with dozens of weapons and bulletproof vests and the robberies could begin.

Their first heist took place on 23 October when

the Central National Bank in Greencastle was cleaned out. Another couple of bank robberies followed before they returned to Chicago to lie low for a while. Christmas 1933 was spent in Florida but they returned to Gary, Indiana, shortly after to hit the First National Bank. In this robbery, Dillinger shot and killed a policeman and gang-member John 'Red' Hamilton was badly wounded. Their luck ran out, however, when they were recognised at a hotel and arrested.

They were wanted in three states, but Dillinger, having killed the police officer in Indiana, was sent back there to face trial, while Pierpont and the others were sent to Ohio where they had killed the sheriff when busting Dillinger out of prison.

Dillinger's fame was now extraordinary and the vehicle transporting him from the airport to prison passed along streets lined with thousands of curious onlookers. Reporters waited for him at the prison and he responded wittily to their questions as he walked in through the gates, like a movie star turning up for a premiere. His trial was set for 12 March. The only problem was that John Dillinger would be long gone by that date.

On the morning of 3 March, Dillinger held up a number of guards with a gun in his hand. It looked real, but had, in actual fact, been carved out of wood. He stole a couple of Thomson submachine guns from the warden's office and he and another prisoner, Herbert Youngblood, drove out of the prison and made for the state border. When he crossed into Illinois, however, Dillinger fatally changed his status. He now came under federal jurisdiction and not only the police but also the FBI, headed by J. Edgar Hoover, would be hunting him.

In Chicago, he put together a new gang that included old colleagues, Homer Van Meter, Red Hamilton, and three new members – the psychopathic killer, 'Baby Face' Nelson and career criminals Eddie Green and Tommy Carroll. Within days of their formation, they robbed a bank in Sioux Falls, Indiana of $49,000.

The Feds were everywhere, though. They almost caught him in St. Paul, Minnesota when someone recognised him while he was staying at the apartment of a girlfriend. He and Van Meter and the girlfriend, Billie Frechette, blasted their way out and escaped.

On another occasion, as the gang hid out at a lodge in Little Bohemia, Boston, the Feds again got wind of their presence and surrounded the building. Once again the gangsters blasted their way through the police cordon and disappeared into the night. Red Hamilton was killed, however, in an ambush later that night but with Dillinger and Van Meter returning fire from their car's running board, they sped off.

Dillinger and Van Meter lay low for a while, Dillinger having plastic surgery carried out on his face, some moles and a scar being removed. Skin was pulled back below his earlobes, pulling it a little tighter over his cheekbones.

Their last bank job was perpetrated on 30 June 1934, when they escaped with meagre takings from the Merchant's National Bank in South Bend, Indiana.

Dillinger disappeared from view for a number of weeks but his car was found in July, parked on a Chicago side street. He had actually been working as a clerk, under the alias of Jimmy Lawrence and was dating a girl named Polly Hamilton.

One of Polly's friends, a Romanian brothel-owner named Anna Sage, whose real surname was Cumpanas, tipped off the authorities about Dillinger, hoping, in return, to have a deportation order on her lifted. She told agents of the FBI that he would be going to see a movie at the Biograph movie theatre on Sunday, 22 July.

As Dillinger entered the cinema that afternoon with Polly Hamilton and Anna Sage, a phalanx of G-Men – 'Government Men' – was watching. A couple of hours later, as the three came out, the Chicago FBI chief, Melvyn Purgis lit a cigar, the signal for the attack on Dillinger to begin. The agents moved in, surrounding the shirt-sleeved bank robber. A nervous Purgis managed to stammer the words, 'Stick 'em up, Johnnie! We have you surrounded'.

As he was not wearing a jacket in the city heat, Dillinger was carrying his pistol in his trousers pocket. As he fumbled for it, the Feds opened fire, catching him in a hail of bullets. He staggered into an alley beside the cinema where he fell to the ground, blood seeping from four wounds. Two bullets had hit him in the chest, while another – the one that killed him – entered at the base of his neck and exited close to his right eye.

Seeking souvenirs, people dipped their handkerchiefs into the pool of Dillinger's blood that was left when they had removed his body to the Cook County Morgue where it was put on display, hundreds of people filing past for a look at the great gangster. He was finally buried in concrete, to deter anyone from stealing his body, or perhaps to ensure that this time he did not escape.

Bugsy Siegel

He was the genuine article – a six foot-tall, dark-haired, handsome A-list celebrity gangster straight from central casting who had climbed his way out of the grimy slums of Brooklyn, New York all the way to the top, mixing with the stars in Hollywood and helping to create the gambling phenomenon of Las Vegas.

He was also a psychopath, a headcase who would let no one and nothing stand in the way of him getting what he wanted. Even his fellow gangsters were wary of his erratic, violent temper, the trait that earned him his nickname 'Bugsy' from the phrase to 'go bugs' – or mad – when things did not go his way. Of course, it was unwise to use the name 'Bugsy' to his face. Ben, Benny or plain Mr. Siegel would ensure that you went home with your health intact. He was fearless. As his boyhood friend and later partner in crime, Meyer Lansky said of him: 'When we were in a fight Benny would never hesitate,' Meyer Lansky once said. 'He was even quicker to take action than those hot-blooded

Sicilians, the first to start punching and shooting. Nobody reacted faster than Benny.'

Benjamin Siegelbaum, as he was born in 1902 to poor Russian parents, grew up in the area known as Hell's Kitchen, a place teeming with Italian, Irish and Jewish immigrants. The young Ben observed the harshness of life when you do not have enough and resolved to do better than that. He began early, teaming up with another Jewish neighbourhood kid on the make, Meyer Lansky. Lansky had observed how the Italians and Irish boys in the neighbourhood had organised themselves and decided that the Jewish kids needed to do the same. He formed a gang and its first member was Benny Siegelbaum. The names of other members of the gang would later go down in American criminal lore – Abner 'Longie' Zwillman, who later ran the New Jersey rackets; Lepke Buchalter, who would become the head of Murder, Inc., the Mob's enforcement wing and who would be the only top gangster to die in the electric chair; and a boy named Arthur Flegenheimer, who would become famous under the name Dutch Schultz. The gang became known as the 'Bugs and Meyer Mob.'

In 1915, they were running street corner gambling games, protection rackets and were dealing in stolen cars. They moved into the murder racket after their Italian friend, Charles 'Lucky' Luciano was released from prison after serving a sentence for narcotics. Luciano had been set up on the drugs charge by the son of an Irish cop and the Italian was bent on revenge. Meyer Lansky told him to leave it to him and Bugsy. They waited a year and told Luciano to get out of town on vacation and ensure that he had a good alibi. The nineteen-year-old cop's son disappeared never to be seen again and although Luciano was the prime suspect, his alibi was strong.

For the next few years, they kept a low profile, with floating craps games, union racketeering and robbery bringing in a good living. In their robberies they were known to be particularly ruthless, having little fear about using knives or fists to get what they wanted.

Unusually, they worked closely with Lucky Luciano and his Italian mob, putting aside some of their ill-gotten gains in a special fund that they hoped would serve them well down the line as they strove to break into the big time. Realising that their luck would not hold forever, they also began to invest in established illegal gambling operations and Lower East Side police officers and politicians were on their payroll. They were so successful that they soon came to the attention of the kingpins of crime in

New York City – Joe 'The Boss' Masseria and Arnold 'The Brain' Rothstein. Masseria wanted to take over the Lower East Side and that meant eradicating Meyer, Bugsy and their gang. Lansky and Siegel were not prepared to hand their operation over, however, and decided to take on Masseria's army of two hundred 'soldiers'. They routed Masseria's men in a huge gun battle and remained in control of the Lower East Side.

Prohibition, in the shape of the 1919 Volstead Act, provided gangsters like Meyer and Bugsy with a major opportunity. It did little to stop the desire to consume alcohol and America's hoodlums were only too happy to be the ones to provide it in speakeasys and the drinking establishments known as blind pigs that flourished in all the major cities.

Arnold Rothstein decided that the men to run his booze operation were Lucky Luciano, Meyer Lansky and Bugsy Siegel. In the next few years, under cover of a car and truck rental business on Cannon Street in Brooklyn, Lansky and Siegel supplied the city with illegal alcohol.

By 1920, business was booming and Siegel, Lansky and Luciano expanded their activities into Chicago where Al Capone, reluctant to get into bootlegging, was happy to let them get on with it as long as he received a cut of the profits. Eventually, however, Bugsy's temper got him into trouble. He and Lansky had gone to war with Waxey Gordon, the boss of Philadelphia, hijacking a large consignment of illegal hootch from him and killing a number of his men. Waxey never forgave them and tried to get even while he was in prison, ordering the Fabrazzo Brothers to plant a bomb in the fireplace of a hideout used by the Bugs and Meyer Mob on Grand Street. Spotting the device, Bugsy hurled it through the window just before it detonated. The two perpetrators did not last long after the incident. Andy Fabrazzo's body was found in a sack in North Jersey and the second brother, Louis, was shot dead in Manhattan. The third brother, Tony, had not been involved, but threatened to go to the police. In autumn 1932, Bugsy informed everyone that he was exhausted and checked into a local hospital for a few days. At the first opportunity, he sneaked out the window of his room, drove to Tony Fabrazzo's house and shot him dead at the door in front of his mother and father.

But, it was a mistake. Everyone knew he had done it and the men at the top were displeased. Furthermore, his relationship with Lansky was deteriorating. Bugs was tired of playing second fiddle to his much smarter friend. Added to this was the fact that Special Prosecutor Thomas Dewey was keeping a close watch on the activities of Lansky and Siegel. The pressure was mounting.

Four years after the murder of Tony Fabrazzo, the Crime Syndicate that Charlie Luciano – now the most powerful gangster in America – had formed, met to discuss Bugsy Siegel. They could easily have declared him too much of a liability and dealt with him in their customary manner, but they decided to give him a break. Bugsy was to be sent to the West Coast to try to grow the Mob's business there.

Arriving in California with his wife and kids, he bought a $200,000 mansion in the upmarket Holmby Hills and began hobnobbing with stars like George Raft, a friend from the old days and now a major movie star. Soon, he was being mentioned in gossip columns and romancing a number of Hollywood starlets, including Jean Harlow, one of the biggest movie stars and sex symbols of the time.

He worked the unions, especially the extras union because without extras there could be no movies. He also set up illegal wire services that provided the results of horse races before they were announced, a racket from which he was making $25,000 a month. When the Syndicate told him they wanted the profits from this operation, Bugsy told them to get lost. It was probably the beginning of the end for Bugsy Siegel.

However, he had one last racket in him but it would be the biggest of them all.

In 1931, the Nevada legislature had legalised gambling in order to raise extra revenue for the state. Bugsy decided to open a casino in the small town of Las Vegas which at the time consisted of no more than a couple of dude ranches and hotels. His hotel was to be named the Flamingo and it would be sufficiently luxurious to entice gamblers from Reno's swanky gaming palaces.

It did not get off to the best of starts, however. Because of the war, building materials were hard to come by and those that were delivered often disappeared out the back gate, being re-delivered and repaid for. Bugsy had borrowed a million dollars from his Mob friends but this quickly grew to six million. The Syndicate grew uneasy about its investment, especially as some of the mobsters, seduced by the thought of quick profits, had volunteered some of their own savings.

The project lagged seriously behind schedule and by 1946 the Flamingo was still a building site. On 22 September, a conference of gangsters, including, amongst others, Meyer Lansky, Frank Costello, Lucky Luciano, Vito Genovese, Joe Bonnano, Albert Anastasia and Joey Adonis discussed Bugsy. Lansky, his friendship with Bugsy having cooled long ago, warned the assembled hoods that he believed that Bugsy had been skimming from the cash the Syndicate had provided and had been depositing it in Swiss bank accounts. When Luciano asked him what he thought they should do, Lansky told them there was no alternative but to issue a contract for his death. The motion was passed unanimously by the meeting and the contract was handed to Charlie Fischetti. He was told, however, that it should not be operated upon until after the casino had opened. And, who knows, Lansky said, it might even be successful and they would all get their money back after all.

Billed as the world's most luxurious hotel, the 105-room Flamingo opened on 26 December 1946. The opening was glamorous with top-notch entertainment including George Raft, Jimmy Durante and Xavier Cugat's orchestra, and the presence of movie stars, Clark Gable, Lana Turner, Joan Crawford and many more. However, after a couple of days the crowds had gone and the gaming tables were empty. The Flamingo was a flop and Bugsy's days were numbered.

On 20 June, he had just returned home to his thirty-five-room mansion at 810 Linden Drive, Beverley Hills, from having a manicure and a haircut. He was relaxing on a chintz sofa, reading a newspaper. Suddenly, a bullet smashed through the window and into his head, knocking out one of his blue eyes. Another four bullets rapidly followed, thudding into his body, smashing his ribs and devastating his lungs.

At the age of just forty-two, Bugsy had received some of his own medicine.

John Lennon

'Mr. Lennon!'

The call rang out from behind the forty-one-year-old rock star and former Beatle as he headed for the entrance to the Dakota building, his home for the past seven years. He turned to see the figure of the man to whom he had just given his autograph, crouching and holding a pistol with both hands, combat style.

John Lennon turned, as if trying to escape, but the man fired five bullets from the gun, four of them ripping into Lennon's body. He did not fall, however, somehow summoning the strength to run up the half-dozen steps that led to the concierge's office. 'I'm shot,' he gasped to the horrified concierge before falling face down.

The doorman, Jose Perdomo, ran at the gunman, screaming, 'Do you know what you done? Do you know what you done,' knocking the gun out of his hand and kicking it away from him. The gunman seemed unperturbed, however. He quickly took off his hat and coat and tossed them onto the pavement. There were going to be police officers there in moments and he wanted them to realise that he was unarmed. Then he took a book from his pocket, a copy of J. D. Salinger's *Catcher in the Rye*, and began to read it as he paced the pavement, waiting for the sirens. When the first police car screeched to a halt, two officers leapt out. They were greeted by the killer who had his hands in the air, and was pleading, 'Don't hurt me, I'm unarmed.'

They threw him against the wall of the Dakota, spreading his legs in order to pat him down. 'I acted alone,' he said as the officers searched him. He was then handcuffed and put into the back of the police cruiser.

'I'm sorry I gave you guys all this trouble,' he said.

Mark David Chapman, one of the most notorious assassins in history, was born on 10 May 1955, in Fort Worth, Texas to a staff sergeant in the United States Air Force and a nurse. Not long after his birth, his father was discharged from the Air Force, enrolling at Purdue University in order to study engineering. The family moved to the Atlanta, Georgia, suburb of Decatur when Mark was seven years old.

It was not a happy childhood. He has claimed that his father was abusive to both him and his mother. He told a psychiatrist after his arrest that he would often wake to the sound of his father beating his mother who would be screaming his name. He would jump out of bed and run in to push his father away. He never received any love or emotional support from his father, he claimed. 'I don't think I ever hugged my father. He never told me he loved me.'

Outside his family, he fared little better. His schoolmates bullied him and nicknamed him 'Pussy' because of his lack of success at sports. As a result, he withdrew into his imagination, inventing imaginary worlds where he was not a failure. He dreamed up a world of 'Little People' of whom he was king and who lived in the walls of his house. In this world, he was a hero, worshipped by his subjects. He could do no wrong.

He was intelligent, with an above-average IQ and, despite his problems, was outwardly a normal little boy, playing with his toys and endlessly listening to the records of The Beatles, his favourite group.

At the age of fourteen, something inside Mark Chapman changed. He grew his hair and began to rebel, skipping school, getting into drugs and arguing with his parents. At one point, he ran away to Miami, living rough for a while before someone, feeling sorry for him, bought him a bus ticket back to Decatur.

He was nothing if not extreme, however, and just as suddenly as his rebellion began, it ended. When he was sixteen, he went to see a meeting featuring an evangelist and experienced a religious conversion. He cut his long hair, began to speak quietly and wore a large wooden cross on a chain around his neck.

He met his first girlfriend, Jessica Blankenship, also a Christian, and began to work at South Kalb YMCA. Working as a counsellor at the YMCA Summer Camp, he demonstrated a talent for interacting with children, earning the nickname 'Nemo' from his charges and being voted best counsellor in the camp.

He had stayed loyal to The Beatles, but when John Lennon uttered his famous statement about The Beatles being more popular than Jesus, Chapman was offended and turned against his former hero.

Around this time, he was introduced to a book that he believed was written just for him. *The Catcher in the Rye* tells the story of Holden Caulfield, a disgruntled teenager who runs away to New York.

He enrolled at South Kalb Community College, aiming to obtain a degree that would help him to get a full-time career with the YMCA. He was thrilled to be selected for the YMCA's international summer programme and flew off to Lebanon. The country was being torn apart, however, by a bloody civil war and proved too dangerous for outsiders. He was evacuated and returned to the States to work with Vietnamese refugees in a resettlement camp in Arkansas. Once again, he proved himself to be adept at working with children.

On the last day of his employment, he had a conversation with a co-worker. 'We're all going to get together again', he said. 'One day one of us is going to be somebody. About five years from now, one of us will do something famous and it will bring us all together.'

It was December 1975, and John Lennon had exactly five years left to live.

Chapman and Jessica Blenkinship were still seeing each other and they enrolled at the strict Presbyterian Covenant College in Lookout Mountain, Tennessee. Chapman's studies did not go well, however. He was crippled by guilt after being seduced by a co-worker at the refugee camp the previous summer. He began to feel suicidal until eventually, at the end of the first semester, he dropped out of college. Jessica broke off their engagement.

Returning to Decatur, he worked at summer camp again before finding work as a security guard during which he took a weapons course that qualified him to be an armed guard. He now knew how to handle a gun.

Still mired in depression, however, he decided to fly to Hawaii where he had decided he would kill himself. He withdrew all his savings – $1,200 – from the bank to buy a plane ticket. In Hawaii, he spent the first few days living like a king, checking into an expensive hotel and spending his evenings in the bar. After a few days he moved into a room at the YMCA and gradually began to realise that he did not want to die. When he called Jessica to explain it all to her, she told him to come home. When he got there, however, he was devastated when he discovered that she had no intention of resuming a relationship with him. After having a furious argument with his parents, he decided to return to Hawaii.

It was May 1977 and he was drinking heavily, living at the YMCA and doing low-paid work. Severely depressed again, he spent most nights on the phone to suicide hot lines. Then, one night, he decided to do it. He rented a car and bought a vacuum cleaner hose. He drove onto a deserted beach, connected the hose to the car exhaust and fed it into the car through the window. Mark Chapman sat back and waited to die.

But he did not die. He awoke to find a Japanese fisherman tapping at the car window – an angel sent by God, he later claimed – and found that the vacuum hose had melted in the exhaust. He went to a nearby mental health clinic and was admitted to Castle Memorial Hospital.

A week later, he seemed better and within a couple of weeks he had been discharged and was working at a local petrol station. He also volunteered at the hospital and was eventually offered a job there as a maintenance man. He entertained the older patients by playing Hawaiian songs on his guitar and socialised with the hospital staff. He was sharing a house with a Presbyterian minister and his life appeared to be back on-track.

In 1978, his thoughts turned to travel. He consulted a travel agent, Gloria Abe about a trip around the world and she organised a trip for him that took in Japan, Korea, China, Thailand, India, Iran and Israel. He ended up in Switzerland before returning to the USA. Waiting for him in Hawaii was Gloria Abe with whom romance had blossomed during the planning of the journey. In June 1979, the two married and Chapman found a job as a printer at Castle Memorial Hospital.

Before long, he lost his job, however, and was working as a night security guard. His old feelings of depression and isolation had returned and he began to become strangely obsessive. Art was one of his obsessions and he purchased a Salvador Dali work for $2,500. He sold this and, with money borrowed from his mother, bought a $7,500 Norman Rockwell painting. He sold his record collection only to replace it with a new one. He bought expensive new stereo speakers but then smashed his turntable. Having watched the movie *Network* one night, he decided that television was evil and sold his TV set. He considered changing his name to Holden Caulfield, the main character in *The Catcher in the Rye*.

He thought he must be slowly losing his mind, a feeling not helped when he began to pray to Satan. Then, after reading a book about John Lennon, he began to splice together lyrics from Beatles songs, the *Wizard of Oz* soundtrack and lines from *Catcher in the Rye*, creating a twisted catalogue of reasons for killing the former Beatle.

Meanwhile, the Little People were back in his life, talking to him and arguing with him about his decision to kill Lennon. But his mind was made up.

In October, John Lennon was staging a comeback, releasing *Double Fantasy*, his first album for five years. Around that time, Mark Chapman quit his job, signing out with the name 'John Lennon' through which he then drew a line. He flew to New York on 30 October, checking into the luxurious Waldorf Hotel. In his luggage was the .38 calibre Charter Arms Special that he had purchased for $169 in Honolulu three days before he left the island. He had no bullets, however, and because of the Sullivan Law that stipulates that New Yorkers require licences for guns small enough to be concealed, he was forced to fly to Atlanta where his friend Dana Reeves, a sheriff's deputy, provided him with five hollow-point cartridges that were designed to do more damage when fired.

Back in New York on 10 November, he called Gloria to tell her he was coming home. When, in a highly-charged conversation, he admitted that he had come to the city to kill John Lennon, she begged him to come home.

It seemed that he had dispensed with his demons but they were not gone for long. His mania led him to start making bomb threats and he began the daily harassment of a Hare Krishna group that sang and danced on the streets of Honolulu. Eventually, he announced to Gloria that he was returning to New York to try to find a new career.

He arrived on 6 December, telling the taxi driver who drove him into the city from the airport that he was a recording engineer there to work on a secret recording session involving John Lennon and his old Beatles cohort, Paul McCartney. He checked into the YMCA and began to hang around the Dakota.

On the 7th, he checked out of his room at the YMCA after having been kept awake by two men having sex in the room next door. He took a room at the Sheraton on Seventh Avenue and 52nd Street. He hung around the Dakota for a few hours but there was nothing happening. Remembering that he had not brought a copy of *Catcher in the Rye*, he visited a bookshop near his hotel. There, however, he spotted a poster of Dorothy and the Cowardly Lion from *The Wizard of Oz*. He bought it as well as the December issue of *Playboy* magazine that had Lennon on the cover and an interview inside.

After reading the interview, he phoned an escort agency. It was something that Holden Caulfield had done in *Catcher in the Rye* and, like the fictional character, he told the girl when she arrived that he just wanted to talk. He did so until three before paying her a generous $190 as she left.

At 10.30 next morning, he woke up and began to construct a strange little tableau on the room's dressing table. He placed a Todd Rundgren audiotape there – he had replaced Lennon as his musical hero with Rundgren – and added the *Gideon Bible* that had been in his room, opened to the Gospel of John and with the word 'Lennon' added after 'John'. To these he added a letter that praised his work at the Vietnamese resettlement camp beside some photographs of him with Vietnamese children. As a backdrop, he added the *Wizard of Oz* poster.

He left the hotel with a copy of Lennon's *Double Fantasy* album and the gun tucked in his pocket, a piece of cardboard over it to conceal the outline of the weapon. He dropped into the bookshop for the copy of *Catcher in the Rye* he had not bought the night before and on its inside cover he signed 'Holden Caulfield'.

Arriving at the Dakota, he leaned against the railings, reading the book, becoming so engrossed that he missed Lennon climbing out of a taxi and slipping into the Dakota. Chapman was irritated but stayed there, chatting to an amateur photographer Paul Goresh who was a regular Lennon-watcher outside the Dakota. Another regular, Jude Stein appeared. Chapman offered to buy her lunch after which they returned to the Dakota. A little later, when Lennon's five-year-old son Sean came out with a nanny, Chapman was introduced to him, shaking the little boy's hand.

For a while, stars came and went – the Dakota was home to many A-listers – but there was no sign of Lennon until much later when he emerged from the building with Yoko and a few members of his staff. Starstruck, Chapman had to be shoved forward by Goresh to have his album autographed. Lennon courteously obliged, writing 'John Lennon, December 1980'.

Chapman later said that after signing, Lennon looked at him and said, 'Is that all you want?' Chapman nervously replied 'Yeah. Thanks John' and Lennon was swallowed up by the large limo parked in the middle of the street.

He was thrilled. He offered Goresh $50 for any photograph he might have taken of Lennon with Chapman beside him and then claims that he prayed, begging God to make him just go home, leaving the rock star to get on with his life. But there was a voice inside his head insisting that he stayed where he was and got on with what he had planned.

Around 8 pm, Goresh decided that as Lennon

would not be back until late from the recording studio, he was going home. Enigmatically, Chapman told him, 'I'd wait. You never know if you'll see him again.'

At 10.50, a white limo pulled up and Yoko Ono clambered out, followed by John. Just then, the voice called out, 'Mr. Lennon'.

Gianni Versace

Born in 1946, Gianni Versace had grown up in Reggio Calabria in southern Italy and began working in fashion at an early age, helping his dressmaker mother find stones and gold braid with which to embroider the dresses she made. At the age of twenty-six, he began to work in fashion design and by his early thirties he was established as one of the world's leading designers.

By 1997, his companies were generating profits of around $900 a year, his clothes gracing the bodies of royalty and movie and rock stars. In July of that year, the fifty-year-old fashion icon had just completed a tour of Europe and was exhausted. He had flown to his house in Miami, the luxuriously appointed Casa Casuarina on 11th Street which had been built in 1930 by architect, philanthropist and political reformer Alden Freeman as a homage to the early sixteenth century palace of Alcazar de Colon in Santo Domingo, in the Dominican Republic. Versace wanted to rest and in Miami he could do just that. He was able to relax in his favourite nightspots, gay bars such as The Twist,

The KGB Club or Liquid and in the mornings, he could sleep late before taking a leisurely stroll, unencumbered by bodyguards or hangers-on, to the News Café on Ocean Drive to sip a coffee and read the newspapers.

What he failed to notice that July, however, was the man who followed him on these carefree walks.

Andrew Cunanan had once been devastatingly handsome. Openly gay since school, his good looks had provided a living for him. He had worked as a male prostitute, the guilty secret of numerous wealthy businessmen who had provided him with apartments, credit cards and cars in return for his time and his body. He had much more going for him than his looks, however. He was a highly intelligent man, spoke seven languages and could debate with the best of them.

By 1997, however, he was in his late twenties and his looks were beginning to fade. His high consumption of alcohol was bolstered by the painkillers he normally sold to make some extra cash but was now using himself. His weight was ballooning and he was letting himself go. His wealthy providers had begun to move on to younger men, leaving Cunanan to sink into a morass of depraved gay porn and even to take part in several porn movies.

The irrational anger that had always lurked just beneath his surface was liable to erupt at any moment. One such eruption occurred when he was rejected by a lover, David Madson. Friends noticed a change in Cunanan around this time, some even believing he was suffering from some kind of breakdown. His fury increased as he began to suspect that Madson was having an affair with another of his old friends, Jeff Trails. The idea of their relationship ate away at him until in April 1997, he decided to do something about it. He bought a plane ticket to Minneapolis where Trails and Madson lived.

It was the beginning of a deadly trip that would end up with Gianni Versace lying dead at the gate of his house in Miami.

Madson met him at the airport and at 9.45 that evening, Cunanan was with Madson and Trails at Madson's apartment. When Cunanan confronted them with his suspicions, they laughed it off, assuring him that there was nothing going on between them. The jealous Cunanan did not believe them, however, and an argument developed, during which a neighbour later reported hearing a commotion and then someone yelling, 'Get the fuck out!' More noises followed before footsteps were heard leaving the apartment.

Cunanan had flown into a monumental rage and had killed Trails with twenty-seven blows with a claw-hammer. He fled with Madson in a red Jeep Cherokee, leaving behind a backpack that was filled with items that identified Cunanan as having been there. But he was now beyond caring. Forty-five miles north of Minneapolis, at Rush Lake, he pulled the Cherokee over, put a pistol to David Madson's head and pumped three bullets into it.

Cunanan's next victim, chosen at random, was the hero of an American success story. Seventy-two-year-old Lee Miglin was a real-estate developer who had been the son of a Lithuanian immigrant coal miner. His wife Marilyn, owner of a cosmetics and perfume company was out of town that night of 4 May when Cunanan came calling.

He probably surprised Miglin before forcing him into his garage where he tied his wrists with duct tape and wrapped it round his face, leaving only a small mouth-hole through which he could breathe. What followed was horrific. Cunanan acted out tortures from his favourite 'snuff' movie, *Target for Torture*. He stabbed him in the chest with a pair of pruning shears and then slowly cut his throat with a garden saw. In a final act of rage, he drove Miglin's 1994 Lexus back and forward over his body.

Cunanan spent the night in the Miglin house watching videos before sleeping in Lee and Marilyn's bed. Early next morning, he drove off in the Lexus, leaving the Cherokee behind, photographs of him strewn across its front seat. He was now taunting the police.

Finn's Point Cemetery in rural Pennsville, New Jersey, is a quiet, remote place, surrounded by marshlands where forty-five-year-old William Reece had worked as caretaker for more than twenty years. Andrew Cunanan found him on 10 May and, wanting his 1995 Chevrolet pick-up, shot him at point-blank range in the back of the head in his kitchen.

There was horror in the media and investigators were baffled. No one knew where this apparently merciless killer was going to turn up next. Furthermore, no one knew what was driving this random murder spree. The gay community postulated that Cunanan might have discovered himself to be HIV-positive and was taking revenge on society. The FBI put him on their Top Ten Most Wanted list.

Meanwhile, Cunanan headed for Miami Beach. He had one more murder in mind – Gianni Versace. The two had met previously. Cunanan had attended a party years before in the company of Eli Gould, a wealthy lawyer who introduced him to Versace. Like many, the designer had been struck by the stunningly handsome young man, suggesting that they had possibly met before although they had not. 'Lago di Como?' he enquired. Cunanan played along, telling Versace that it was sweet of him to remember.

Now he looked everywhere for Versace, hanging out in the bars and clubs he knew he frequented while in Miami. But he was nowhere to be seen.

Cunanan had checked into the Normandy Hotel but he was not at all careful about keeping his whereabouts secret and in fact there were three ways that he might have been apprehended before killing Versace. The first time was during a visit to a sandwich bar where an employee recognised him from the picture that had been shown in the media. He told him he would have to wait while he made up his order and slipped into the back room where he called the police. Tragically, while he was doing this, another employee served Cunanan who left the shop before officers arrived on the scene.

There was also a great deal of criticism of police concerning William Reece's pick-up that was parked in a public garage close to his hotel for a considerable time. Following Versace's murder, the media and the public were outraged that no search of garages or side streets had been made for the vehicle.

The worst piece of police negligence, however, occurred after Cunanan went to the Cash on the Beach pawnshop on 7 July in order to pawn a gold coin he had stolen from the Miglin house. The coin was worth $200 but in order for the transaction to be processed, Cunanan, by law, had to provide two forms of identification. These would be sent to the Miami Police Department to be checked against their fugitives list. Cunanan realised that it was a risk he had to take because he was now flat broke. He gave the clerk a signature and an address – his hotel – received the cash and the details were sent off. Unfortunately, however, the document sat untouched on a desk at police headquarters for the next eight days.

He began to follow Versace on his morning stroll. On the morning of 15 July, he followed him to the café and then back along 11th Street to the ornate gate of his magnificent house.

Versace pulled the key from his pocket and reached out to put it in the lock. At that moment, Cunanan stepped up behind him, put Jeff Trails' .40 calibre pistol to the Italian's head and pulled the trigger. The designer, although mortally wounded, instinctively spun round to face his assassin, but Cunanan coolly pointed the gun and fired a second bullet into Versace's tanned, handsome face. He crumpled to the ground and Cunanan calmly walked away, horrified eyewitnesses looking on.

Andrew Cunanan was found a short while later on a houseboat on which he had been hiding. Hundreds of police flooded the quayside area, marksmen taking aim from neighbouring rooftops and vantage points. But they were too late. His body lay on a sofa, a bullet hole just behind his left ear where he had shot himself. No one would ever know what had motivated his murderous cross-country spree.

Tupac Shakur

He always wore a bulletproof vest. The world he had come from, and still moved in, was a dangerous and violent one and it paid to take precautions. As his fiancée, Kidada Jones, model, actor and designer daughter of musician Quincy Jones, packed his suitcase at his house in Calabasas in Los Angeles in September 1996, however, the rapper and promising actor Tupac Shakur told her to leave the vest behind. It would be too hot in Las Vegas to wear it.

It was a decision that would cost him his life.

He had grown up in the East Harlem area of New York City and was named after the eighteenth-century Inca leader Tupac Amaru II. His mother Afeni and father Billy Garland were activists in the African-American revolutionary organisation, the Black Panther Party.

Tupac was surrounded by trouble from the start, family members and friends always being incarcerated for violent acts but he was a good student, showing a particular talent for acting. He also developed rapping skills that won him numerous rapping competitions.

His family moved to Marin City in California and his career as a rapper began to flourish. So, too, did his conflict with the authorities. Gun violations, driving incidents and accusations of sexual assault dogged him in the years leading up to his death.

During his trial for the sexual assault of a woman in a hotel room, in 1994, Tupac was shot five times as he entered the lobby of a recording studio in Manhattan. He accused rappers Sean Coombs (who would gain fame as Puff Daddy), Biggie Smalls (Notorious B.I.G.) and record label boss Andre Harrell of setting him up. Later, he also suspected his close friend, Randy 'Stretch' Walker. Stretch was shot dead a year later. Meanwhile, Tupac was sentenced to 1½–4½ years in prison for the sexual assault. He went to prison as his multi-platinum album, *Me Against the World* went to number one, the only artist to have a number one album on the Billboard chart while serving a prison sentence.

After serving eleven months, he was released on bail, pending an appeal, the $1.4 million surety being put up by Death Row Records owner Suge Knight in return for Tupac making three albums on the Death Row label.

He got straight into recording when he came out, delivering his fourth solo album, *All Eyez on Me*, a double album representing his first two albums for Death Row. He would go on to record hundreds of tracks at Death Row, many of which were released posthumously.

The Vegas trip in September 1997 was so that he could be ringside with Suge Knight at the Mike Tyson-Bruce Seldon boxing match but Suge irritated Tupac by leaving it to the last minute to arrive.

Tyson won convincingly and Tupac was thrilled by his performance. 'Tyson did it to him!' he told anyone listening. 'Did ya'll see that? We bad like that. Come out of prison and now we running shit.' He went back to meet and congratulate Tyson after the fight. A short while later, however, he was involved in an altercation with a man in the lobby of the MGM Grand where the fight had taken place. Orlando 'Baby Lane' Anderson was a member of the Southside Crips, a Los Angeles gang while Tupac and his entourage were members of the rival gang, the Bloods. Earlier that year, Anderson and other Crips had robbed a Death Row employee and on seeing him Tupac launched himself at him, the others joining in. Anderson was badly beaten.

Tupac, riding in Knight's BMW and followed by a convoy of ten vehicles containing his entourage, left the Grand with the intention of going to a club

– the 662 – that was owned by Suge. Playing on the car's sound system was Tupac's new album – *The Don Killuminati: The 7 Day Theory*. En route to the club, however, at around eleven o'clock, they were stopped on Las Vegas Boulevard by police officers for playing the car stereo too loud and for not having licence plates on their vehicle. The plates were located in the boot of Suge's BMW 750 and they were allowed to continue on their journey without paying the requisite fine.

Ten minutes later, while stopped at a red light at Flamingo Road close to the intersection of Koval Lane in front of the Maxim Hotel, a car pulled up alongside them. There were two women inside and Tupac, standing up with the upper part of his body out through the car's sunroof, turned to them and invited them to join him at Club 662. As he was talking, a new, white, four-door Cadillac drew up alongside the BMW on the other side from the two women. A window was rolled down and a volley of shots suddenly rang out. Tupac was hit in the chest, pelvis, right hand and thigh. Most seriously, one of the bullets had penetrated his right lung. Suge was grazed by a bullet and slightly wounded by bullet fragments and although he later claimed to have a bullet from the incident lodged in his skull, medical reports later contradicted this. There was no one else in the car with the two men. In another fatal mistake that night, Tupac had asked his bodyguard, Frank Alexander, to ride behind them in Kidada's car.

Immediately after the shooting, the Cadillac sped south on Koval while Suge made a u-turn from Flamingo and headed west towards Las Vegas Boulevard, away from the nearest hospital. When he told Tupac that he would get him to a hospital as quick as he could, the bleeding rapper told him, 'I need a hospital? You're the one shot in the head!'

Police officers, answering a call at the Maxim Hotel, heard the gunshots and summoned back-up. They followed the BMW as it headed onto Las Vegas Boulevard South, finally catching it up when it stopped in traffic at the intersection of Las Vegas Boulevard and Harmon Avenue. An ambulance was called to the beleaguered vehicle. Its interior looked like a battlefield.

Tupac was complaining that he was unable to breathe as he was placed on a stretcher before being rushed to University Medical Center. He lost a huge amount of blood en route to the Medical Center and as he was being carried to the emergency room, he moaned, 'I'm dying.'

His condition was, indeed, critical. He had been

shot in the chest and had a massive haemothorax – blood accumulated around his lungs. Just before midnight, he was conveyed to the hospital's trauma centre where he was resuscitated before being put on a life support machine. The two litres of blood that had gathered in his chest cavity were removed before he underwent emergency surgery, a procedure that was completed at 2.35 in the morning.

Four hours later, he was back in the operating theatre where his punctured right lung was removed in order to stop internal bleeding. At 7.45, he was put in a barbiturate-induced coma and back on life support.

Away from the hospital, the talk was of who had carried out the shooting and of revenge. Yafeu Fula of Tupac's backing group the Outlaws Immortalz – who was, himself, fatally shot at a later date – had been in the car behind them. He told the police that he could do a photo line-up, but everyone immediately suspected that the man they had beaten earlier, Orlando Anderson, was behind the shooting.

The Bloods met to talk about retaliation against the Southside Crips and at just before three that afternoon, a man who Las Vegas police later said might have been in the white Cadillac, was shot in the back and killed.

Before he died, Tupac Shakur opened his eyes just once, while Kidada was putting Don McLean's song *Vincent* into a cassette player beside his bed. She said that if he could hear her he should move his feet. His feet moved. She then asked if he knew that she loved him. He nodded and sank back into his coma.

On 11 September, Bobby Finch, a Southside Crip who police also identified as possibly having been in the white Cadillac died in a hail of bullets.

The following day doctors unsuccessfully tried several times to resuscitate Tupac but his mother Afeni asked them not to try again. He was pronounced dead at 4.03 on Friday, 13 September.

Notorious B.I.G.

It was 7 March 1997, six months after rapper Tupac Shakur had been gunned down in Las Vegas. Tupac's rival from the east coast, the Notorious B.I.G., aka Biggie Smalls, was in Los Angeles to present an award at the 11th Annual Soul Train Awards at the Shrine Auditorium and Expo Center. When he appeared onstage, however, a chorus of boos rang out and persisted throughout his presentation of an award to singer Toni Braxton. Smalls, embarrassed at the reception he had received, leaned into the microphone and, trying to lighten the mood in the hall, smiled and said, 'What's up Cali?' It only made the booing louder.

The East-West Coast hip-hop rivalry had arisen out of an accusation in *Vibe* magazine by rapper Tupac Shakur, a former associate of the Notorious B.I.G., that B.I.G., Andre Harrell, founder of Uptown Records and Sean Coombs, later to become famous as Puff Daddy and then P. Diddy, had been behind a November 1994 robbery in a Manhattan recording studio in which he had lost thousands of dollars worth of jewellery. Shakur, speaking from Clinton

Correctional Facility where he was serving time for sexual assault, noted that on the night that two men in army fatigues had robbed him and shot him five times, Smalls and his entourage were in the same recording studio.

Smalls, however, always denied any involvement. 'It just happened to be a coincidence that he was in the studio,' he said. 'He just, he couldn't really say who really had something to do with it at the time. So he just kinda' leaned the blame on me.'

He had been born Christopher George Latore Wallace and grew up in Clinton Hill in Brooklyn, the only child of a Jamaican pre-school teacher, Violet Wallace and her husband, welder and minor Jamaican politician, George Latore. Latore had walked out on the family when Christopher was only two years old and his mother had to work hard to bring up her son, but, already nicknamed 'Big' because of his size, even before the age of ten, he did well at school. He followed the same path as many local kids, however, and was selling drugs at an early age.

He attended the George Westinghouse Information Technology High School, the same school as Jay-Z and Busta Rhymes, but dropped out at seventeen becoming more involved in criminal activity. In

1989, after being arrested on weapons charges, he was sentenced to five years' probation. In 1990, he went to prison for nine months for dealing crack cocaine.

He was already rapping as a teenager, performing on the streets of Brooklyn as well as with local groups. Released from prison, he recorded a demo tape under the name of Biggie Smalls, an ironic reference to his six feet three, 350-pound stature. The tape was heard by the editor of the magazine *The Source* and in March 1992, there was a piece about him in the magazine. He was asked to make another demo that was heard by Sean Combs, at the time A&R and record producer for Uptown Records. Combs signed him to the label and he appeared on a track on an album by Heavy D & the Boyz. By this time, his long-term girlfriend had given birth to his daughter and he was selling drugs again to make ends meet, but Combs persuaded him to stop in order to focus on his music career.

He began to come to wider attention when he featured on a remix of a Mary J. Blige track, by this time calling himself the Notorious B.I.G. because the name Biggie Smalls was already being used. The track rose to number seven on the Billboard chart and other successes quickly followed.

In 1994, he married singer Faith Evans and enjoyed his first solo success with *Juicy/Unbelievable*, a double A-side that reached number 27. His album *Ready to Die* was released in September 1994, reaching number thirteen. It would eventually sell more than four million copies.

From that time forward, it was million sellers and gold and platinum records all the way. At the Source Awards in August 1995, he was named Best New Solo Artist, Lyricist of the Year, Live Performer of the Year, while album *Ready to Die* won debut Album of the Year. At the Billboard Awards, he was named Rap Artist of the Year.

The recording of his second album was hampered by legal wrangles, injury and the dispute with Tupac but he also worked with Michael Jackson on his *History* album. Then, in March 1996, after being arrested for beating up an autograph hunter he was sentenced to a hundred hours of community service.

When Tupac was shot in September, dying six days later, rumours of B.I.G.'s involvement were rife but he, of course, denied it and the claims of his guilt were disproved.

The booing in California that night was, therefore, deeply disappointing to the rapper, especially as he had been making strenuous efforts to extricate himself from the feuds and bad behaviour that had long poisoned rap music.

The night after the awards, he and his entourage attended a party hosted by *Vibe* magazine and Qwest Records at the Peterson Automotive Museum on Wiltshire Boulevard. Smalls had been reluctant to go – he was walking with a cane following a car accident six months earlier and the boos of the previous night still rankled with him. However, he had an album about to be released – *Life After Death … 'Til Death Us Do Part* and Sean Coombs convinced him that his attendance at the party would provide some excellent promotion for the album.

The party was the event of the night in L.A. with around 2,000 people crowded into the museum while hundreds milled about in the streets outside trying to get in. Smalls was enjoying himself, meeting old friends and being accosted by beautiful women. At 12.53 am, however, fire marshals declared that the building was dangerously overcrowded and ordered the party to be closed down.

As guests headed for the doors, Smalls and his party remained behind. Unable to walk very fast because of his injury, he wanted to avoid the crush. Eventually, with the exit clear of people, they walked out to the two GMC Suburbans – a dark green one and a black one – they had rented which they had been forced to park on the street as the valet parking lots were full when they had arrived.

B.I.G climbed into the black Suburban, sitting in the front passenger seat. Also in the car were his friends, Damion 'D-Roc' Butler, rapper Lil' Cease and the driver, Gregory 'G-Money' Young. In the other car Sean Coombs travelled with some friends.

Combs' vehicle was first to pull away from the kerb into the flow of traffic, the black Suburban containing the rapper following closely behind. Behind that was a Ford Blazer carrying their three bodyguards, all off-duty Inglewood police officers. They drove to the junction of Fairfax Avenue and Wiltshire Boulevard where the traffic light had turned red and stopped.

As they waited for the light to change, B.I.G.'s forthcoming album by this time booming from the car stereo, a man called out to the green Suburban containing the rap star from a dark Chevrolet Impala that had pulled up alongside it. B.I.G., presuming it was a fan who wanted to say hello, casually wound down his window. The driver of the other vehicle, an African American man in a suit and a bow tie, suddenly raised a 9mm automatic pistol, pointed it at B.I.G. and opened fire, hitting the rapper four times in the chest. As the Impala sped away, Sean Combs rushed from his car to the other. B.I.G. had already lost consciousness, however, and by the time he arrived at Cedars-Sinai Medical Center, it was too late. He was pronounced dead at 1.15 am.

The murder of the Notorious B.I.G. remains unsolved to this day. Many have tried to put the blame on Marion 'Suge' Knight, owner of Death Row Records, for whom Tupac Shakur recorded. Alleged to be a member of the Bloods gang, it has been suggested that he and David Mack, a Los Angeles policeman and alleged Death Row Security employee, killed B.I.G in order to make it look like a part of the East Coast-West Coast rivalry in order to cover up his murder of Tupac which he is said to have ordered so that he and his company could benefit from the renewed interest that an artist's death inevitably creates. After all, in his vaults he had around two hundred unreleased Tupac Shakur tracks. He may even have been angered by losing his best-selling artist and wanted Sean Combs' label, Bad Boy Records to suffer the same fate. The fact remains, however, that Knight was only a few feet from the gunman and was actually hit by a bullet. Is it likely that he would have put himself at risk like that?

Some said that there was a gang element to the murder. David Mack was also, it is alleged, a member of the Bloods and some believe the rival gang the Crips were responsible for the killing. According to this theory, B.I.G had agreed to pay the Crips to murder Tupac, but had then reneged on his promise to pay them. They were simply punishing him for that.

Mack, serving a fourteen-year sentence for bank robbery by the time police got to him, refused to cooperate with the investigation. The gunman, said to have been Amir Muhammad – also known as Harry Billups simply vanished.

Fifteen days after his death the Notorious B.I.G.'s second album, now titled *Life After Death*, went to number one on the Billboard chart.

Many consider him to have been the greatest rapper of all time and his lyrics have been sampled by a wide range of hip hop, R&B and pop artists including Jay-Z, 50 Cent, Alicia Keys, Nelly, Ja Rule, Eminem, Lil Wayne, Game, Michael Jackson and Usher.

JILL DANDO

She was the BBC's poster girl, a vivacious blonde who was known as the 'Sunshine Girl', host of the BBC's *Holiday* programme and, with Nick Ross, the presenter of *Crimewatch*, the show that explored unsolved crimes and asked viewers to help solve them.

She had started her career as a journalist in her hometown of Weston-super-Mare with the *Weston Mercury*, five years later launching her television career with the regional news magazine show, *Spotlight South West*. In 1988, she moved onto national television, presenting the prestigious BBC television news. She worked on *Breakfast News*, the BBC *One O'Clock News* and the *Six O'Clock News* while occasionally presenting the Sunday evening religious programme, *Songs of Praise*. Her uncontroversial, girl-next-door style led to her being voted BBC Personality of the Year and by 1999, aged thirty-eight she was at the pinnacle of her career.

Away from the screen, her life was also going well. She had enjoyed several relationships, notably one with BBC producer Bob Wheaton that had lasted from 1989 until 1996. In 1997, however, she had met gynaecologist Alan Farthing and the two were set to marry in September 1999. She was scaling down on her work commitments in advance of her wedding.

On April 25, Jill had presented the first programme of a brand-new BBC1 series, *Antiques Inspectors*. She had then gone to her fiancé's home in the West London suburb of Chiswick where she had been spending much of her time recently. The following morning – 26 April – she got into her car and drove to the house she owned in Gowan Avenue, in the West London area of Fulham. She had put it up for sale and nowadays visited it rarely.

At around 11.32, as she was standing at the door of the Gowan Avenue house, about to put the key in the lock, she was grabbed from behind, her assailant holding her tight and forcing her to the ground. With her face close to the tiled step of the porch, he put a gun, held in his left hand to her temple. He pulled the trigger, firing a single shot into her head, the bullet entering just above the left ear and exiting on the right side of her head, lodging in the front door.

Jill's next-door neighbour, Richard Hughes, said afterwards that he heard a cry that he described as surprise, 'like someone greeting a friend', but he did not hear the report of the gun. Nonetheless, the sound prompted him to go to the front window of his house and look out. He saw the killer, a well-dressed man, in front of the house but by the time he opened his front door to get a better look, the man was gone. He was horrified, however, by the sight that greeted him – his next-door neighbour lying on the doorstep unconscious and covered in blood.

An ambulance was called but Jill Dando died a short while later en route to Charing Cross Hospital.

It was a brutal slaying of one of Britain's best-loved personalities and the nation was horrified at the senselessness of it. The question was, however, why would anyone do such a thing?

The investigation started immediately. Named 'Operation Oxborough', it was led by Detective Chief Inspector Hamish Campbell and involved experts from every investigative discipline – criminologists, psychologists and forensic scientists as well as countless police officers.

The initial forensic sweep of the area surrounding the immediate area around the murder scene revealed a single Remington brand cartridge that had been fired from a rare short version 9mm semi-automatic Browning pistol. It was described by one expert as the type of gun that would normally be used by 'drug dealers and professional killers.'

Police initially believed that her killer could have been either a stalker or a professional hitman, but the investigation was to prove tricky.

A number of people came forward following the murder to report what seemed to be suspicious events around Gowan Avenue that morning. A ten-year-old boy who had been in a car driving him to school, told investigators that he had spotted a 'weird' man outside Jill Dando's house. He had been wearing an old suit and a cap and had been pacing up and down the street. He had almost walked out in front of the car in which the boy was being driven. Disappointingly, however, neither the boy nor his mother who had been driving managed to see the suspect's face.

A man had been seen outside the house by a window cleaner about an hour before the murder. And another witness reported seeing a man wearing large glasses in the area around the house not long before the shooting.

Still more people had seen a man running away with what looked like a mobile phone in his hand, although it was probably the murder weapon they had seen, while another report had a Range Rover parked near the house that morning. Traffic cameras showed a Range Rover speeding down Fulham Road not far from the house just twenty-two minutes after the shooting.

From information gathered from witnesses, a composite picture of the suspect was created but time passed and the leads dried up. A new man was put in charge, Detective Chief Superintendent Brian Edwards and a new team of forty-four inspectors was assembled, but in spite of massive media coverage and 2,500 interviews, the trail had gone completely cold.

Numerous theories were put forward and police followed these lines of enquiry. Some suggested that Jill Dando had been killed by a jealous ex-boyfriend or an unknown lover. Interviews of all her friends and associates quickly made police dispense with this line. Could an assassin have been hired to kill her perhaps in revenge for a crime that had been exposed on Crimewatch? Detectives thought it unlikely that a professional hitman would wait at an address that she visited only rarely. It was also felt from the forensic evidence of the shell casing and bullet that it had come from a replica or decommissioned gun. It seemed highly improbable that a professional gunman would have used such a poor quality weapon. Could it have been a deranged fan of Jill Dando, a stalker, who, spurned by her, had turned his love into hate, a common occurrence with stalkers. Making this line of enquiry credible was the report from her brother that a man had been pestering her in the days leading up to her death. Police also considered the chance that it could have been a case of mistaken identity but this seemed highly unlikely, given that she had pointedly been killed on her own doorstep.

Suddenly, more than a year after Jill Dando's murder, on 25 May 2000, police announced the arrest of a suspect. They had begun to focus on him after interviewing him following the murder, setting up surveillance cameras outside his home. New circumstantial evidence had been found in his home and there had been numerous tip-offs about him in the days following the murder.

His name was announced as Barry Bulsara but he also went by the names of Steve Majors and Tom Palmer. His real name was Barry Michael George; he had borrowed the name Bulsara from the lead singer of the rock group Queen, Freddy Mercury, whose real surname was Bulsara. George lived half a mile from Jill Dando's house.

Eight months after his arrest, when the case came to trial a picture was created of a man obsessed with fame and celebrity who, it was also learned, was a member of a pistol club.

One of the most important pieces of evidence in the case was a coat that was found at his flat that was similar to the one worn by the killer. Crucially, one of its pockets was found to contain discharge residue. Forensic scientists had matched this to particles found in Jill Dando's hair. A piece of fibre had also been found at the scene of the murder that matched a pair of trousers found at George's flat. He was also recognised by a witness as having been standing across the street from Jill Dando's house on the morning in question.

In the fourth week of the trial, George's QC, Michael Mansfield, posited another theory for Jill Dando's murder. It had been reported, he told the jury, that her life had been taken in retaliation for NATO's bombing of Belgrade. Her death had been ordered by the notorious Serbian paramilitary leader Arkan and carried out by a professional Yugoslavian hitman. He further insisted that there was no real evidence linking his client with Jill Dando's murder.

It was to no avail, however. On 2 July 2001, Barry George was found guilty and sentenced to life in prison. At this point, George's past record could be made public. It emerged that he had previously been arrested for indecent assault and attempted rape. He had also, in 1983, been arrested for trespassing in the London property of Diana, Princess of Wales. Wearing combat fatigues, carrying a gas mask, a length of rope and with a knife in his belt, he was discovered hiding in bushes. On that occasion, no charges had been brought against him.

Barry George was in jail, but seven years later, he was re-tried after lengthy appeals questioned the forensic evidence at his first trial. With this evidence inadmissible in 2008, he was found not guilty.

The real killer of Jill Dando remains unknown to this day.